PIG OUT

COOKBOOK

Selected Recipes from The Junior League
of Waterloo–Cedar Falls, Iowa

WCF Publications
Waterloo-Cedar Falls, Iowa

The purpose of the Junior League is exclusively educational and charitable and is to promote voluntarism; to develop the potential of its members for voluntary participation in community affairs; and to demonstrate the effectiveness of trained volunteers.

Proceeds from the sale of PIG OUT will be returned to the community through projects sponsored by The Junior League of Waterloo-Cedar Falls, Iowa, Inc.

For additional copies, use the coupons at the back of this book, or write:

WCF Publications
The Junior League of Waterloo-Cedar Falls,
   Iowa, Inc.
Box 434
Waterloo, Iowa 50704

PIG OUT may be obtained for fundraising projects or by retail outlets at special rates. Write to the above address for further information.

Copyright © 1986 by The Junior League of Waterloo-Cedar Falls, Iowa, Inc.
First Edition
First Printing: 10,000 copies, April, 1986
Second Printing: 10,000 copies, October, 1986
Third Printing: 15,000 copies, July, 1989
The Library of Congress Catalog Code Number: 85-051884
International Standard Book Number: 0-9615904-0-8

Printed by S. C. Toof and Company
Memphis, Tennessee

I owa. We are the heartland. America's bread-
basket. Our fields produce a rich harvest of
golden corn. Our farmers raise the choicest beef
and pork. Like the Iowa Chop . . . an Iowa
original.

And originality is what this cookbook is all
about. Between its covers you will find the best
of eating pleasure. We present country whole-
some — with class. That extra special touch that
turns good food into great entertainment.

Our recipes — collected and painstakingly
tested by our best cooks — are guaranteed to
pique your palate . . . whether it's a delicious
appetizer, that perfect entree, savory salad or
marvelous dessert.

So, we invite you to PIG OUT . . . not by
eating out of gluttony, but rather by eating "out
of the ordinary" — country style!

PIG OUT is a collection of "praise-winning" recipes submitted by League members and friends. Among this selection are country favorites, treasured for many years, as well as original creations. Each recipe has been tested at least twice by one of our 11 testing teams and enthusiastically endorsed by these accomplished cooks.

 For your convenience, we have emphasized those recipes that feature pork ingredients. Look for the tiny pig to the right of those titles.

 Recipes that are easy to prepare or contain convenience foods are noted by the small fleur-de-lis to the right of those titles.

Our sincere appreciation to all League members and friends who willingly shared their recipes, inspiration and enthusiasm, and generously contributed their time and talents. And to our families, who have been so patient and supportive during the past three years, we express our love and special thanks.

The Cookbook Committee

About our artist...

Jim Erkel's interpretation of classic country is reflected in the fleur-de-lis pattern and bold pig stenciled on our cover. An Iowa farm boy himself, Mr. Erkel received an associate of applied arts degree from Hawkeye Institute of Technology. He has repeatedly been honored for his artistic work by the Marketing and Advertising Club of Northeast Iowa. He is art director for Cooper and Associates advertising agency.

C O N T E N T S

COOKBOOK COMMITTEE

General Co-Chairmen
Linda Johnston Rust
Kate Della Maria Weidner

Editor/Design & Format Chairman
Susie Kaldor Heaton

Testing Chairman
Cynthia Staley Kenyon

Section Chairmen

Menus
Cynthia Staley Kenyon

Beverages & Appetizers
Karen Karman Gartelos
Becky Peet Martens

Soups & Sandwiches

Eggs, Cheese & Pasta
Marty McNutt Port

Breads
Linda Monroe Hoel

Salads, Dressings & Condiments

Vegetables
Carol Hayes Steckelberg
Connie Stroh Werner

Entrees
Jane Walker Christensen
Barbara Dunn McDonald

Desserts
Judy Mathews Arnold
Diane Drewis Good

Special Occasions
Jane Rife Field

Typing Coordinator
Susan Young Peters

Manuscript/Proofreading Coordinator
Cathie Pederson Miehe

Index Coordinators
Karen Buck Garvin
Jeri Mixdorf Jenner

Marketing Chairman
Sally Brees Young

Promotions Co-Chairmen
Marcy O'Bryon Coontz
Sandy Smith Ritland

Ex-Officio Members
Dianne Brink Warren, 1983-84
Peg Zeis McGarvey, 1984-85
Junean Goschke Witham, 1985-86

Special Acknowledgements
Jan Danielsen Andersen
Linda Schaedler Hoskins
Marilyn Stephenson Hurley
Linda Hexom Lott
Anna Griffith Randall
Jan McDonough Taylor
Linda Lu Smith Thompson

MENUS

Recipes for these selected menus can be found within our cookbook.

Sunday Brunch

Eggnog Mold with Raspberry Sauce   *Asparagus Roll-Ups*
Sensational Shrimp Salad
Ground Pork Quiche

Poppy Seed Bread   *Ensaymadas*
Chocolate Peppermint Brownies

Rhubarb Bars   *Swedish Cream Wafers*
Slices of Heaven   *Bloody Dill Mary*

Elegant Brunch

Glazed Fruit Salad
Chicken Artichoke Salad   *Broccoli-Cheddar Timbales*
Shrimp-Crabmeat Scrambled Eggs

Cheese-Filled Coffeecake   *Bread Sticks*
Strawberry Puffs with Raspberry Cassis Sauce

Reception Chocolate   *Rhubarb Punch*

Ladies Summer Luncheon

Frosted Strawberry Soup

Asparagus Vinaigrette

Cherry Chicken Salad   *Layered Salmon Salad*

5 P.M. Rolls

Meringue Pie

Apricot Brandy Slush

Midnight Supper

Lemonade Your Grandmother Never Made

Orange Cheese Dip

Sticky Ham Balls   *Mushrooms Stuffed with Crab*

Steak Soup

Savory Cheese Loaf

Glazed Pears   *Irish Cream Liqueur*

Candlelight Dinner

Chairheads

Hot Gouda Cheese   *Crabmeat Mold*

Asparagus-Leek Soup

Spinach Salad Supreme

Champagne Sherbet

Carrot-Zucchini Casserole   *Gourmet Potatoes*

Individual Beef Wellingtons

Stockbridge Twists

Angel Pie

Celebration Dinner

Lemon Champagne Punch

Mushroom Strudel   *Party Wedges*

Cream of Broccoli Soup

Mixed Greens and Artichoke Salad

Watermelon Granite

Cauliflower Pie   *Layered Broccoli-Wild Rice Casserole*

Pork Loin Roast with Orange Glaze Cups

Swedish Rye Bread

Valentine Tarts

Tailgate Party

Guacamole Supreme

Springtime New Potato-Bean Salad　　　　　　　*Avocado Salad*

Hearty Iowa Beans

Turkey Pockets

Lemon Cheese Bars　　　　　　　*Peppermint Brownies*

Fruit Cooler "With"

Picnic in the Park

Crab Sticks

Million Dollar Salad　　　　　　　*Pasta Salad Italiano*

Ham and Breast of Chicken en Croute

Chocolate Cream Cheese Cupcakes　　　*Grandma's Frosted Creams*

Beer Daiquiris　　　　　　　*Angel Wings*

Fruited Tea

Children's Party

Poppycock

Fresh Fruit Kabobs　　　　　　　*Bacon-Stuffed Cherry Tomatoes*

Calico Burgers

Cookie Pizzas　　　　　　　　　　*Twinkie Cake*

Fruited Cooler "Without"

After-the-Game Teen Party

Vegetable Pizza

Calico Corn Salad　　　　　　　*Strawberry Frozen Fruit Salad*

Saucy Ham and Cheese Sandwiches

Popcorn Cake　　　　　　　　　*The Ultimate Chocolate Bar*

Fruited Tea

BEVERAGES

BEVERAGES

Cold Beverages

Angel Wings	17
Apricot Brandy Slush	16
Beer Daiquiri	15
Bloody Dill Mary	17
Chairheads	15
Fruit Cooler "With or Without"	21
Fruited Tea	20
Irish Cream Liqueur	20
Lemon Champagne Punch	15
Lime Summer Freeze	19
Rhubarb Punch	20
Slices of Heaven	18
Summer Slush Cooler	16

Hot Beverages

Christmas Apple Cider	22
Hot Buttered Rum	19
Lemonade Your Grandmother Never Made	18
Reception Chocolate	22

Lemon Champagne Punch ⚘

Planning: Can be made ahead
Preparation Time: 10 minutes

Quantity: 50 servings
Chilling Time: 2-3 hours

2 12-ounce cans frozen lemonade
2 12-ounce cans frozen pineapple
    juice
1 1/2 quarts cold water
2 quarts gingerale, chilled
1 quart sparkling water
6 fifths dry champagne,
    chilled

1. Mix juices and water. Cover and chill.   2. Just before serving, add gingerale, sparkling water, and champagne.

Margie Lahey Skahill
(Mrs. Timothy)

Chairheads ⚘

Planning: None
Preparation Time: 1 minute

Quantity: One 8-ounce glass
Chilling Time: None

Southern Comfort
pineapple juice
ice

1. Fill 8-ounce glass with ice.   2. Pour 1 jigger Southern Comfort slowly over ice.   3. Shake pineapple juice well and fill glass.   4. Stir carefully.

Hint: Garnish with a cherry and fresh pineapple or canned pineapple chunk.

Dee Reinhart Vandeventer
(Mrs. David)

Beer Daiquiri ⚘

Planning: Can be prepared ahead
Preparation Time: 2 minutes

Quantity: 6 servings
Chilling Time: None

1 6-ounce can frozen lemonade
6 ounces gin (use empty lemonade
    can to measure)
ice
1 12-ounce can of beer

1. In a blender, combine lemonade, gin and enough ice to fill 1/2 blender. Blend well.   2. Add beer and blend again. 3. If necessary, add more ice and blend to make drink thick.

Hint: Drink can be prepared ahead of time and kept in the freezer.

Mary Waldon Gabrick
(Mrs. David)

Summer Slush Cooler ❧

Very refreshing.

Planning: Must be made ahead
Preparation Time: 15 minutes

Quantity: 10-12 servings
Chilling Time: Overnight until frozen

1 cup sugar (or less to taste)
1 cup hot tea
1 12-ounce can frozen orange
   juice, thawed
1 12-ounce can frozen lemonade,
   thawed
3 cups water
1 1/2 cups liquor
(suggestions: vodka, rum, whisky,
   apricot brandy)
clear, carbonated soft drink

1. Mix all ingredients, except carbonated soft drink, thoroughly.   2. Freeze in a large plastic container (tightly sealed)   3. To serve mix 2/3 parts slush to 1/3 part clear, carbonated soft drink.

Sheryl Belden Bewyer
(Mrs. David)

Apricot Brandy Slush ❧

Planning: Must be made ahead
Preparation Time: 10 minutes

Quantity: Sixty 8-ounce servings
Freezing Time: 24 hours

1 12-ounce can frozen lemonade
1 12-ounce can frozen orange
   juice
1 32-ounce can apricot nectar
1 46-ounce can pineapple juice
2 cups vodka
2 cups apricot brandy
lemon-lime carbonated beverage

1. Combine all ingredients except carbonated beverage.   2. Stir thoroughly in large container.   3. Store in freezer, stirring several times the first couple hours.   4. To serve, fill glass half full of slush and add carbonated beverage.

Mary Ludlow Alfrey
(Mrs. Gary)

Angel Wings ❧

Planning: Mixture can be made ahead
Preparation Time: 5 minutes

Quantity: 12 servings
Chilling Time: None

1 cup gin or vodka
1 cup powdered sugar
1 cup whipping cream
¹/₂ cup lemon juice
white cream soda

1. Mix togehter first four ingredients.
2. Place one shot glass of this mixture in a glass.   3. Add cream soda to fill glass.   4. Ice cubes may be added (optional).   5. Refrigerate remaining mixture.

*Carol Irgens Hellman
(Mrs. James)*

Bloody Dill Mary ❧
Great variation of a Bloody Mary.

Planning: None
Preparation Time: 5 minutes

Quantity: Four 8-ounce drinks
Standing Time: 10 minutes

2 teaspoons dried dill weed
6 ounces vodka
1¹/₂ cups tomato juice
4 drops red hot pepper sauce
¹/₂ teaspoon salt
light grinding of pepper

1. Rub dill between fingers to powder and drop into a pitcher.   2. Pour in vodka and tomato juice.   3. Let stand 10 minutes.   4. Add red hot pepper sauce and salt; stir.   5. Strain through fine mesh strainer over ice cubes into four 8-ounce bar glasses. Stir until chilled. Grind a light sprinkle of black pepper over top.

*Marty McNutt Port
(Mrs. Dale)*

Lemonade Your Grandmother Never Made ❧

But Grandpa and everyone else loves this tummy-warming concoction.

Planning: None
Preparation Time: 15 minutes

Quantity: Twenty-four 1-cup servings
Cooking Time: 15 minutes

4 quarts water
juice of 12 lemons
4 cups sugar
2 teaspoons salt
light rum, 1 fifth
24 cinnamon sticks

1. In a stainless steel or enameled pan, combine water, lemon juice, sugar, and salt. Heat to very hot, but not boiling. **2.** Add the rum. **3.** Serve in cups or mugs that each contain one cinnamon stick.

Janet Rohlf Holden
(Mrs. L. Sam)

Slices of Heaven ❧

A truly heavenly drink.

Planning: Can not be made ahead
Preparation Time: 10 minutes

Quantity: 5 1/2 cups
Chilling Time: None

1 6-ounce can orange juice
   concentrate
1 quart vanilla ice cream
1 raw egg
1/3 pint of whipping cream
1/3 cup vodka
crushed ice (desired thickness)

1. Blend all ingredients in blender.
2. Pour into glasses and serve.

Hint: Can float mandarin orange slice on top.

Susie Kaldor Heaton
(Mrs. Robert)

APPETIZERS

APPETIZERS

Dips And Spreads

Boursin Cheese Spread	46
Caviar Supreme	26
Chili Dip	48
Crabmeat Mold	25
Elegant Baked Crab Appetizer	25
Guacamole Supreme	48
Horseradish Spread	50
Nutty Ham Ball	37
Orange Cheese Dip	47
Shrimp or Crabmeat Dip	30

Hot Appetizers

Artichoke Parmesan Strudel	42
Asparagus Roll-Ups	44
Chicken Sate	41
Crab Sticks	30
Crescent Roll Pinwheels	49
Double Hot Hors d'oeuvres	38
Ham and Chutney Canapes	36
Hot Gouda Cheese	46
Magnificent Mushrooms	33
Marie's Piquant Cocktail Meatballs	34
Mushroom Strudel	32

Mushrooms Stuffed with Crab	31
Paul's Stuffed Bread	49
Pork Sausage Balls	39
Rumaki	40
Spinach Balls	45
Sticky Ham Balls	36
Sweet and Sour Meatballs	39
Sweet Hot Mushroom Appetizer	31
Tex-Mex Wontons	35
Tiropites (Cheese Triangles)	47

Cold Appetizers

Bacon Poles	40
Bacon-Stuffed Cherry Tomatoes	45
Cucumber Delights	41
Deviled Ham Cornucopias	37
Dilled Scallops and Shrimp	29
Party Wedges	34
Pickled Pigs	38
Poppycock	50
Salmon Balls	29
Smoked Salmon Cheesecake	28
Spinach Squares	44
Vegetable Pizza	43

Elegant Baked Crab Appetizer

Unbelievably delicious—your guests will rave.

Planning: Can be made ahead
Preparation Time: 15 minutes

Quantity: 6-10 servings
Baking Time: 20-30 minutes, 350°

3/4 cup finely diced green onion
1/2 cup finely diced celery
1/2 cup butter
1/3 cup flour
1/2 teaspoon garlic salt
1 1/2 pints half and half cream
1 cup processed cheese, diced
1 pound fresh or frozen crabmeat
  or crab stix
1/2 cup Parmesan cheese, grated
1/2 teaspoon paprika
crackers

1. Sauté onions and celery in butter. Add flour, garlic salt, half and half cream, and cheese.   2. After cheese has melted, add crabmeat. Stir crabmeat into cheese mixture.   3. Pour mixture into greased 9" x 9" baking dish. Sprinkle Parmesan cheese and paprika over top of crabmeat mixture.   4. Bake 350° for 20 to 30 minutes and serve with crisp cracker rounds.

Linda Bjornstad Martin
(Mrs. James)

Crabmeat Mold

For crab lovers.

Planning: Must be made ahead
Preparation Time: 30 minutes

Quantity: One 2-quart mold
Chilling Time: 24 hours

1 8-ounce package cream cheese
1 10 3/4-ounce can tomato soup,
  undiluted
1 1-ounce envelope unflavored
  gelatin
1/2 cup cold water
1 small onion, diced
1 cup diced celery
1/8 teaspoon pepper
1/2 teaspoon salt
2 teaspoons lemon juice
1 tablespoon barbecue sauce,
  ketchup, or chili sauce
2 packages frozen crabmeat,
  drained and shredded

1. Soften cream cheese in small saucepan over low heat.   2. Add tomato soup and bring to boil just until bubbly and smooth.   3. Add gelatin which has been dissolved in the water.   4. Add onion, celery, salt, pepper, lemon juice and chili sauce. Mix well.   5. Add crabmeat and stir. Pour into a 2-quart mold which has been rinsed in very cold water—do not dry!   6. Refrigerate 24 hours before serving. Serve with crackers or party rye.

Sue Willett Sawyer
(Mrs. Gary)

Sue Willett Sawyer
(Mrs. Gary)

Caviar Supreme
A gourmet's delight.

Planning: Must be made ahead
Preparation Time: 1 1/2 hours

Quantity: 12-16 servings
Chilling Time: Refrigerate overnight

Homemade Mayonnaise:
1 egg
1 teaspoon fresh lemon juice
1 teaspoon red wine vinegar
1 teaspoon Dijon mustard
1 teaspoon salt
freshly ground white pepper
1 1/2 cups safflower oil with
    3 tablespoons olive oil

Homemade Mayonnaise:
1. In food processor or blender, combine egg, lemon juice, vinegar, mustard, salt, and pepper with 3 tablespoons oil and mix 5 seconds. With machine running, begin adding oil in steady thin stream through top opening until mayonnaise thickens. Add remaining oil more quickly. **2.** Taste and adjust seasonings.

Gelatin:
oil
1 1-ounce package unflavored
    gelatin
1/4 cup cold water

Gelatin:
1. Line bottom of 1-quart souffle dish with foil extending beyond rim of dish on 2 sides. Oil lightly. **2.** Soften gelatin in cold water in measuring cup. Liquefy gelatin by setting cup in pan of hot water or in microwave for about 20 seconds at lowest setting. This gelatin will be divided among the three layers.

Egg Layer:
4 hard cooked eggs, chopped
1/2 cup homemade mayonnaise
1/4 cup minced parsley leaves
1 large green onion, minced
3/4 teaspoon salt
dash of red hot pepper sauce
dash of white pepper

Egg Layer:
1. Combine all ingredients with 1 tablespoon of gelatin. Taste and adjust seasoning. **2.** Neatly spread egg mixture into prepared dish with spatula, smoothing top. Wipe any egg mixture from foil with paper towel.

Continued...

Avocado Layer:
1 medium avocado, pureed just
    before adding
1 medium avocado, diced just
    before adding
1 large shallot, minced
2 tablespoons fresh lemon juice
2 tablespoons homemade
    mayonnaise
¹/₂ teaspoon salt
dash of red hot pepper sauce
dash of ground black pepper

Sour Cream and Onion Layer:
1 cup sour cream
¹/₄ cup minced onion
1 3¹/₂ to 4-ounce jar black or red
    caviar
fresh lemon juice
1 loaf thinly sliced pumpernickel
    bread

Avocado Layer:
1. Combine all ingredients with 1 tablespoon dissolved gelatin. Taste and adjust
seasoning.   **2.** Gently spread mixture
evenly over egg layer.

Sour Cream and Onion layer:
1. Mix sour cream and onion with remaining 2 tablespoons gelatin. Spread
carefully over avocado layer.   **2.** Cover
dish tightly with plastic wrap and refrigerate overnight.   **3.** Just before serving,
place caviar in fine sieve and rinse
gently under cold running water. Sprinkle with lemon juice and drain. Lift
mold out of dish using foil extensions as
"handles." Transfer mold to serving
dish, cut away foil. Spread caviar over
top. Serve with thin slices of dark
pumpernickel.

Sue Willett Sawyer
(Mrs. Gary)

Smoked Salmon Cheesecake
Very elegant and rich.

Planning: Must do ahead
Preparation Time: 20 minutes

Quantity: 12-16 servings
Baking Time: 30 minutes, 325°

Pan Coating:
1 1/2 tablespoons butter
1/2 cup fine bread crumbs
1/4 cup Gruyere cheese, grated
1 teaspoon fresh dill (or 1/4
   teaspoon dried)

Pan Coating:
1. Butter 9″ springform pan. 2. Mix bread crumbs, 1/4 cup Gruyere cheese and dill. Sprinkle into pan and coat well. Refrigerate.

Filling:
3 tablespoons butter
1 small onion, minced
3 1/2 8-ounce packages cream
   cheese, softened
4 eggs
1/2 cup Gruyere cheese, grated
1/3 cup half and half
1/2 teaspoon salt
8 ounces smoked salmon,
   coarsely chopped

Filling:
1. Melt butter in skillet and cook onion until translucent. 2. Mix cream cheese in food processor until smooth. Blend in onion, eggs, Gruyere cheese, half and half and salt. 3. Add salmon (mixture should retain texture). 4. Pour into prepared pan. Set pan in roasting pan and add enough hot water to come half way up side of springform pan.
5. Bake for 30 minutes at 325.° Turn oven off and cool 1 hour with door ajar.
6. Transfer to rack and cool to room temperature before removing from springform pan and serving. Serve at room temperature.

Hint: 1. This recipe can be frozen after baking. Cut into individual servings to freeze. Wrap each one separately in zip-lock bag. Defrost in refrigerator 2 days before serving. **2.** To serve, cut into 12 sections, place on small doilies and put back in circle shape (as in pan).

Sally Brees Young
(Mrs. Jeff)

Salmon Ball ♣

Planning: Can be made ahead and frozen
Preparation Time: 30 minutes

Quantity: Serves many
Chilling Time: Minimum 1 hour

1 16-ounce can red salmon
1 8-ounce package cream cheese
1 tablespoon lemon juice
1 teaspoon horseradish sauce
1/4 teaspoon salt
2 teaspoons onion, grated
scant 1/4 teaspoon liquid smoke
1 cup pecans, chopped
crackers or party bread

1. Mix all ingredients except pecans.
2. Cover and chill for a minimum of 1 hour. 3. Shape into a ball and roll in pecans. Serve with crackers or party bread.

Noreen Hermansen

Dilled Scallops and Shrimp

Planning: Must do ahead
Preparation Time: 30 minutes

Quantity: 8-10 servings
Chilling Time: Overnight

1 1/2 cups mayonnaise
1/4 cup sugar
1/3 cup lemon juice
1/2 cup dairy sour cream
1 large red onion, thinly sliced
2 tablespoons dried dill weed
1/4 teaspoon salt
1 pound shrimp, cooked
1 pound sea scallops, cooked

1. In a large bowl mix all ingredients except shrimp and scallops. 2. Stir in shrimp and scallops, cover and refrigerate overnight. Stir only once.

Marion Fiebig Clay
(Mrs. Charles)
Sandra Tuinstra Pearson
(Mrs. Thomas)

Shrimp or Crabmeat Dip

Planning: None
Preparation Time: 30 minutes

Quantity: 2½ cups
Chilling Time: 1 hour

1 6½-ounce can crabmeat or
  shrimp, deveined and chopped
1 8-ounce package cream cheese,
  softened
⅛ teaspoon salt
¼ teaspoon curry powder
1 tablespoon grated onion
2 teaspoons lemon juice
½ teaspoon Worcestershire sauce
¾ cup sour cream
crackers

1. Clean and chop crabmeat or shrimp. Set aside. **2.** Allow cream cheese to reach room temperature, then mash. Add salt, curry powder, grated onion, lemon juice, Worcestershire sauce and sour cream to cream cheese. Beat at low speed with mixer until smooth. **3.** Fold in shrimp or crabmeat. **4.** Refrigerate at least 1 hour. **5.** Serve with crackers.

Carol Irgens Hellman
(Mrs. James)

Crab Sticks ✿

Planning: Can be made ahead and
  frozen
Preparation Time: 35 minutes

Quantity: 48 sticks
Baking Time: 15 minutes, 375°

1 6-ounce jar Old English cheese
  spread
½ cup butter, softened
½ teaspoon seasoned salt
¼ teaspoon garlic powder
1 tablespoon mayonnaise
1 7½-ounce can crabmeat,
  drained and flaked
6 English muffins

1. Mix cheese and butter together until smooth. Add seasonings and mayonnaise. Stir in crabmeat. **2.** Spread mixture generously onto split untoasted English Muffins. **3.** Freeze for 10 minutes. **4.** Cut each half into 4 lengthwise sticks. **5.** May now be frozen for later use or baked, at 375° for 15 minutes. Serve warm.

Hint: Great to have in freezer for unexpected company.

Carol Hayes Steckelberg
(Mrs. Randy)

Mushrooms Stuffed with Crab

Easy, elegant and delicious.

Planning: Can be made ahead and refrigerated
Preparation Time: 30 minutes

Quantity: 12 servings
Baking Time: 18-20 minutes, 350°

24 large fresh mushrooms
$^1/_2$ cup milk
1 tablespoon butter
$^1/_2$ cup cracker crumbs
1 teaspoon dry mustard
1 teaspoon fresh minced onion
$^1/_4$ teaspoon salt
$^1/_2$ teaspoon prepared horseradish
dash of pepper
1 6$^1/_2$-ounce can crabmeat,
    drained and flaked
2 tablespoons butter, melted

1. Clean mushrooms and remove stems. Set mushroom caps aside. 2. Combine milk and 1 tablespoon butter in small saucepan. Cook over low heat until butter melts. 3. Remove from heat. Stir in cracker crumbs, mustard, onion, salt, horseradish, pepper and crabmeat. 4. Spoon crabmeat mixture into mushroom caps. 5. Place in a lightly greased 13" x 9" baking dish and brush tops lightly with butter. 6. Bake for 18 to 20 minutes at 350° and serve.

Jane Walker Christensen
(Mrs. Samuel)

Sweet Hot Mushroom Appetizer 🐖

Planning: Can be made ahead
Preparation Time: 15 minutes

Quantity: 4-6 servings
Broiling Time: 3-4 minutes

12 large mushrooms, stemmed
1 3-ounce package cream cheese,
    softened
6 slices bacon, cut in half

1. Clean and stem mushrooms. 2. Fill mushroom caps evenly with cream cheese. 3. Pre-cook bacon until partially done. Wrap each mushroom with $^1/_2$ slice bacon and secure with toothpicks. 4. Arrange mushrooms (cream cheese side down) on baking sheet. Broil until bacon is crisp (1 to 2 minutes). Turn mushrooms over and continue broiling until second side is done.

Sauce:
$^1/_2$ cup pineapple preserves
$^1/_2$ cup apple jelly
2 tablespoons horseradish
1 tablespoon dry mustard

Sauce:
1. Combine remaining ingredients in small bowl and blend. 2. Serve mushrooms hot, passing sauce separately.

Cheryl Hansen Galehouse
(Mrs. Leon)

Mushroom Strudel

Impressive, well worth the time for this gourmet delight.

Planning: Can be made one or two days ahead and refrigerated
Preparation Time: 1 hour

Quantity: 2 strudels, 8 servings each
Baking Time: 25-30 minutes, 375°

3 tablespoons butter
1 pound fresh mushrooms, sliced
3/4 teaspoon onion salt
1 tablespoon dry sherry
1 8-ounce package cream cheese cut into small pieces, room temperature
1 cup fine bread crumbs
1/2 cup plain yogurt
1/2 cup sour cream
1/3 cup dried parsley leaves
1/2 teaspoon freshly ground pepper
3 tablespoons water chestnuts, (about 10) chopped
1/8 teaspoon garlic powder
juice of 1 small lemon
20 phyllo pastry sheets
1 cup butter, melted
2 to 3 teaspoons poppy seeds

1. Melt 3 tablespoons butter in large skillet over medium high heat. Add mushrooms and sauté until mushroom juices have evaporated. **2.** Stir in onion salt and sherry and cook until all of sherry is absorbed. Remove from heat and drain. **3.** Return mushroom mixture to skillet. Add cream cheese to mushrooms and stir until melted (warm up if necessary). **4.** Blend in bread crumbs, yogurt, sour cream, parsley, water chestnuts, garlic powder, lemon juice and pepper. Set aside. **5.** Open phyllo and cover stack with plastic wrap to prevent drying. **6.** Place 1 phyllo sheet on work surface and brush with melted butter. Top with second phyllo sheet, and brush with butter. Repeat steps with 8 more sheets, totalling 10 sheets of phyllo, brushing each with butter. **7.** Spoon half of mushroom filling in strip along 1 long edge of phyllo, leaving 3″ margin at each end. Tuck long edge over phyllo, then fold over ends, rolling in jelly-roll fashion to enclose filling. **8.** Transfer to greased jelly-roll pan, seam side down. Brush with butter. Sprinkle top with half of poppy seed. **9.** Repeat with remaining phyllo and filling to form second roll. **10.** Bake strudels until crisp and golden brown, about 25 minutes. Cut each roll into 8 pieces. Serve immediately.

Carol Hinson Driver
(Mrs. Craig)

Magnificent Mushrooms ❧
Elegant.

Planning: Can be made ahead
Preparation Time: 15 minutes

Quantity: 6-8 servings
Baking Time: Microwave 3 minutes
or broil 3 to 5 minutes

8 ounces large fresh mushrooms
¼ cup butter
4 large green onions
½ teaspoon garlic powder
¼ teaspoon dry mustard
1 teaspoon soy sauce
⅛ teaspoon oregano
1½ tablespoons grated Parmesan
cheese
1½ tablespoons grated Romano
cheese
3 tablespoons Italian seasoned
bread crumbs

Topping:
grated Parmesan
grated Romano

1. Wash mushrooms carefully and remove stems. Chop finely, half of the stems.   2. Melt butter in saucepan, or glass dish if using microwave. Add chopped mushroom stems and sauté.   3. Separate green onions into bulbs and stems. Wash and then chop bulbs finely. Chop stems finely.   4. Add green onion bulbs, garlic powder, and dry mustard to mushroom stems. Sauté on high heat, 2 minutes.   5. Stir in soy sauce, green onion tops, oregano, cheeses, and bread crumbs. Heat over high heat, 1 minute.   6. Stuff mushroom caps with mushroom stem mixture and place in buttered 9" pie plate (glass for microwave). Sprinkle with grated Parmesan and Romano cheese.   7. Cover with plastic wrap and refrigerate until ready to serve.   8. When ready to serve, microwave on high heat for 3 minutes or broil until lightly browned and heated, 3 to 5 minutes.

Linda Johnston Rust
(Mrs. Larry)

Party Wedges

Planning: Can be made ahead
Preparation Time: 25 minutes

Quantity: 10-12 small servings
Chilling time: 1 hour

¹/₂ cup pecans, chopped
¹/₄ teaspoon salt
2 tablespoons butter
1 8-ounce package cream cheese, softened
2 teaspoons milk
1 tablespoon grated onion
¹/₂ teaspoon garlic salt
¹/₄ teaspoon black pepper
¹/₂ cup sour cream
1 2¹/₂-ounce package dried beef, finely chopped
¹/₄ cup finely chopped green pepper
8 crepes, cooked

1. In small skillet, combine pecans with salt and butter. **2.** Cook over medium heat until golden brown, stirring several times. Set aside. **3.** In small mixing bowl, mix cream cheese with milk, onion, garlic salt, black pepper, and sour cream until smooth. **4.** Stir in beef and green pepper. **5.** Spread 3 to 4 tablespoons beef mixture over each crepe. **6.** Make a stack 8 crepes high. **7.** Sprinkle toasted pecans on top of stack. **8.** Refrigerate at least one hour. **9.** Cut into wedges and serve.

Susan Walker Crouse
(Mrs. James)

Marie's Piquant Cocktail Meatballs 🌿

Great anytime—especially at holidays!

Planning: Can be made ahead
Preparation Time: 45 minutes

Quantity: 60 meatballs
Baking Time: 30 minutes, 350°

2 pounds ground round steak
1 cup corn flake crumbs
2¹/₂ tablespoons dried parsley flakes
2 eggs
2 tablespoons soy sauce
¹/₄ teaspoon pepper
¹/₂ teaspoon garlic powder
¹/₃ cup ketchup
1 tablespoon instant minced onion
1 16-ounce can jellied cranberry sauce
1 12-ounce bottle chili sauce
2 tablespoons brown sugar
1 tablespoon lemon juice

1. In large bowl, combine beef, crumbs, parsley, eggs, soy sauce, pepper, garlic powder, ketchup, and onion. Blend well. **2.** Form into small balls and arrange in a 10¹/₂" x 15¹/₂" pan. **3.** Combine cranberry sauce, chili sauce, brown sugar, and lemon juice. **4.** Cook sauce over medium heat, stirring until mixture is smooth. **5.** Pour sauce over meatballs. **6.** Bake uncovered for 30 minutes at 350° **7.** Serve in a chafing dish.

Marie Shipman Spears
(Mrs. Jon)

Tex-Mex Wontons

Planning: Can be made ahead if kept
  warm in oven
Preparation Time: 45 minutes

Quantity: 48 appetizers
Cooking Time: 2 minutes in hot
  oil, 375°

¹/₂ **pound ground beef**
¹/₄ **cup chopped onions**
¹/₂ **of a 15-ounce can refried beans**
¹/₄ **cup Cheddar cheese, shredded**
1 **tablespoon taco sauce**
1¹/₂ **teaspoon chili powder**
¹/₄ **teaspoon cumin**
4 **dozen wonton skins**
**cooking oil or shortening for deep
  frying**
**taco suace, sour cream, or
  guacamole**

1. In a large skillet, cook ground beef
and onion until meat is brown and onions are tender. Drain off fat.   2. Stir
beans, cheese, taco sauce, and spices
into meat mixture. Mix well.   3. Place
a wonton skin with one point toward
you.   4. Spoon a generous teaspoon of
meat mixture onto center of skin.
5. Fold bottom of skin over filling; tuck
point under filling. Fold side corners
over forming an envelope shape. Roll up
toward remaining corner. Moisten point
and press to seal. Repeat.   6. Fry a few
at a time in deep hot fat, 375,° for about
1 minute per side.   7. Use a slotted
spoon to remove. Drain.   8. Serve
warm with taco sauce, sour cream, or
guacamole.

*Sue Willett Sawyer
(Mrs. Gary)
Marty McNutt Port
(Mrs. Dale)*

Ham and Chutney Canapes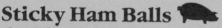

Serve either hot or cold.

Planning: Can do ahead
Preparation Time: 15 minutes

Quantity: 30 canapes
Broiling Time: 3-5 minutes

2 cups ground cooked ham
³/₄ cup chutney, chopped
¹/₂ cup mayonnaise
¹/₈ teaspoon curry powder
1 3-ounce package cream cheese, softened
1 5-ounce package melba toast

1. Mix ham, chutney, mayonnaise, and curry powder well.   **2.** Spread toast with thin layer of cream cheese.
3. Place small amount of ham mixture on toast.   **4.** For hot canapes, place under broiler for 3 to 5 minutes.

Marty Gillam Clark
(Mrs. Mark)

Sticky Ham Balls

Great for large parties.

Planning: Can be made ahead
Preparation Time: 30-45 minutes

Quantity: 20-24 servings
Baking Time: 1¹/₂ hours, 325°

2 pounds ground ham
2 pounds ground pork
2 cups fine graham cracker crumbs
2 eggs, slightly beaten
1¹/₂ cups milk
1 10.75-ounce can condensed tomato soup
1¹/₂ cups brown sugar
¹/₂ cup vinegar
1 teaspoon dry mustard

1. Combine ground meats, cracker crumbs, eggs, and milk. Mix thoroughly.   **2.** Shape into 1″ balls and place in two 9″ x 13″ pans.   **3.** Blend soup, brown sugar, vinegar, and dry mustard together until smooth.
4. Bake for 1¹/₂ hours in 325° oven, covering pans with foil for the first ¹/₂ hour. Uncover and baste three times during last 1 hour of baking.   **5.** Serve in large casserole or chafing dish that will keep meatballs warm.

Marty McNutt Port
(Mrs. Dale)

Nutty Ham Ball

Planning: Can be made ahead
Preparation Time: 30 minutes

Quantity: 1 large ball
Chilling Time: Until firm

4 cups ham, finely chopped
1 8-ounce package cream cheese, softened
3/4 cup mayonnaise
1 cup almonds, blanched, slivered and toasted
1/3 cup thinly sliced green onions
1/4 cup pickle relish
crackers or party rye bread

1. Combine ham, 4-ounces softened cream cheese, 1/2 cup mayonnaise, 1/2 cup almonds, onion and pickle relish. Mix well and chill.   2. Shape into a ball or cone-shaped mound.   3. Combine remaining 1/4 cup mayonnaise and remaining cream cheese; mix well.
4. Frost hamball with cream cheese mixture. Chill slightly; cover with remaining slivered almonds.

Judy Mathews Arnold

Deviled Ham Cornucopias

Too pretty to pass up.

Planning: Make filling ahead
Preparation Time: 30 minutes

Quantity: 20 pieces
Baking Time: 12-15 minutes, 350°

20 slices of thin sliced white bread
mayonnaise for spreading

1. Cut each slice of bread with a round cookie cutter, discarding crusts.
2. Flatten each bread circle with a rolling pin. Spread mayonnaise on both sides. Roll up to form cornucopias and fasten with toothpicks.   3. Bake on ungreased cookie sheet for 12 to 15 minutes, or until lightly brown, at 350.° Remove toothpicks.

Filling:
3 tablespoons mayonnaise
1 4 1/2-ounce can deviled ham
2 eggs, hard-boiled and finely chopped
1 tablespoon prepared mustard

Filling:
1. Combine filling ingredients and chill.   2. Fill each cornucopia with 1 generous teaspoon and serve.

Barb Burnham Paxson
(Mrs. Richard)

Double Hot Hors d'oeuvres

Great served with taco sauce.

Planning: Can be doubled and frozen
Preparation Time: 15-20 minutes

Quantity: 18 squares
Baking Time: 45 minutes, 350° to 375°

1/4 cup salad oil
4 eggs
1/2 cup flour
1/2 teaspoon baking powder
1/2 teaspoon seasoning blend
2 cups Monterey Jack cheese, shredded
1 cup low-fat cottage cheese
2 4-ounce cans green chilies, chopped
3 slices bacon, crisp, cooled, drained, and crumbled or 4 tablespoons cooked ham, chopped

1. Use the oil to grease 11" x 7" x 1/2" baking dish, reserve oil.   2. Beat eggs until light.   3. Beat in flour, baking powder and seasoning blend.
4. Blend in oil, Monterey Jack cheese and cottage cheese.   5. Stir in chilies and bacon or ham, mix well.   6. Pour into baking dish.   7. Bake 375° for 15 minutes. Reduce oven to 350°. Bake 30 minutes more.   8. Cut into 2" squares and serve hot.

Hint: To freeze, place squares on baking sheet. Freeze solid and put into bags. Reheat to serve.

Marty McNutt Port
(Mrs. Dale)

Pickled Pigs

Planning: Can be made ahead
Preparation Time: 30 minutes

Quantity: Many
Chilling Time: Until ready to serve

1 tablespoon parsley
1 teaspoon sweet basil
1 8-ounce package cream cheese, softened
1 8-ounce package boiled ham, thin sliced
1 22-ounce jar dill pickles

1. Blend parsley and basil with cream cheese.   2. Blot ham dry. Spread a thin layer (1/8") of cream cheese on each ham slice.   3. Place each dill pickle lengthwise along one side of ham. Roll up pickle in ham slice.   4. Refrigerate.   5. Before serving, slice (1/4" to 1/2" thick) ham/pickle crosswise. Arrange on platter and serve.

Several League Members

Sweet and Sour Meatballs

Men love these.

Planning: Can be made ahead
Preparation Time: 15 minutes

Quantity: 3 dozen
Cooking Time: 15 minutes

1 pound bulk pork sausage
1/2 cup saltine crackers, finely crushed
1/3 cup milk
1 egg, beaten
1/4 teaspoon dried sage, crushed
1/2 cup water
1/4 cup ketchup
2 tablespoons brown sugar
1 tablespoon vinegar
1 tablespoon soy sauce

1. Combine sausage, cracker crumbs, milk, egg, and sage. Mix until well blended.   **2.** Shape into 1 1/4" balls (wet hands to shape). Brown on all sides in ungreased skillet. Pour off excess grease.   **3.** Combine water, ketchup, brown sugar, vinegar and soy sauce. Pour over meatballs in skillet.
4. Cover and simmer 15 minutes, stirring occasionally.

Linda Schaedler Hoskins
(Mrs. Richard)

Pork Sausage Balls

Made for a man's taste.

Planning: Can be made ahead and frozen
Preparation Time: 30 minutes

Quantity: 75-100 balls
Baking Time: 15-18 minutes, 375°

1 pound pork sausage
3 cups pancake mix
3/4 cup sharp Cheddar cheese, grated
3/4 cup milk
1 tablespoon Worcestershire sauce
1/4 cup minced onion
1/4 cup minced celery
2 tablespoons parsley or cilantro flakes

1. Mix all ingredients together.   **2.** Roll into small balls and place on greased cookie sheet.   **3.** Bake 15 to 18 minutes at 375°.   **4.** Serve hot with cocktail picks.

Hint: If you desire to freeze them, freeze on cookie sheet before cooking and when frozen put in plastic bags. Thaw before baking.

Ann Frisby Callahan
(Mrs. William)

Bacon Poles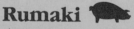
Crisp and flavorful.

Planning: Can do ahead
Preparation Time: 10 minutes

Quantity: 20
Cooking Time: Microwave on high
2 minutes

10 strips bacon
20 long, thin garlic breadsticks
or sesame breadsticks

1. With scissors, cut bacon strips in half lengthwise, making two long, thin strips from each slice. 2. Wrap one strip in a spiral "barber pole" fashion around each breadstick. 3. Place two paper towels in bottom of 13" x 9" x 2" dish. Distribute wrapped breadsticks so they don't touch each other. Cover with paper towel. 4. Microwave at high 2 minutes, rotating dish ½ turn after 1 minute, until bacon is cooked.

Hint: Can use cheese or onion flavored breadsticks too.

Barbara Ehmen Miller
(Mrs. Lee)

Rumaki
A new twist to a bite size favorite.

Planning: Can be made ahead
Preparation Time: 30 minutes

Quantity: 18-24 appetizers
Baking Time: 2 hours, 300°

1 8-ounce can water chestnuts
12 ounces bacon
¹/₂ cup sugar
¹/₃ cup ketchup

1. Drain water chestnuts. 2. Wrap ½ slice of bacon around a water chestnut and secure with a toothpick. 3. Bake, on a broiler pan, one hour at 300.° 4. Mix sugar and ketchup together. Dip chestnuts and bacon into this mixture. 5. Bake for one more hour, at 300.°

Diane Kunz Solberg
(Mrs. John)

Chicken Sate

Planning: Uses bamboo skewers
Preparation Time: About 7 to 8 hours, including the marinating time

Quantity: 12-16 skewers
Broiling Time: 15-20 minutes

2 tablespoons vegetable oil
1 garlic clove, crushed
1 tomato, peeled, seeded and chopped
¼ cup chunky-style peanut butter
1 cup chicken broth or bouillon
½ teaspoon salt
½ teaspoon crushed dried red pepper
1 pound boneless chicken breasts

1. In a small skillet, heat oil and garlic. Stir in tomato, peanut butter, broth or bouillon, salt and red pepper. Simmer about 10 minutes, stirring occasionally; set aside to cool. **2.** Remove skin from chicken breasts; cut into 1" pieces. Thread 3 or 4 pieces on each of 12 to 16 bamboo skewers. Arrange in a 7" x 12" baking pan. Pour peanut butter marinade over skewered chicken; cover and refrigerate 5 to 6 hours. **3.** Preheat broiler if necessary. Place oven shelf 3" to 4" from heating element. Broil in oven or on barbecue grill until browned. Brush with marinade; turn and broil other side until browned and tender.

Carol Hayes Steckelberg
(Mrs. Randy)

Cucumber Delights

Planning: Can be made ahead
Preparation Time: 45 minutes

Quantity: 36
Chilling Time: 2 hours

1 5-ounce can white chicken
1 hard-boiled egg, chopped
½ cup mayonnaise
¼ cup finely chopped onion
¼ cup finely chopped green pepper
2 tablespoons finely chopped pecans
dash of salt and pepper
1 loaf party rye bread
butter, softened
2 to 3 medium cucumbers, thinly sliced
36 pecan halves

1. Mix chicken, egg, mayonnaise, onion, green pepper, chopped pecans and salt and pepper. Refrigerate 2 hours, minimum. **2.** Butter bread on one side. **3.** Slice cucumbers thinly. Place a cucumber slice on each bread slice. **4.** Top with 1 teaspoon chicken mixture. **5.** Top with pecan half.

Marion Fiebig Clay
(Mrs. Charles)
Sandra Tuinstra Pearson
(Mrs. Thomas)

Artichoke Parmesan Strudel

Planning: Can be made ahead and frozen

Preparation Time: 1 hour

Quantity: 2 rolls, 10 to 15 servings
Baking Time: 25-30 minutes, 400°

2 9-ounce packages frozen artichoke hearts (can use same amount canned)
1 ½ cups small curd cottage cheese
1 ½ cups Parmesan cheese, freshly grated
3 eggs, slightly beaten
½ cup minced green onion
½ cup fresh bread crumbs
¾ teaspoon dried tarragon, crumbled
½ teaspoon pepper, freshly ground
1 pound phyllo sheets
1 cup butter, melted

1. Simmer artichoke hearts in lightly salted water to cover for 3 minutes. Drain, pat dry, and cut into bite-size pieces. (If using canned artichokes, drain and cut into pieces.) Transfer to medium bowl and cool. **2.** Add cheeses, eggs, green onion, bread crumbs, tarragon, and pepper. Mix well and set aside. **3.** Open phyllo. Cut stack into 12″ x 16″ rectangle. Cover phyllo stack with a damp towel while working with each sheet. **4.** Lift 1 sheet from stack, place on work surface, and brush with melted butter. Top with another sheet, brush with butter, and continue with 6 more sheets, totaling 8 sheets of phyllo. **5.** Mound scant 2 cups filling crosswise 3″ in from one short end of phyllo, leaving 1″ border at each end. Cover filling with 3″ phyllo border. Fold over 1″ ends to enclose filling and roll jelly-roll fashion. Arrange seam side down on baking sheet. Brush top with butter. Repeat, making second roll. **6.** Strudels can be refrigerated one day ahead or frozen at this point. If frozen, reduce oven to 375° and bake for an extra 10 minutes, or until golden brown and a knife inserted in center comes out hot after being inserted 2 seconds.

Hint: Wonderfully elegant for a sit-down appetizer or as a first course.

Susan Walker Crouse
(Mrs. James)

Vegetable Pizza ✤
Attractive and colorful.

Planning: Can be made ahead
Preparation Time: 20 minutes

Quantity: 20 servings
Baking Time: 10 minutes, 400°

2 8-ounce packages refrigerated
   crescent rolls
2 8-ounce packages cream cheese,
   softened
²/₃ cup mayonnaise
1 teaspoon dill weed
¹/₄ teaspoon onion salt
¹/₄ teaspoon garlic powder
¹/₄ teaspoon prepared mustard
Use some or all of fresh
   vegetables:
chives
fresh mushrooms
broccoli
cauliflower
radishes
carrots
green pepper
black olives
grated cheese (optional)

1. Spread rolls on ungreased cookie sheet. Push together to cover cookie sheet. **2.** Bake at 400° for 10 minutes. Cool. **3.** Mix cream cheese, mayonnaise, dill weed, onion salt, garlic powder and mustard. Spread over cooled crust. **4.** Cut assorted vegetables into pieces. Place onto cheese mixture. **5.** May form into flower shapes or scatter. Different combinations will give different flavors and looks. **6.** Top with grated cheese (optional). **7.** If not served immediately, it should be refrigerated.

Hint: Very suitable for hors d'oeuvre buffets. Can be served for brunch as well as other meals.

Marcy O'Bryon Coontz
(Mrs. James)
Marty McNutt Port
(Mrs. Dale)

Asparagus Roll-Ups

Planning: Can be made ahead
Preparation Time: 25 minutes

Quantity: 60 pieces
Baking Time: 10-15 minutes, 400°

1 8-ounce package cream cheese
3 ounces blue cheese, or any
  special cheese you like
1 egg
1/2 teaspoon salt
1/4 teaspoon pepper
20 slices soft sandwich white
  bread
1 10½-ounce can asparagus
  spears, drained
1/2 cup butter, melted

1. Mix cream cheese and blue cheese together. 2. Beat in egg, salt, and pepper, until fluffy. 3. Cut crusts off bread. 4. Roll slices with a rolling pin until thin. 5. Spread each slice with one tablespoon cheese mixture. 6. Put an asparagus spear on bread slice and roll up. 7. Brush with melted butter. 8. Cut each roll-up into 3 pieces and bake for 10 to 15 minutes at 400° until brown.

Hint: Can be frozen on a cookie sheet after brushing with butter and slicing. After pieces are frozen, put in a plastic bag.

Karen Klemme Stelmacki
(Mrs. Sonny)
Susan Walker Crouse
(Mrs. James)

Spinach Squares

For those of you who don't like spinach.

Planning: Can be made ahead
Preparation Time: 20 minutes

Quantity: 108 1" squares
Baking Time: 45 minutes, 350°

1 cup milk
1 cup flour
3 eggs, beaten
1/2 teaspoon baking powder
1 clove garlic, finely chopped
1 pound Monterey Jack cheese,
  shredded
4 10-ounce packages frozen
  spinach, thawed and well
  drained
1/4 cup butter

1. In a large bowl, combine milk, flour, eggs, baking powder and garlic. Mix well. 2. Add cheese and spinach. 3. Melt butter in bottom of 9" x 13" baking pan. 4. Pour spinach mixture into pan. 5. Press down in pan, especially in corners. 6. Bake at 350° for 45 minutes. 7. Cool completely before cutting.

Hint: These can be frozen before baking. Do not thaw before baking.

Carol Hinson Driver
(Mrs. Craig)

Spinach Balls 🌿

Planning: Can be made ahead
Preparation Time: 15 minutes

Quantity: 36 appetizers
Cooking Time: 10 minutes, 350°

2 10-ounce boxes frozen spinach,
   cooked and drained well
1 box chicken flavored stuffing
6 eggs, beaten
1 cup Parmesan cheese
2 onions, finely chopped
³/₄ cup butter, melted

1. Be sure spinach is squeezed and drained well. 2. Mix all ingredients together and drop by spoonfuls onto ungreased cookie sheet. 3. Bake 10 minutes at 350.°

Hint: Can be cooked in microwave. Great served with champagne or with a meal.

Mary Waldon Gabrick
(Mrs. Dave)

Bacon-Stuffed Cherry Tomatoes 🐷

A pop-in-your-mouth BLT sandwich.

Planning: Should be made ahead
Preparation Time: 60 minutes

Quantity: 24 cherry tomatoes
Chilling Time: 2-24 hours

1¹/₂ pounds bacon
¹/₂ cup green onion, finely
   chopped
¹/₂ cup mayonnaise
24 cherry tomatoes

1. Fry bacon until very crisp. Drain and cool on paper towels. Crumble bacon. 2. In medium bowl, combine bacon, chopped green onions, and mayonnaise. Refrigerate. 3. Wash and remove stems from tomatoes. On cutting board cut a thin slice off of bottom of tomatoes and scoop out insides. 4. Invert tomatoes on a paper towel for at least 30 minutes. 5. Fill tomatoes with bacon mixture just before serving.

Cheryl Hansen Galehouse
(Mrs. Leon)

Boursin Cheese Spread 🌱

Elegant peppery taste.

Planning: Must be made ahead
Preparation Time: 15 minutes

Quantity: 3 cups
Chilling Time: Overnight

1 cup butter, room temperature
2 cloves garlic, pressed
2 8-ounce packages cream cheese
¹/₂ teaspoon oregano
¹/₄ teaspoon basil
¹/₄ teaspoon thyme
¹/₄ teaspoon marjoram
¹/₄ teaspoon dill weed
¹/₄ teaspoon black pepper
crackers

1. Blend all ingredients, except crackers, using electric mixer or food processor. **2.** Chill overnight to blend flavors. **3.** Serve with crackers at room temperature for easier spreading.

Sue Willett Sawyer
(Mrs. Gary)

Hot Gouda Cheese 🌱

Planning: Can be prepared ahead up to baking
Preparation Time: 10 minutes

Quantity: 10-12 wedges
Baking Time: 20 minutes, 350°

¹/₂ package refrigerated crescent rolls
3 tablespoons Dijon mustard
7 ounces Gouda cheese
1 egg white
¹/₈ cup sesame seeds or poppy seeds

1. Flatten crescent rolls, pressing seams together making a square. **2.** Spread with mustard and place the cheese in the center. **3.** Pull edges of dough to the top of the cheese and press together. **4.** Place cheese in an ovenproof dish, with seams down. Brush lightly with egg white. **5.** Sprinkle with sesame seeds or poppy seeds. **6.** Bake at 350° for 20 minutes or until brown. **7.** Let cool 10 minutes.

Hint: Serve with plain crackers, apple or pear wedges.

Tricia McArthur Elmer
(Mrs. Clark)

Tiropites (Cheese Triangles)

Planning: Can be made ahead and frozen
Preparation Time: 1 hour

Quantity: 36-40 pieces
Baking Time: 15-20 minutes, 350°

¹/₂ pound Feta cheese, crumbled
1 3-ounce package cream cheese, softened
¹/₂ cup cottage cheese
¹/₄ cup Kefalotiri or fresh Parmesan, grated
¹/₈ teaspoon nutmeg
2 eggs, beaten
¹/₂ pound phyllo
¹/₂ pound unsalted butter, melted

1. Blend Feta, cream cheese, cottage cheese, Kefalotiri or Parmesan, and nutmeg. Mix thoroughly. 2. Add eggs and mix well. Set aside cheese mixture while you prepare phyllo. 3. Cut phyllo into 2″ strips, lengthwise. (Keep remaining phyllo covered with plastic wrap). 4. Brush one strip with melted butter; place second strip on top of first and brush with butter. 5. Roll triangle by placing 1 teaspoon of cheese mixture at one end of 2″ buttered strip. Lift corner of the strip closest to the filling and fold over to form a triangle. Continue folding flag-style, maintaining a triangle shape. 6. Brush tops lightly with butter. (Triangles may be frozen at this point.) 7. Bake for 15 to 20 minutes, until crisp and golden. If frozen, place frozen triangles directly into 350° oven. Bake for 20 to 25 minutes. 8. Serve warm.

Karen Karman Gartelos
(Mrs. Peter)

Orange Cheese Dip ❧

Planning: Can do ahead
Preparation Time: 5 minutes

Quantity: 1¹/₂ cups
Chilling Time: None

1 8-ounce package cream cheese, softened
1 11-ounce can mandarin oranges, drained
Tortilla chips or fresh vegetables

1. Combine cream cheese and oranges in blender. 2. Serve with chips or vegetables.

Donna Robinson Brown
(Mrs. Gary)

Guacamole Supreme ❧
Light and fluffy.

Planning: Can be made ahead
Preparation Time: 20 minutes

Quantity: Nine ¼-cup servings
Chilling Time: Up to 48 hours

2 ripe avocados, peeled and
   chopped
1 8-ounce package cream cheese,
   softened
4 ounces sour cream
1 tablespoon lemon juice
1 tablespoon milk
4 to 6 drops hot red pepper sauce
¹/₈ teaspoon salt
¹/₈ teaspoon pepper
1 large tomato, chopped
4 salad onions, chopped
1 cup Cheddar cheese, grated
¹/₂ cup black olives, sliced
nacho or taco chips

1. In blender (or bowl using high speed on mixer), blend together avocados, cream cheese, sour cream, lemon juice, milk, hot red pepper sauce, salt and pepper until creamy. **2.** Spoon into 9" pie plate or quiche dish. **3.** May be refrigerated at this time—no longer than 48 hours. **4.** Just before serving top with tomato, onions, cheese, and olives. **5.** Serve as a dip with nacho or taco chips.

Cary Willoughby Euchner
(Mrs. James)

Chili Dip ❧
Men like this one.

Planning: Must make ahead
Preparation Time: 15 minutes

Quantity: 9" x 13" pan
Cooking Time: 15-20 minutes

2 pounds hamburger
1 cup chopped onion
2 15¹/₂-ounce cans kidney beans,
   mashed
1 bottle hot ketchup
¹/₈ teaspoon garlic salt
4 tablespoons chili powder
¹/₂ cup green olives, chopped
¹/₂ pound Cheddar cheese, grated
corn or taco chips

1. Brown hamburger and ¹/₂ cup onion. Add beans, ketchup, garlic salt and chili powder. **2.** Spread on deep platter or cake pan. Top with remaining ¹/₂ cup onion, green olives and Cheddar cheese. **3.** Serve warm with corn or taco chips.

Barbara Burnham Paxson
(Mrs. Richard)

Paul's Stuffed Bread ⚜

Planning Time: None
Preparation Time: 15 minutes

Quantity: 2 cups
Cooking Time: 1¹/₂ hours, 300°

1¹/₂ pound round loaf dark rye bread (unsliced)
1 8-ounce package cream cheese, softened
1 cup sour cream
1 4-ounce can chilies, chopped
1 2¹/₂-ounce package dried beef, shredded
1¹/₂ cups Cheddar cheese, grated

1. Cut off top of bread and scoop out center. Break into pieces to be used to dip later. 2. Mix remaining ingredients. 3. Put dip mixture into hollow loaf. Wrap in foil. 4. Bake at 300° for 1¹/₂ hours. 5. Serve with broken bread pieces.

Hint: As dip disappears, break bread shell and use to dip also.

Peg Zeis McGarvey
(Mrs. Thomas)

Crescent Roll Pinwheels ⚜
Circles of deliciousness.

Planning: Can be made ahead
Preparation Time: 20 minutes

Quantity: 12-15 pieces
Baking Time: 10-12 minutes, 375°

1 package refrigerator crescent rolls
2 3-ounce packages cream cheese
1 4-ounce can mushrooms, chopped
¹/₄ cup green pepper, chopped
2 to 3 dashes hot red pepper sauce
garlic salt, to taste
poppy seeds

1. Put triangle slices of dough on cookie sheet. Pinch together perforations to make long rectangle. 2. Mix cheese, mushrooms, green pepper, hot red pepper sauce and garlic salt. Spread mix on dough. 3. Roll into a log starting at long side of rectangle. Slice into individual servings (about ¹/₂″ thick) and place cookie style on baking sheet. 4. Sprinkle with poppy seeds. Bake at 375° for 10 to 12 minutes, or until light golden brown.

Susan Walker Crouse
(Mrs. James)

Horseradish Spread ❧

Planning: Keeps for weeks in covered jar in refrigerator
Preparation Time: 10 minutes

Quantity: 3³/₄ cups
Chilling Time: Until ready to serve

1 18-ounce jar pineapple
  preserves
1 18-ounce jar apple jelly
1 5-ounce jar prepared
  horseradish, drained (can use
  any amount from tablespoon to
  whole jar depending on
  preference)
1 1.12-ounce can dry mustard
1 tablespoon cracked black
  pepper
3 8-ounce packages cream cheese
crackers

1. Combine all ingredients, except cream cheese, in a bowl and mix well.
2. To serve, place cream cheese on serving plate and spoon sauce generously over cheese. Serve with crackers.

Hint: Sauce keeps for weeks refrigerated in a covered jar.

Linda Johnston Rust
(Mrs. Larry)

Poppycock ❧
Guaranteed not to last.

Planning: Can be made ahead
Preparation Time: 30 minutes

Quantity: 4¹/₂ quarts
Cooking Time: 20 minutes

4 quarts popped popcorn
1¹/₃ cups dry-roasted peanuts,
  pecans or almonds
1¹/₃ cups sugar
¹/₂ cup white corn syrup
1 cup (2 sticks) butter
1 teaspoon vanilla

1. Put popped corn and nuts in big bowl. 2. Combine sugar, syrup, and butter in 1¹/₂-quart pan. 3. Bring to boil over medium heat, stirring constantly. 4. When mixture turns caramel color, test. Should be at hard-ball stage on a candy thermometer.
5. Remove from heat and stir in vanilla. 6. Pour over popcorn and nuts and mix.

Susan Walker Crouse
(Mrs. James)

SOUPS & SANDWICHES

SOUPS & SANDWICHES

Soups

Asparagus-Leek Soup	55
Avgolemono Soup	58
Beer Cheese Soup	53
Bobbie's Spring Garden Soup	54
Chick-Chick Soup	59
Chunky Tomato Soup	53
Clam or Seafood Chowder	57
Corn Potato Chowder	56
Cream of Broccoli Soup	54
Frosted Strawberry Soup	59
Lamb Stew	57
Potato Cheese Chowder	56
Steak Soup	56

Sandwiches

Deluxe Grilled Cheese	64
French Bread Farci	62
French Dip Sandwiches	60
Italian Beef Sandwiches	61
Monte Cristo Sandwiches	63
Muenster Cheese Bread	63
Pork Rites	62
Saucy Ham and Cheese Sandwiches	64
Turkey Pockets	60

Beer Cheese Soup

Planning: Can do ahead
Preparation Time: 20 minutes

Quantity: 12-16 servings
Cooking Time: 30 minutes

1/4 cup (1/2 stick) butter
1 cup diced carrots
1 cup diced celery
1 cup diced onions
1 cup diced green pepper
2 quarts chicken broth
2 16-ounce jars cheese sauce
2 cans warm beer
1/2 cup grated Parmesan cheese
1/2 pound Cheddar cheese, grated
4 tablespoons cornstarch
popcorn for garnish

1. Melt butter in soup kettle.   2. Sauté carrots, celery, onions and green pepper in the butter. Do not brown.   3. To vegetables add chicken broth, cheese sauce, 1 1/2 cans beer, and the Parmesan and Cheddar cheese.   4. Combine and bring back to simmer.   5. Thicken with cornstarch dissolved in the remaining 1/2 can beer.   6. Reheat to boiling point, garnish with popcorn.

Mary Jean Adams Clark
(Mrs. Craig)

Chunky Tomato Soup ❧

A good way to use a lot of fresh tomatoes.

Planning: Can do ahead
Preparation Time: 15-20 minutes

Quantity: 4 servings
Cooking Time: 20 minutes

4 cups tomatoes, blended but still
    chunky
1 10³/4-ounce can chicken broth
1 teaspoon dried oregano
2 teaspoons thyme
2 teaspoons basil
1/4 teaspoon garlic powder
1/4 cup onions, diced
1/2 teaspoon salt
1/2 teaspoon sugar
1/4 teaspoon pepper
sour cream

1. Combine all ingredients except sour cream and cook until onion are transparent and practically disappear.
2. Serve hot with a dollop of sour cream.

Hint: For a low calorie soup use plain yogurt instead of sour cream.

Linda Lichty Anderson
(Mrs. Robert)

Cream of Broccoli Soup

Planning: Can do ahead
Preparation Time: 45-60 minutes
Quantity: 8-10 servings
Cooking Time: 1 hour

1 medium carrot, scraped and
    chopped
1 stalk of celery, chopped
1 medium onion, peeled and
    chopped
1 small potato, peeled and finely
    chopped
2 bay leaves
4 cups chicken stock or 3
    10¹/₂-ounce cans chicken broth
1 large head broccoli, cut in
    flowerets and chopped or 2
    10-ounce packages frozen
    chopped broccoli
1¹/₂ cups half and half, scalded
salt and white pepper

1. Combine carrot, celery, onion, potato, bay leaves and stock in large saucepan. Bring the liquid to a boil. Reduce heat and simmer the vegetables covered, for 25 minutes or until very tender. **2.** Chop fresh broccoli and add to the contents of the saucepan and boil covered, for 20 minutes.   **3.** In the container of a food processor, whirl the mixture, 2 cupfuls at a time, until it is smooth.   **4.** Combine and blend the puree and half and half. Bring soup to serving temperature. Season the soup to taste with salt and pepper.

Susan Kersten Cortright
(Mrs. Steven)

Bobbie's Spring Garden Soup

Planning: Can do ahead
Preparation Time: 45 minutes
Quantity: Seven 1-cup servings
Cooking Time: 20 minutes

1 cup potatoes, thinly sliced and
    unpeeled
1 cup onion, chopped
2 tablespoons butter
2 13³/₄-ounce cans chicken broth
1 large cucumber, peeled and
    diced
1 teaspoon dill weed
1 teaspoon salt
2 cups lettuce, shredded
dash of pepper
1 8-ounce carton plain yogurt

1. Cook potatoes and onion in butter over medium heat for 5 minutes.
2. Stir in all remaining ingredients except yogurt and bring to a boil.
3. Reduce to simmer and cook and stir for 15 minutes.   **4.** Add yogurt. Put in blender and blend.

Hint: Serve with hot bread.

Linda Schaedler Hoskins
(Mrs. Richard)

Asparagus-Leek Soup
A wonderful blending of flavors.

Planning: Can do ahead, can be
frozen
Preparation Time: 40 minutes

Quantity: Six 2/3-cup servings
Cooking Time: 30 minutes

4 cups chicken broth
3 medium potatoes, peeled and
quartered
3 medium leeks, diced
1 1/2 pounds fresh asparagus,
diced
1 teaspoon dried dill weed
1 teaspoon salt (optional)
1/2 to 1 cup half and half

1. In 3-quart saucepan bring broth to
boiling.. **2.** Add potatoes and leeks.
Simmer covered, 15 minutes. **3.** Add
asparagus, dill weed and salt (optional).
Simmer, covered, about 10 minutes.
4. Add 2 cups of the vegetable mixture
to blender or food processor bowl (steel
blade). Process until very smooth. Remove. Repeat with remaining mixture,
processing 2 cups of vegetable mixture
at a time. **5.** Return smooth vegetable
mixture to saucepan. Stir in cream. Heat
thoroughly.

Hint: Serve with fruit salad, boiled new red buttered potatoes with skins on,
barbequed chicken, pork loin or beef steak.

Linda Bjornstad Martin
(Mrs. James)

Potato Cheese Chowder

Planning: Can do ahead; cannot be
frozen
Preparation Time: 30 minutes

Quantity: 4-6 servings
Cooking Time: 20 minutes

1/2 cup potatoes, pared and diced
2 chicken bouillon cubes
2 tablespoons butter
1/4 cup green pepper, diced
2 tablespoons flour
1 teaspoon salt
1/8 teaspoon pepper
2 cups milk
1 1/2 cups grated Cheddar cheese
parsley, finely chopped

1. Simmer potatoes in 2 cups boiling
water until tender. **2.** Drain potatoes,
reserving 1 1/2 cups liquid. Add bouillon
cubes and dissolve. **3.** Melt butter in
same saucepan. Sauté green pepper.
4. Remove from heat. Stir in flour, salt,
pepper. Gradually stir in potato liquid
and milk. **5.** Bring to boiling and
simmer 2 minutes. **6.** Remove. Add
cheese and potatoes. Stir until melted.
Sprinkle with parsley.

Cindy Poyser Spragg
(Mrs. John)

Corn Potato Chowder 🌿 🐷

Planning: Can be prepared ahead, should not be frozen

Preparation Time: 30 minutes

Quantity: 6-8 servings

Cooking Time: 30 minutes

5 slices bacon

2 cups potatoes, diced

1 cup onion, chopped

1 17-ounce can whole kernel corn, with liquid

1 17-ounce can cream style corn

1 10³/₄-ounce can cream of mushroom soup

2 cups milk

1 teaspoon salt

dash of pepper

1. Cook bacon until crisp. Crumble. Drain off fat, reserving 3 tablespoons. **2.** Bring 1 cup water to boiling. Add potatoes and onion and cover. Cook until potatoes are tender (10 to 15 minutes). **3.** Do not drain. Add reserved drippings and remaining ingredients; bring to a boil and simmer at least 5 minutes, stirring often. **4.** Top with crumbled bacon.

Ruth Lutz Buck
(Mrs. David)

Steak Soup

Planning: Can do ahead of time; can be frozen

Preparation Time: 30 minutes

Quantity: 2¹/₂ to 3 quarts

Cooking Time: 2-3 hours

³/₄ cup butter

1¹/₂ cups flour

2 quarts water

2 pounds ground round or round steak, cubed

¹/₂ teaspoon salt

¹/₄ teaspoon garlic powder

1 cup cubed onions

1 cup cubed carrots

1 cup cubed celery

1 10-ounce package frozen mixed vegetables

1 cup canned tomatoes

2 tablespoons beef concentrate

1 teaspoon pepper

2 tablespoons parsley

1 teaspoon basil

1. Melt butter and whip in flour. Slowly stir in 2 quarts water. **2.** Sauté beef and season with salt and garlic powder. **3.** Drain grease and add meat to soup. **4.** Parboil onions, carrots and celery. Drain and add to soup. **5.** Add remaining ingredients and bring to a boil. **6.** Simmer until vegetables are done.

Hint: Add French bread, salad, and dessert for a great winter meal.

Cynthia Staley Kenyon
(Mrs. James)

Lamb Stew

Planning: May be frozen
Preparation Time: 30 minutes

Quantity: 6 servings
Cooking Time: 1½ hours

2 tablespoons oil
2 pounds boneless lamb, cut into
  2" cubes
2 tablespoons flour
2 cups water
1 16-ounce can tomato sauce
1 tablespoon lemon juice
1 large onion, chopped
1 clove garlic, minced
1 teaspoon salt
³/₄ teaspoon oregano leaves
³/₄ teaspoon basil
¹/₈ teaspoon pepper
2 cups diced raw potatoes
2 cups cubed raw carrots

1. In large, heavy dutch oven, heat oil. Add lamb and brown well on all sides. 2. Stir in flour. Cook and stir 2 minutes. Add water, tomato sauce, lemon juice, onion, garlic salt, oregano, basil and pepper. Simmer, covered, until meat is almost tender, about 1 hour. 3. Add vegetables, cover and simmer until vegetables are tender.

Hint: Serve with a green salad and French bread.

Dorothy Hostetter Plager
(Mrs. Vernon)

Clam or Seafood Chowder

Planning: None
Preparation Time: 15 minutes

Quantity: 12 servings
Cooking Time: 45 minutes

1 cup onion, diced
1 cup celery, diced
¹/₄ cup butter
4 cups potatoes, diced
4 cups hot water
6 chicken bouillon cubes
1 to 2 teaspoons salt
¹/₄ teaspoon pepper
4 cups chopped clams or 3 pounds
  seafood (shrimp, clams,
  haddock)
3 cups powdered milk
4 cups hot water
2 cups cream
1¹/₂ cups instant potato flakes

1. Sauté onion and celery in butter until tender. 2. Add potatoes, water, bouillon, salt and pepper. 3. Bring to a boil and simmer 15 minutes. 4. Add seafood, simmer 10 minutes. 5. Mix powdered milk with hot water and add to the rest. 6. Add cream and then potato flakes. Continue to simmer until potato flakes are cooked.

Margie Lahey Skahill
(Mrs. Timothy)

Avgolemono Soup

Planning: Broth can be made ahead
Preparation Time: 1 1/2 hours

Quantity: 8-10 servings
Cooking Time: 1 hour

1¾ pound chicken, cut up or whole
2½ quarts water
1 stalk celery
1 carrot, whole or halved
1 small onion, whole
1 teaspoon salt
1 cup orzo (rose marina) or rice

Avgolemono:
4 eggs, separated
juice of 1½ to 2 lemons, strained

1. Cover chicken with 2½ quarts water. Add celery, carrot and onion. Bring to boil. 2. Lower heat and simmer, covered, about 1 hour or until chicken is tender. 3. Remove chicken and vegetables from broth. Strain broth and skim off extra fat. (Cooked chicken can be saved for future use.) 4. Add salt to broth and bring to boil. Add orzo or rice and cook until tender. (Rice requires about 15 to 20 minutes cooking time, orzo about 10 minutes.) Remove from heat. 5. In a large bowl beat egg whites until thick. Add egg yolks and continue beating until creamy. 6. Slowly add strained lemon juice, while continuing to beat. 7. Very slowly add ladles of hot broth to egg/lemon mixture, beating constantly until egg mixture is about same temperature as broth. 8. Now add egg/lemon broth mixture, slowly, to remaining broth and stir quickly until thickened.

Hint: Broth can be made ahead. Bring to boil, add rice or orzo, and finish with avgolemono sauce. If necessary to reheat soup, do not allow to boil.

Karen Karman Gartelos
(Mrs. Peter)

Chick-Chick Soup

When served with fresh fruit, this is a complete meal.

Planning: None
Preparation Time: 45 minutes

Quantity: Four 2-cup servings
Cooking Time: 35 minutes

4 cups chicken broth
4 garlic cloves, minced
²/₃ cup brown rice
1 15-ounce can cooked garbanzo
    beans/chick peas, drained
1 cup celery, sliced
1 cup carrots, sliced
1 or 2 small bay leaves
¹/₂ teaspoon leaf thyme
1 teaspoon salt
¹/₂ cup water
¹/₂ cup sliced onions
2 tablespoons fresh parsley,
    chopped or ¹/₂ tablespoon dry
2 cups chicken, cooked and cut in
    chunky pieces

1. Combine and simmer for 15 minutes the chicken broth, garlic, brown rice and chick peas. **2.** Add and simmer for 15 minutes more the celery, carrots, bay leaves, thyme, salt, water, onions and parsley. **3.** Add chicken and heat. **4.** Remove bay leaves and serve.

Marjorie Van Hoesen Butler
(Mrs. Wallace)

Frosted Strawberry Soup ❧

Planning: Must be prepared ahead;
    can be frozen
Preparation Time: 15 minutes

Quantity: Five 1-cup servings
Chilling Time: 1 hour

1 quart strawberries, hulled
1 cup sour cream
¹/₂ cup burgundy wine
2 tablespoons sugar

1. Puree strawberries in blender.
2. Add sour cream, wine and sugar; blend. **3.** Chill well before serving.
4. Garnish with thinly sliced lemons or sliced strawberries.

Deborah Prust Adams
(Mrs. David)

Turkey Pockets

Delicious luncheon dish or family meal.

Planning: If using frozen turkey roast, allow baking time

Preparation Time: 1 hour, not including roasting time

Quantity: 8-10 servings

Cooking Time: 45 minutes

1 2-pound frozen turkey roast, or leftover turkey, cut into bitesized pieces
$^1/_2$ cup butter, divided
1 large onion, chopped
2 green peppers, chopped
6 stalks celery, chopped
1 15$^1/_2$-ounce can pitted black olives, sliced
1 package pita bread, halved and cut open
1 16-ounce carton sour cream

1. Cook turkey roast according to package directions and let cool enough to handle. Cut into bitesized piece. 2. In large saucepan, sauté onion, peppers and celery in $^1/_4$ cup butter until tender. Remove from pan. Add $^1/_4$ cup butter to pan and sauté turkey pieces. 3. Return vegetables to pan and add black olives. Simmer 15 minutes. 4. During this time, warm pita halves in oven. Spoon turkey mixture into pita pockets. Top with spoonful of sour cream and serve remaining sour cream at table.

Connie Stroh Werner
(Mrs. Charles Jr.)

French Dip Sandwiches

Planning: Can be done ahead in a crock pot

Preparation Time: 15 minutes

Quantity: 8-10 depending on roast size

Cooking Time: 3-4 hours

10 beef bouillon cubes
1 teaspoon oregano
3 bay leaves
3 garlic buds, crushed
2 tablespoons sugar
2 large onions, thinly sliced
$^1/_2$ teaspoon seasoned salt
coarse ground pepper
1 can of beer
3 beer cans of water
3 to 5 pound rump roast
8 to 10 French bread style rolls

1. Combine all ingredients, except for the roast and rolls, in a large soup pot. 2. Add meat. 3. Cover and simmer for at least 3 hours depending on size of roast, until meat is tender. 4. Slice meat thinly. Serve on rolls which can be dipped in remaining juice in individual dishes.

Marilyn Daily Strubel
(Mrs. James)

Italian Beef Sandwiches

A nice change.

Planning: Can be made ahead
Preparation Time: 20 minutes

Quantity: 8-12 sandwiches
Cooking Time: 4-6 hours, 275°,
2 hours, 250°

**4 to 5 pound beef roast (chuck,
arm, rump)**
2 onions, halved
1 package dry onion soup mix
1 beef bouillon cube
salt
pepper
1 tablespoon Worcestershire sauce
1 teaspoon garlic powder
1 tablespoon oregano
1 tablespoon basil
mozzarella cheese, shredded
**8 to 12 crusty French bread style
rolls**

1. Place roast with water to cover and halved onions in covered Dutch oven. Bake 4 to 6 hours at 275° until very well done.   **2.** Remove meat from roasting pan and shred.   **3.** Return shredded meat to Dutch oven after discarding broth and onions.   **4.** Cover with water.   **5.** Except for the rolls, add the remaining ingredients (more or less according to taste).   **6.** Cover and return to 250° oven for 2 hours. Serve on hot crusty individual French bread with a generous handful of shredded mozzarella cheese.

Hint: If making ahead of time, shred meat and refrigerate. Puree cooked onion and place with meat. Refrigerate the broth. When you're ready to prepare the dish, skim off the fat and use the original broth instead of new water.

Joan Dawson Huhn
(Mrs. Kenneth)

French Bread Farci

Planning: Can be frozen
Preparation Time: 45 minutes

Quantity: 24 pieces
Baking Time: 10-15 minutes, 400°

1 14-ounce package French rolls
 (12 per package)
²/₃ cup water
¹/₂ cup minced parsley
¹/₄ cup Dijon mustard
2 eggs, slightly beaten
¹/₂ teaspoon oregano
¹/₂ teaspoon pepper
1 pound bulk pork sausage (can
 use Italian sausage)
1 pound lean ground beef
1 medium onion, chopped
¹/₂ teaspoon garlic powder
6 tablespoons butter, melted

1. Halve rolls lengthwise using fork or fingers. Carefully remove soft centers, leaving shells about ¹/₄″ thick. Let centers dry a bit, then place dried bread in batches in a blender and reduce to a finer consistency. Transfer to a medium bowl. 2. Add water, parsley, mustard, eggs, oregano, and pepper. 3. Brown sausage, beef, onion, in skillet over medium-high heat until sausage is cooked through. Drain well. 4. Combine meat and crumb mixture, blending thoroughly. 5. Fill rolls with mixture, packing slightly. Place on ungreased baking sheet. Can be frozen at this point. 6. Stir garlic powder into melted butter or margarine. Brush over filling and edges of bread. 7. Bake 10 to 15 minutes or until hot and browned. Serve immediately.

Hint: Put two halves together and you've got a delicious meal.

Jane Schneider Overbeeke
(Mrs. John)

Pork Rites

Better than a sloppy joe.

Planning: Can do ahead
Preparation Time: 10 minutes

Quantity: 10-12 sandwiches
Cooking Time: 20 minutes

2 pounds 75 to 80% lean ground
 pork
2 tablespoons vinegar
¹/₂ cup water
1 cup ketchup
1 tablespoon brown sugar
1 teaspoon dry mustard
1 teaspoon salt
2 tablespoons onion, chopped
12 hamburger buns

1. Brown pork and drain. 2. Combine remaining ingredients and add pork. 3. Simmer 20 minutes. 4. Serve on a bun.

Marty McNutt Port
(Mrs. Dale)

Monte Cristo Sandwiches

A superior sandwich.

Planning: Cannot be made ahead
Preparation Time: 30 minutes

Quantity: 4-6 sandwiches
Cooking Time: 6-8 minutes

Batter:
1 ½ cups flour
1 tablespoon baking powder
1 egg yolk
1 ⅓ cups water
1 egg white, beaten stiff

Batter:
1. Mix flour and baking powder.
2. Beat together yolk and water and add dry ingredients.   3. Fold in stiffly beaten egg white.

Sandwich:
firm white bread, crusts trimmed
sliced Monterey Jack cheese
sliced ham
sliced turkey
powdered sugar

Sandwich:
1. Make sandwiches starting with bread, then layering cheese, ham, cheese, turkey, cheese and the other slice of bread.   2. Trim fillings so they do not fall over edges.   3. Slice diagonally and secure with toothpick.   4. Dip in batter and fry in 2" of oil, 3 to 4 minutes per side, turning once.   5. Sprinkle generously with powdered sugar and serve hot.

Hint: Tastes great served with warm blackberry or any other jelly.

Joan Dawson Huhn
(Mrs. Kenneth)

Muenster Cheese Bread

Planning: Can do ahead; can be frozen
Preparation Time: 40 minutes

Quantity: Many
Broiling Time: 5 minutes

⅓ cup butter
1 loaf Italian bread, ⅜" slices
8 ounces Muenster cheese, shredded
1 tablespoon prepared mustard
1 teaspoon Worcestershire sauce
1 egg

1. In frying pan, melt butter. Brown one side of bread until golden. Remove from pan.   2. Top the other side of bread with mixture of cheese, mustard, Worcestershire sauce and egg.   3. Broil 5 minutes until brown and bubbly.

Janie Stivers Mast
(Mrs. Steven)

Saucy Ham and Cheese Sandwiches

A great after-the-game meal.

Planning: Must be made ahead; can be frozen
Preparation Time: 10-15 minutes

Quantity: 8-10 servings
Chilling Time: Overnight
Baking Time: 15 minutes, 375°

1/2 cup butter
1/4 cup onion, chopped
3 tablespoons pickle relish
1 tablespoon poppy seed
1/4 cup mayonnaise
2 tablespoons prepared mustard
1/2 teaspoon Worcestershire sauce
8 to 10 kaiser rolls
sliced ham
Swiss cheese

1. Melt butter. Add chopped onion and sauté. 2. Add pickle relish, poppy seed, mayonnaise, mustard and Worcestershire sauce. Mix well. 3. Refrigerate overnight or until very thick. 4. Spread generously on both sides of kaiser roll. 5. Pile ham and cheese in roll. 6. Wrap in foil. Bake at 375° for 15 minutes.

Hint: The onion kaiser rolls are great for this.

Catherine Zach Shaw
(Mrs. John)

Deluxe Grilled Cheese

Very easy to make and good to eat.

Planning: Cannot be frozen
Preparation Time: Varies according to number made

Quantity: Depends on how many are needed
Cooking Time: 5 minutes

Texas toast
butter
Swiss cheese
Monterey Jack cheese
Longhorn Cheddar cheese
red Bermuda onion, chopped
ripe olives, sliced
tomatoes, chopped

1. Prepare Texas toast by buttering outer sides. 2. Layer the three kinds of cheeses, onion, ripe olives and tomatoes. 3. Place on a griddle or frying pan. Toast on low heat until cheese is melted. (You may want to place them in a warm oven until cheeses are thoroughly melted.)

Hint: Pieces of cooked bacon may be added for a variation.

Mary Jane McNutt Miller
(Mrs. Charles)

BREADS

BREADS

Yeast Breads And Rolls

Quick Breads

Coffeecakes and Sweet Rolls

Pancakes and Waffles

Ensaymadas

A fabulous roll recipe from the Philippines.

Planning: Allow maximum rising time

Preparation Time: 1 hour (over an 8 hour period)

Quantity: 12 rolls

Baking Time: 10 minutes, 350°

¹/₂ cup lukewarm water
1 teaspoon sugar
1 teaspoon yeast
1 cup flour
6 egg yolks
9 tablespoons sugar
6 tablespoons butter, softened
2 cups flour
extra butter, softened
1¹/₄ cups Edam cheese, grated
extra sugar

1. Mix water, 1 teaspoon sugar and yeast in a bowl. Let stand for 10 minutes.
2. Add 1 cup flour and mix with wooden spoon. Cover with a towel and let rise in warm place until doubled (about 40 minutes to 1 hour). 3. Add egg yolks, 9 tablespoons sugar and 6 tablespoons butter to flour mixture and mix. 4. Add 2 cups flour, mix, and knead (add slightly more flour if dough is too sticky). Let rise again until doubled (about 3 hours). 5. On a floured board, roll dough into a circle with a 12″ diameter. Spread with butter and sprinkle with 1 cup grated cheese. Cut into 12 pie-shaped pieces. Starting with the wide end, roll up each piece. Place on cookie sheet with point under dough. 6. Let rise until doubled (about 4 hours). Bake at 350° for 10 minutes until light brown. Brush with butter and sprinkle with ¹/₄ cup grated cheese and sugar. Best if served warm.

Cathy Foster Young
(Mrs. Rick)

Jalapeño and Cheese Rolls
Rolls with a lot of character.

Planning: Allow rising time
Preparation Time: 2¹/₂ hours

Quantity: 30 rolls
Baking Time: 1 hour, 325°

8 cups all purpose flour
1 pound Cheddar cheese, grated
³/₄ cup fresh jalapeño peppers, minced
¹/₂ cup sugar
1¹/₂ teaspoons salt
2 cups hot water (105°-115°)
3 packages active dry yeast
2 tablespoons plus 2 teaspoons oil

1. In a very large bowl, combine 7 cups flour, cheese, jalapeño peppers, 7 tablespoons of the sugar, and salt; mix well.   **2.** In separate bowl, combine the water, yeast, and remaining 1 tablespoon sugar. Let sit 10 minutes; stir until yeast granules are thoroughly dissolved.   **3.** Add oil to the liquid mixture.   **4.** Add half the liquid mixture to the flour mixture. Mix with hands to moisten flour as much as possible. Add remaining liquid mixture to dough and knead by hand until smooth and elastic, about 15 minutes (gradually adding enough flour to keep dough from sticking).   **5.** Place in large greased bowl, cover and let rise in warm place until doubled (about 1 hour).   **6.** Punch down dough. Shape into 2" rolls, rolling smooth. Place in a greased 9" x 13" pan with rolls snugly touching each other. Cover, let rise until doubled (about 45 minutes).   **7.** Bake at 325° until dark brown (about 1 hour); rotate pan after 25 minutes for even browning.
8. Cool 10 minutes in pan; then turn out and complete cooking.

Dianne Rowland Gearhart
(Mrs. Stephen)

5 P.M. Rolls

A basic roll recipe that is adaptable to several roll variations.

Planning: Allow from 5 P.M. to 10
P.M. for hourly stirring
Preparation Time: 14 1/2 hours

Quantity: 6-7 dozen rolls
Baking time: 25-35 minutes, 350°

1 tablespoon dry yeast
3 cups very warm water
1 cup sugar
1/2 cup vegetable shortening
3 eggs, slightly beaten
8 cups flour
1 tablespoon salt

1. Dissolve yeast in warm water; let stand 5 minutes, stir in sugar and shortening until melted. Add beaten eggs and mix thoroughly.   **2.** Combine 4 cups flour and salt in large mixing bowl. Add yeast mixture to flour mixture and mix at medium speed on mixer until blended. Gradually mix in remaining flour to form soft dough.   **3.** Cover bowl and let stand from 5 P.M. to 10 P.M. Each hour, on the hour, briefly stir the dough from 5 P.M. to 10 P.M. **4.** Shape rolls as desired, (dinner rolls, cloverleaf rolls, crescent rolls, cinnamon rolls). Place rolls in three greased 13" x 9" baking pans. Cover and let sit on counter at room temperature overnight, (approximately 8 to 9 hours). **5.** Bake for 25 to 35 minutes at 350°

Linda Monroe Hoel
(Mrs. Roger)

Orange Rolls

Planning: Allow rising time
Preparation Time: 4¹/₂-5 hours

Quantity: 24 rolls
Baking Time: 20 minutes, 350°

¹/₈ cup warm water (110°)
¹/₈ cup warm orange juice
  concentrate (110°)
1 package active dry yeast
1 cup sugar
1 teaspoon salt
2 eggs
¹/₂ cup sour cream
3¹/₄ cups flour
3 tablespoon orange rind, grated
¹/₄ to ¹/₂ teaspoon cinnamon
  (optional)
¹/₂ cup butter, melted

1. Combine water and orange juice and warm to 110.° Dissolve yeast in water/ orange juice mixture.   **2.** Using an electric mixer, add ¹/₄ cup of the sugar, salt, eggs, sour cream and 6 tablespoons of the melted butter to the yeast mixture.   **3.** Gradually add 1¹/₂ cups of flour; beat until smooth. Knead in rest of flour. Cover and let rise until doubled (2 to 3 hours).   **4.** Punch down; divide dough in half. Roll each dough half into a 1 foot diameter circle.   **5.** Combine remaining ³/₄ cup sugar, orange rind and cinnamon. Brush each circle with 1 tablespoon of the melted butter, then sprinkle with the sugar mixture.
6. Cut 12 equal pie-shaped pieces in each circle. Roll each piece from wide end to point to form a crescent roll. Place the rolls point-side down in rows in a greased large rectangular pan. Cover and let rise 1 hour.   **7.** Bake for 20 minutes at 350.°

Glaze:
3 tablespoons orange juice
  concentrate
2 tablespoons butter
2 cups powdered sugar

Glaze:
1. Make glaze by heating orange juice and butter together, then mixing in powdered sugar.   **2.** Pour warm glaze over hot rolls.

Cathy Foster Young
(Mrs. Rick)

Whole Wheat Potato-Onion Bread

An excellent sandwich bread.

Planning: Allow rising time
Preparation Time: 2 1/2 hours

Quantity: 2 loaves
Baking Time: 35-40 minutes, 375°

1 3/4 cups white flour
2 packages active dry yeast
1 cup milk
1/2 cup water
2 tablespoons butter
2 tablespoons sugar
1 tablespoon salt
1 1/2 cups prepared instant mashed
  potatoes, prepared
1/2 cup sour cream
1/2 cup fresh onion, minced
2 teaspoons tarragon
1 teaspoon garlic powder
5 to 6 cups whole wheat flour
1 tablespoon oil

1. Stir together the white flour and yeast. 2. Heat the milk, water, butter, sugar and salt over low heat until warm (120 to 130°), stirring to blend. 3. Add liquid mixture to the flour mixture and beat until smooth (about 3 minutes). 4. Add the potatoes, sour cream, onion, tarragon and garlic powder; beat until smooth. 5. Add enough of the whole wheat flour to make a moderately stiff dough. Turn out on a surface floured with whole wheat flour and let rest 4 minutes. 6. Knead until smooth (6 to 8 minutes). 7. Let rise in covered bowl until doubled in size (about 1 hour). Punch down. 8. Divide the dough in half and shape into 2 loaves. 9. Place in 2 greased 8 1/2" x 4 1/2" loaf pans; let the dough rise until almost double (about 30 minutes). 10. Bake at 375° for 35 to 40 minutes. After removing loaves from oven, brush tops with oil. Cool.

Joan Dawson Huhn
(Mrs. Kenneth)

Swedish Rye Bread

Planning: Allow rising time
Preparation Time: 2½-3 hours

Quantity: 2 loaves
Baking Time: 45-50 minutes, 375°

2 cakes fresh yeast
½ cup sugar
3 tablespoons molasses
2 cups warm water
2 cups rye flour
4 cups white flour
2 teaspoons salt
½ cup vegetable shortening, melted

1. Combine yeast, sugar, molasses and water in large mixing bowl. When yeast and sugar are dissolved, add rye flour. 2. Add white flour and mix thoroughly. 3. Add salt and shortening. Knead until shortening is completely worked in. 4. Cover dough in bowl and let rise until doubled. 5. Knead lightly. Shape into 2 loaves. Place loaves in greased 9" x 5" loaf pans. Let rise until doubled. 6. Bake for 45 to 50 minutes at 375.°

Peg Zeis McGarvey
(Mrs. Thomas)

Root Beer Rye Bread

An excellent sandwich bread and superb bun for bratwurst and kraut sandwiches.

Planning: Allow rising time
Preparation Time: 4 hours

Quantity: 3 loaves
Baking Time: 40-50 minutes, 375°

2¼ cups root beer
2 packages dry yeast
1½ cups rye flour
⅓ cup sorghum
1 tablespoon salt
¼ cup shortening or lard
1 tablespoon caraway seed
5 cups white flour

1. Warm the root beer to 100 to 110°; dissolve yeast in warm root beer. 2. Add rye flour, sorghum, salt, shortening, caraway seed and 2 cups of white flour. Beat until smooth. Add remaining flour. 3. Knead 10 minutes. Cover and let rise until doubled. 4. Punch down; let rest 15 minutes. Shape into 3 loaves and place in greased 8" x 4" loaf pans. Let rise until doubled. 5. Bake for 40 to 50 minutes at 375.°

Marilyn Daily Strubel
(Mrs. James)

Stockbridge Twists

Planning: None
Preparation Time: 40 minutes

Quantity: 5 dozen twists
Chilling Time: 2 hours
Baking Time: 15 minutes, 375°

1 package dry yeast
¹/₄ cup lukewarm water
3¹/₂ cups flour
1¹/₂ teaspoons salt
1 cup butter
2 eggs, beaten
¹/₂ cup sour cream
1 teaspoon vanilla

1. Dissolve yeast in water. **2.** Sift together flour and salt in mixing bowl; cut in butter. **3.** Blend together eggs, sour cream, vanilla and the softened yeast mixture. **4.** Add yeast mixture to flour mixture and blend. **5.** Chill dough 2 hours. **6.** Roll out chilled dough on sugared "coating" surface. Fold into 3 layers and roll again and fold. **7.** Roll to ¹/₄" thickness. Cut into 4" x 1" strips and twist. **8.** Place on ungreased cookie sheets and bake for 15 minutes at 375° Remove immediately from pan to cool.

Coating:
1¹/₂ cups sugar
2 teaspoons vanilla

Coating:
1. Combine sugar and vanilla.
2. Cover rolling surface with sugar mixture.

Jane Schneider Overbeeke
(Mrs. John)

Bread Sticks

Planning: Allow rising time
Preparation Time: 2-3 hours

Quantity: 16 breadsticks
Baking Time: 10-12 minutes, 350°

²/₃ cup warm water
1 package dry yeast
1 teaspoon salt
1 tablespoon sugar
¹/₄ cup salad oil
2¹/₄ cups flour
poppy seeds, sesame seeds, or
    seasoning salt

1. Dissolve yeast in water in large bowl. 2. Add salt, sugar, oil and flour; mix completely. Knead dough until smooth (about 8 to 10 minutes). Let rise until doubled. 3. Divide dough in half; then divide each half into 8 pieces. Roll each piece into a pencil shape about 8" long. 4. Place on greased baking sheet 2" apart. Brush with egg wash. Sprinkle sticks with poppy seeds, sesame seeds or seasoning salt. Let rise until doubled. 5. Bake for 10 to 12 minutes at 350°

Egg Wash:
1 egg, beaten
1 tablespoon water

Egg Wash:
1. Beat egg and water together.
2. Brush sticks with egg wash before baking.

Marilyn Daily Strubel
(Mrs. James)

Onion-Dill Ring 🌿

Planning: Thaw frozen dough in refrigerator 1 day ahead

Preparation Time: 15-20 minutes; 3 hours to allow dough to rise

Quantity: 8-10 servings

Baking Time: 20-25 minutes, 350°

1 1-pound loaf of frozen bread dough

3 tablespoons butter, melted

2 teaspoons dill weed

1 to 2 tablespoons onion, minced

1. Allow frozen dough to thaw: 24 hours in the refrigerator or according to package directions. At room temperature, approximately 8 hours.   **2.** Cut loaf into 24 equal pieces.   **3.** Place 12 pieces of dough in one layer in a buttered ring mold (glass or metal). **4.** Brush layer with ¹/₂ of butter. **5.** Sprinkle with 1 teaspoon of dill weed and ¹/₂ to 1 tablespoon of onion. **6.** Place remaining dough pieces on top to form second layer.   **7.** Brush with butter and sprinkle with remaining dill and onion.   **8.** Let rise until doubled in size, approximately 3 hours.   **9.** Bake at 350° for 20 to 25 minutes, or until golden brown.

Hint: Excellent to serve with brunch egg dish. To add a holiday touch, make a red fabric bow and place at bottom of ring to imitate a "wreath."

Marsha Kohler Fisher
(Mrs. Michael)

Savory Cheese Loaf

Excellent accompaniment to steak—can also be served as a snack.

Planning: Can do ahead to point of heating
Preparation Time: 20-30 minutes

Quantity: 1 loaf
Baking Time: 20-30 minutes, 350°

1 loaf Vienna or French bread, unsliced
¹/₂ cup butter, softened
6 to 8 green onions, chopped (greens too)
1¹/₂ tablespoons poppy seed
5 tablespoons prepared mustard
8 slices Swiss cheese, sliced in triangles
4 slices bacon, uncooked

1. Trim all crusts from bread. Cut diagonally about every 1" to 1¹/₂", cutting almost through the loaf.   **2.** Mix the rest of the ingredients, except the Swiss cheese and bacon.   **3.** Butter outside of the loaf and between slices with the butter mixture. Fill each slice with a triangle of Swiss cheese.   **4.** Press the loaf together.   **5.** Cut bacon slices in fourths and arrange on top of loaf.
6. Place uncovered on greased cookie sheet.   **7.** Bake 20 to 30 minutes at 350°, until loaf is lightly browned and bacon is done.

Susie Kaldor Heaton
(Mrs. Robert)

Cheese Pillows

Serve with chunky tomato soup.

Planning: Cannot be made ahead
Preparation Time: 25 minutes

Quantity: 12 pillows
Baking Time: 25 minutes, 375°

¹/₂ cup milk
4 tablespoons butter
³/₄ cup flour
4 eggs
4 ounces Swiss cheese, shredded
1 teaspoon oregano
¹/₈ teaspoon salt
¹/₈ teaspoon pepper

1. In a small saucepan, heat milk and butter until butter melts.   **2.** Add flour and stir vigorously with a wooden spoon until mixture forms a ball and leaves the sides of the pan. Remove from heat.   **3.** Add eggs, one at a time, beating thoroughly until blended.
4. Stir in cheese and seasonings.
5. Spray regular sized, non-stick muffin cups with cooking spray. Divide mixture evenly into 12 cups. Bake 25 minutes at 375°.

Bonnie Nelson Anderson
(Mrs. Larry)

Irish Soda Bread

Good for an Irish celebration.

Planning: None
Preparation Time: 30 minutes
Quantity: 1 loaf
Baking Time: 1 hour, 20 minutes, 375°

4 cups unsifted all-purpose flour
1 tablespoon salt
3/4 teaspoon baking soda
3/4 teaspoon baking powder
2 cups buttermilk
1/2 cup raisins or currants
2 teaspoons caraway seeds
1 tablespoon butter, melted

1. Combine flour, salt, baking soda and baking powder in mixing bowl. Make a well in the center and pour in buttermilk. Mix well. **2.** Add raisins and caraway seeds. Knead lightly on well-floured surface, adding more flour, if necessary, to form a soft dough. **3.** Shape into a 6" round loaf. Place on a greased baking sheet. Cut a cross on top of loaf with sharp knife, cutting in 1/4." **4.** Bake for 1 hour and 20 minutes at 375.° **5.** Place on wire rack; brush top with melted butter. Cool thoroughly. To serve, slice thinly.

Kate Della Maria Weidner
(Mrs. Steven)

Honey Corn Bread

Planning: None
Preparation Time: 20 minutes
Quantity: 9 squares
Baking Time: 20-25 minutes, 425°

1 1/2 cups stone-ground yellow corn meal
1/2 cup unbleached flour
1/2 teaspoon baking soda
1 cup milk
1/4 cup butter, melted
1/3 cup honey

1. Mix corn meal, flour and soda together in a blender for food processor. **2.** Combine milk, butter and honey. **3.** Add to flour mixture and blend thoroughly. **4.** Pour batter into greased 8" square pan. **5.** Bake for 20 to 25 minutes at 425.°

Several League Members

Cinnamon Puffs

Planning: None
Preparation Time: 2¹/₂-3 hours

Quantity: 32 puffs
Baking Time: 20-25 minutes, 375°

1¹/₄ **cups scalded milk**
2 **packages quick-rise yeast**
1 **teaspoon sugar**
1 **cup quick oatmeal**
¹/₄ **cup butter, softened**
¹/₄ **cup sugar**
1¹/₂ **teaspoons salt**
1 **egg, beaten**
3¹/₂ **to 4 cups flour**

Topping:
¹/₂ **cup butter, melted**
1 **cup sugar**
1 **teaspoon cinnamon**

1. Cool ¹/₄ cup scalded milk to luke-warm; add yeast and 1 teaspoon sugar. Stir to dissolve yeast.   2. Pour 1 cup hot milk over oatmeal, butter, ¹/₄ cup sugar and salt; stir until mixed.   3. Add beaten egg, then the yeast mixture to the oatmeal mixture.   4. Add 2 cups flour and mix; then add remaining flour as needed to make soft dough.
5. Knead for 5 minutes; let rise in covered bowl for 1 hour. Punch down and let rest for 20 minutes.   6. Form into one large ball; divide into quarters, then divide each quarter into eight equal parts. Form into balls; place on greased cookie sheet and let rise (about 45 minutes).   7. Bake at 375° for 20 to 25 minutes, or until light brown (do not overbake).   8. Roll in melted butter, then sugar mixture. Serve warm.

Mary Esther Harper Pullin
(Mrs. Ron)

Cheese-Filled Coffeecake

Planning: Can do ahead
Preparation Time: 35 minutes

Quantity: 1 large coffeecake
Baking Time: 30-35 minutes, 350°

2 packages active dry yeast
1/4 cup warm water (105° to 115°)
2 1/2 cups all purpose flour
1 tablespoon sugar
1 teaspoon salt
1 cup butter
4 egg yolks

1. Soften yeast in warm water. Let stand 5 minutes. 2. Mix flour, sugar, and salt together. 3. Cut in butter. 4. Add egg yolks and mix well. 5. Add yeast and mix well. 6. Refrigerate two hours. 7. Divide chilled dough in half. 8. Roll out 1/2 dough to measure 10" x 15". 9. Press dough into lightly greased 10" x 15" pan. 10. Cover with filling. 11. Roll out remaining dough to 10" x 15". Place over filling. Seal edges. 12. Brush slightly beaten egg white over dough. Sprinkle with nuts. 13. Let rise in warm place one hour. 14. Bake for 30 to 35 minutes at 350.° 15. Let cool slightly.

Filling:
2 8-ounce packages cream cheese, softened
1 cup sugar
1 egg yolk
1 teaspoon lemon juice

Filling:
1. Beat filling ingredients together until smooth. 2. Set aside.

Topping:
1 egg white, slightly beaten
1/2 cup nuts, finely chopped

Frosting:
1 cup powdered sugar
water or milk

Frosting:
1. Mix powdered sugar with enough water or milk, so it can be drizzled over the coffeecake. 2. Drizzle topping over baked coffeecake.

Hint: Also serve as a dessert.

Jane Schneider Overbeeke
(Mrs. John)
Cynthia Staley Kenyon
(Mrs. James)

Maple Cream Coffeecake

Planning: None
Preparation Time: 30 minutes

Quantity: 1 coffeecake
Baking Time: 30-40 minutes, 350°

1 cup brown sugar
3/4 cup chopped nuts
1/2 cup maple syrup
1/4 cup butter, melted
1 8-ounce package cream cheese
1/4 cup powdered sugar
2 teaspoons butter, softened
1/2 cup coconut, shredded
2 8-ounce packages extra-thick
   refrigerator biscuits

1. Mix together brown sugar, nuts, maple syrup and 1/4 cup butter; pour over bottom of ungreased 9" x 13" pan.
2. Blend cream cheese, powdered sugar and butter until smooth. Stir in coconut.   3. Separate biscuits (20); press each biscuit into a 4" circle. Spoon 1 tablespoon of the cream cheese mixture into the center of each biscuit.   4. Lap the side biscuit edges together over filling, forming finger-shaped rolls.
5. Place rolls, seam side down, in two rows of ten over the syrup mixture in the pan.   6. Bake 30 to 40 minutes at 350°; cool 3 minutes and invert. Serve warm.

Marcy O'Bryon Coontz
(Mrs. James)

Jewish Coffeecake

Planning: Can be frozen
Preparation Time: 15 minutes

Quantity: 10-12 servings
Baking Time: 40-45 minutes, 350°

Cake:
1 box yellow cake mix (without
   pudding added)
2 3 1/2-ounce boxes instant vanilla
   pudding
1/2 cup vegetable oil
4 eggs
2 teaspoons vanilla
1 cup water

Topping:
1/2 cup brown sugar
1/2 cup nuts, chopped
1 teaspoon cinnamon

Cake and Topping:
1. Mix cake mix, pudding, oil, eggs, vanilla and water.   2. Pour 1/2 of batter in a well-greased bundt pan.   3. Mix topping ingredients together.   4. Sprinkle 1/2 of the topping on cake.   5. Pour in last half of batter and sprinke with the rest of the topping.   6. Take a knife and swirl through mixture.   7. Bake for 40 to 45 minutes in a bundt or tube pan at 350.° Cool for 10 minutes and remove from pan.

Debra Grubb Gray
(Mrs. Steve)

Pecan Rolls

Planning: None
Preparation Time: 15 minutes

Quantity: 20 rolls
Baking Time: 35-45 minutes, 350°

1/2 cup orange marmalade
1 cup pecans, whole or chopped
1 cup brown sugar
1 teaspoon cinnamon
1/2 cup butter, melted
2 8-ounce packages refrigerator
  biscuits, country style

1. Spread marmalade and pecans in botton of bundt pan. 2. Combine the brown sugar and cinnamon in a bowl. 3. Dip each biscuit in the melted butter, then in the brown sugar mixture. 4. Place the biscuits snugly side by side on top of the marmalade/pecan layer. Pour the extra butter and brown sugar mixture over the biscuits. 5. Bake at 350° for 35 to 45 minutes. After removing from oven, wait 5 to 10 minutes, then invert pan with rolls onto a plate. Serve warm.

Kathy Wettengel Welch
(Mrs. John)

Fruited Eggnog Bread

Planning: None
Preparation Time: 30 minutes

Quantity: 1 loaf
Baking Time: 1 hour, 350°

2 3/4 cups flour
3/4 cup sugar
1 tablespoon baking powder
1 teaspoon salt
1/2 teaspoon mace
1 1/2 cups eggnog
1/4 cup butter, melted
1 egg, beaten
1 tablespoon rum (optional)
3/4 cup pecans, chopped
3/4 cup mixed candied fruits

1. In large bowl mix flour, sugar, baking powder, salt and mace. Stir in eggnog, butter, egg and rum just until flour is moistened (batter will be lumpy). 2. Fold in nuts and fruit. 3. Spread batter in a greased 5″ x 9″ loaf pan. 4. Bake 1 hour at 350.° Cool bread in pan on wire rack for 10 minutes. Remove from pan to complete cooling. 5. Serve warm.

Hint: After bread is cooled, wrap and freeze (this bread may be frozen 3 months prior to use). About 3 hours before serving, thaw the wrapped bread at room temperature, then slice.

Martha Gillam Clark
(Mrs. Mark)

Poppy Seed Bread ❧

Planning: None
Preparation Time: 15 minutes

Quantity: 3 loaves
Baking Time: 50-55 minutes, 350°

3 eggs, beaten
2¹/₂ cups sugar
1¹/₂ cups milk
1 cup plus 2 tablespoons oil
1¹/₂ teaspoons vanilla
1¹/₂ teaspoons almond extract
1¹/₂ teaspoons imitation butter
  extract
3 cups flour
1¹/₂ teaspoons salt
1¹/₂ teaspoons baking powder
2 tablespoons poppy seeds

Glaze:
¹/₂ teaspoon vanilla
¹/₂ teaspoon almond extract
¹/₂ teaspoon imitation butter
  extract
³/₄ cup sugar
¹/₄ cup orange juice, ready to
  drink

1. Beat together eggs, sugar, milk, oil, vanilla, almond extract and butter. **2.** Mix in the flour, salt, baking powder and poppy seeds. **3.** Pour batter into 3 greased 3" x 7" loaf pans. **4.** Bake at 350° for 50 to 55 minutes. **5.** Mix together glaze ingredients. Put glaze on loaves while still hot and in the pans. When cool, remove loaves from pans.

Hint: Bake bread in various size cans (soup cans, coffee cans) to produce a different shape: good gift-giving idea. This recipe freezes well.

Mary Kay Gallagher Beecher
(Mrs. John)

Coconut Carrot Bread

For coconut lovers.

Planning: None
Preparation Time: 15 minutes

Quantity: 1 loaf
Baking Time: 70 minutes, 350°

3 eggs
1/2 cup vegetable oil
1 teaspoon vanilla extract
2 cups carrots, finely shredded
1 7-ounce package flaked coconut
1 cup walnuts, chopped
1 cup raisins
2 cups all-purpose flour
1 cup sugar
1 teaspoon baking powder
1 teaspoon soda
1 teaspoon cinnamon
1/2 teaspoon salt

1. In a large bowl beat eggs with electric mixer until light. Stir in oil, vanilla, carrots, coconut, walnuts and raisins. 2. In a separate bowl, mix flour, sugar, baking powder, soda, cinnamon, and salt. Stir this mixture into the first mixture. 3. Spread batter in a greased 9" x 5" x 3" loaf pan. Bake on low rack at 350° for 70 minutes. 4. Let stand for 10 minutes, then remove from pan. Cool thoroughly before slicing.

Hint: No milk or other liquid is needed.

Karen Rasmussen Mukai
(Mrs. Teruo)

Belgian Waffles 🌿

Planning: Can be prepared ahead and frozen
Preparation: 15 minutes

Quantity: 8 waffles
Cooking Time: 2-3 minutes

2 cups biscuit mix
1 egg
3 tablespoons oil
1 1/3 cups club soda

1. Mix together all the ingredients. 2. Make sure the mixture is thick; add extra biscuit mix if necessary. 3. Spray waffler with vegetable spray and preheat. 4. Pour about 2/3 cup of the batter into the waffler and cook 2 to 3 minutes. 5. This batter will not keep, so make it all into waffles. 6. Freeze any unused waffles to reheat in the toaster at another time. 7. Serve waffles with your favorite syrup or garnish.

Several League Members

Strawberry Bread ❧

Planning: None
Preparation Time: 25 minutes

Quantity: 2 loaves
Baking Time: 45-50 minutes, 350°

2 cups frozen, unsweetened,
  whole strawberries
3 cups plus 2 tablespoons flour
2 1/4 cups sugar
1 tablespoon cinnamon
1 teaspoon salt
1 teaspoon baking soda
1 1/4 cups oil
4 eggs, beaten
1 1/4 cups chopped pecans
2 tablespoons superfine or regular
  sugar

1. Place strawberries in medium bowl; sprinkle lightly with 1/4 cup sugar. Let stand until thawed, then slice.
2. Combine flour, 2 cups sugar, cinnamon, salt and baking soda in large bowl; mix well.   3. Stir oil and eggs into strawberries; add strawberry mixture to flour mixture; add pecans and blend until dry ingredients are just moistened (do not overmix).   4. Divide batter between two 4 1/2" x 8 1/2" pans that have been greased and floured.
5. Bake 45 to 50 minutes at 350°.
6. Cool bread in pans for 10 minutes, then turn loaves out and cool completely.   7. Sprinkle tops of loaves with sugar.

Dianne Rowland Gearhart
(Mrs. Stephen)

Golden Delight Pancakes

Planning: Cannot be done ahead; can
  be frozen after pancakes are cooked
Preparation Time: 10 minutes

Quantity: Twenty 4" pancakes
Cooking Time: 2-3 minutes

1 cup cream-style cottage cheese
6 eggs
1/2 cup sifted flour
1/4 teaspoon salt
1/4 cup vegetable oil
1/4 cup milk
1/2 teaspoon vanilla

1. Put all ingredients in a blender. Blend at high speed one minute, stopping once to stir.   2. Bake on a greased griddle (or frying pan), using 1/4 cup batter per pancake.

Hint: Batter can be used to make waffles, too. Pancakes or waffles can be frozen and reheated in toaster or microwave. This recipe makes great light pancakes with much more protein than the regular variety. The recipe may also be halved.

Marty Gillam Clark
(Mrs. Mark)

SALADS, DRESSINGS & CONDIMENTS

SALADS, DRESSINGS & CONDIMENTS

Sensational Shrimp Salad ❧

Planning: Must be made ahead
Preparation Time: 20 minutes

Quantity: 6 servings
Chilling Time: Overnight

1 cup uncooked macaroni rings
   or ringo noodles
1 8-ounce package small frozen
   shrimp
1 small green pepper, chopped
3 green onions, minced (include
   tops)
1 10-ounce package frozen green
   peas
2 stalks celery, chopped
³/₄ cup mayonnaise
¹/₂ tablespoon seasoned salt

1. Cook noodles according to package directions; drain thoroughly. **2.** Rinse shrimp with cold water according to package directions. **3.** Combine noodles, shrimp, and remaining ingredients. **4.** Refrigerate overnight. **5.** Serve on bed of lettuce.

Hint: Serve with fresh fruit and muffins for an elegant luncheon.

Susie Kaldor Heaton
(Mrs. Robert)

Layered Salmon Salad

Planning: Can be done ahead
Preparation Time: 45 minutes

Quantity: 6-8 servings
Chilling Time: 1 hour

Dressing:
1¹/₂ cups mayonnaise
1 tablespoon chopped onion
¹/₂ teaspoon dill weed
¹/₄ cup milk

Salad:
2 cups tomatoes, chopped
2 cups cucumber slices, halved
1 15-ounce can red salmon,
   drained and flaked
2 cups lettuce, shredded
2 cups cooked shell macaroni,
   drained
¹/₂ cup pitted black olives, halved
dill

1. Combine mayonnaise, onion, dill and milk. Chill. **2.** Combine tomatoes, cucumber and salmon. **3.** In a clear glass 3-quart bowl, beginning at bottom of bowl, layer lettuce, macaroni, olives and the combined tomatoes, cucumber and salmon. **4.** Top with dressing and garnish with dill.

Dianne Brink Warren
(Mrs. Adelor)

Shrimp and Lobster Salad ❧

Very elegant.

Planning: None
Preparation Time: 20 minutes

Quantity: 8 servings
Chilling Time: Overnight

8 slices white sandwich bread
butter, softened
1/2 cup onion, minced
2 eggs, hard-boild and chopped
1/2 pound shrimp, cooked
1/2 pound lobster, cooked
1/2 cup celery, finely diced
1 1/2 cups mayonnaise
lettuce

Garnish:
tomatoes
cucumbers
ripe olives

1. Remove crusts from bread. Butter bread and cube.   2. Mix bread cubes, onion and eggs. Chill overnight.
3. Add shrimp, lobster, celery and mayonnaise. Chill.   4. Serve on a bed of lettuce and garnish with tomatoes, cucumbers and ripe olives.

Margie Lahey Skahill
(Mrs. Timothy)

Chicken Salad for Twenty-five

Planning: Can be made up to 2 days
     ahead
Preparation Time: 4 hours

Quantity: 25 servings
Chilling Time: Several hours

Dressing:
3 cups mayonnaise (or
     homemade)
3 tablespoons red wine vinegar
1 scant tablespoon curry powder
1/2 cup western salad dressing
3 tablespoons sugar

Salad:
8 cups cooked chicken, cubed
3 cups chopped celery
2 8 1/2-ounce cans water chestnuts,
     drained and sliced
1 15 1/2-ounce can pitted ripe
     olives, sliced in rings
4 cups seedless white grapes
1 cup slivered almonds, toasted

1. Combine dressing ingredients and mix well.   2. Toss with remaining ingredients except almonds.   3. Refrigerate several hours or overnight to allow flavors to blend.   4. Sprinkle with almonds and serve.

Jane Rife Field
(Mrs. Hugh)

Cherry Chicken Salad
Fresh bing cherries make this recipe elegant.

Planning: Can make ahead
Preparation Time: 45 minutes

Quantity: 6 servings
Chilling Time: 2 hours

Dressing:
1 tablespoon lemon juice
³/₄ cup sour cream
¹/₄ cup mayonnaise
2 tablespoons sugar
¹/₂ teaspoon curry powder
³/₄ cup fresh bing cherries, pitted
   and sliced

Dressing:
1. Combine lemon juice, sour cream, mayonnaise, sugar, and curry; mix. Toss cherries in the dressing. Chill.

Salad:
¹/₄ cup slivered almonds
¹/₄ teaspoon salt
2¹/₂ cups cooked chicken, diced
   (3 or 4 large breasts)
¹/₂ cup chopped celery
¹/₃ cup diced green pepper
lettuce liners (optional)

Salad:
1. Combine remaining ingredients. Add a little dressing to hold it together.
2. To serve, scoop chicken salad with an ice cream scoop onto a plate lined with lettuce. Top with creamy cherry dressing.

Sue Willett Sawyer
(Mrs. Gary)

Chinese Chicken Salad

This is truly unique—and delicious.

Planning: Can be prepared ahead
    except for tossing
Preparation Time: 45 minutes

Quantity: 6 servings
Cooking Time: 45 minutes

Dressing:
2 tablespoons sugar
3 tablespoons Japanese rice
    vinegar
1 teaspoon salt
1 teaspoon MSG
1/4 teaspoon pepper
1/4 cup salad oil
1 tablespoon sesame oil

Dressing:
1. Whisk vinegar, sugar, salt, MSG, and pepper until dissolved.   **2.** Add the salad and sesame oil, whisking a little at a time to emulsify. Set aside.

Salad:
2 chicken breasts, cooked
1 package medium long rice sticks
    (Chinese noodles)
oil
3 large green onions, slivered
2 tablespoons sesame seeds,
    toasted
1 medium head lettuce, sliced
1 4-ounce package slivered
    almonds
3 tablespoons cilantro, chopped

Salad:
1. Finely shred chicken by hand.
2. Fry Chinese noodles in hot oil until they puff—2 to 5 seconds. Drain.
3. Toss chicken, Chinese noodles, green onions, sesame seeds, lettuce, almonds and cilantro.   **4.** Add dressing and serve immediately.

Helen Suzuki Nutting
(Mrs. Joe)

Chicken Artichoke Salad
Delightful served hot or cold.

Planning: Can be made ahead
Preparation Time: 30-45 minutes

Quantity: 6 servings
Baking Time: 35-45 minutes, 350°

1 8-ounce package chicken flavored rice mix
¼ teaspoon curry powder
½ cup mayonnaise
2 green onions, chopped
½ green pepper, chopped
8 green olives, sliced
3 to 4 chicken breasts, baked and cut into small pieces
2 6-ounce jars marinated artichoke hearts, undrained and chopped
parsley (optional)

1. Prepare rice mix according to package directions. Chill if serving cold.
2. Blend curry powder into mayonnaise. Add rice mix and remaining ingredients to mayonnaise and mix together. 3. Chill if serving cold; serve on lettuce. 4. If serving hot, bake for 35 to 45 minutes at 350° 5. Garnish with parsley, if desired.

Mary Strack Kabel
(Mrs. David)

Tropical Luncheon Salad

Planning: Chicken mixture may be done ahead
Preparation Time: 2 hours

Quantity: 16-20 servings
Chilling Time: Several hours

3 cups mayonnaise
2 teaspoons curry
2 tablespoons soy sauce
2 quarts chicken (mostly white meat), cooked and cut in large pieces
2 pounds of green seedless grapes, cut in half if desired
2 8-ounce cans pineapple chunks, drained
1 20-ounce can of water chestnuts, drained and sliced
2 cups celery, diced or sliced
2 to 3 cups slivered almonds, toasted
2 to 3 heads of lettuce for cups or beds

1. Combine mayonnaise, curry, soy sauce. 2. Mix this with chicken pieces (may be done and refrigerated day ahead). 3. Add grapes, pineapple, chestnuts, celery and half of the almonds. 4. Chill several hours.
5. Spoon into lettuce cups and sprinkle with the remaining almonds.

Jane Reed Buck
(Mrs. Dennis)

Pasta Salad Italiano

Colorful and delicious—sure to impress your guests.

Planning: Can be made a day ahead
Preparation Time: 4 hours
  (including refrigeration time)

Quantity: 8-10 servings
Chilling Time: 3 hours

1 8-ounce bottle Italian dressing
  (not creamy)
1 cup broccoli, cut into bite size
  pieces
1/2 cup cauliflower, cut into
  flowerets
1/2 cup fresh mushrooms, sliced
  (optional)
1 can water chestnuts, sliced
1 carrot, diced
1/4 cup olives, sliced (ripe, green,
  or both)
3/4 cup cherry tomatoes, halved
4 ounces spaghetti noodles,
  cooked, drained and chilled
1/4 cup Parmesan cheese
1/4 cup real bacon bits

1. In medium size bowl, pour dressing over vegetables. Cover and marinate in refrigerator at least 3 hours. 2. Cook spaghetti noodles according to package directions. Drain and chill. 3. Drain the marinade from the vegetables. Reserve it. 4. Combine the reserved marinade with the noodles and Parmesan cheese. Toss lightly. 5. Place noodles in a 7" x 11" glass dish or large platter, adding the vegetables to it. 6. Sprinkle with additional cheese and the bacon bits.

Hint: If the spaghetti noodles are broken, it is easier to serve and eat.

Beverly Bergstrom Moser
(Mrs. Larry)

Straw and Hay Salad

Planning: Can be made 4 to 5 days ahead

Preparation Time: About 3 hours

Quantity: 40-50 servings

Cooking Time: About 30 minutes to cook pasta

Pasta Salad:

1 16-ounce package kluski (egg noodles)

1 12-ounce package spinach noodles

1 bunch green onions, coarsely chopped

2 15 1/2-ounce cans seedless black olives, sliced

2 1/2 cups Parmesan cheese, freshly grated, if possible

1 1/2 pounds Genoa salami, cut in 1/4" x 1 1/2" julienne strips

1 recipe vinaigrette dressing

Pasta Salad:

1. Cook kluski in boiling salted water until just tender.   **2.** Drain, rinse, and toss with 1 to 2 tablespoons of oil.
3. Repeat procedure for spinach noodles.   **4.** Place cooked noodles and remaining ingredients into very large mixing bowl and toss with dressing.

Dressing:

3/4 cup red wine vinegar

3 teaspoons salt

1/4 to 1/2 teaspoon pepper, freshly ground

4 teaspoons Dijon mustard

1 1/2 teaspoons basil

1 1/2 teaspoons tarragon

1 1/2 teaspoons thyme

3 cloves garlic, crushed

2 1/4 cups oil (1/2 good grade olive oil and 1/2 corn oil)

Dressing:

1. Whisk vinegar and salt together until salt is dissolved. (Do not add oil until salt is dissolved).   **2.** Whisk in remaining ingredients except oil.   **3.** Whisking constantly, drizzle oil into vinegar-herb mixture until all oil is added.

Jane Rife Field
(Mrs. Hugh)

Spinach Salad Supreme

Planning: Dressing must be made
ahead
Preparation Time: 20 minutes

Quantity: 8 servings
Standing Time: 1 hour or refrigerate
overnight

Spicy Oil and Vinegar Dressing:
3 tablespoons white wine vinegar
1 tablespoon dry vermouth
³/₄ teaspoon sugar
³/₄ teaspoon salt
¹/₂ clove garlic, minced
¹/₂ teaspoon prepared mustard
¹/₈ teaspoon ground pepper
¹/₂ cup olive or salad oil

Spicy Oil and Vinegar Dressing:
1. In a small mixing bowl, combine all
ingredients except the oil. Stir well to
blend.   **2.** Gradually beat in the oil.
3. Cover and let stand 1 hour before
serving or refrigerate overnight.

Salad:
3 bunches of spinach, cleaned,
drained and chilled
1 bunch of watercress, cleaned,
drained and chilled
2 green apples, peeled and
coarsely chopped
1 ripe avocado, peeled and diced
1 cup walnuts, coarsely chopped

Salad:
1. Tear spinach leaves and watercress
into bite-size pieces; put into a bowl.
2. Add prepared apple pieces, avocado
pieces and walnuts. Toss to mix.
3. Pour on dressing. Toss again.
4. Serve on chilled plates.

Margie Lahey Skahill
(Mrs. Timothy)

Spinach and Nut Salad

Very colorful and delicious—almost a meal in itself.

Planning: Can be made ahead, but toss at the last minute

Preparation Time: 20-25 minutes

Quantity: 10-12 servings

Chilling Time: 2-3 hours

1 12-ounce package fresh spinach, cleaned, no stems

¹/₂ to 1 cup fresh chopped parsley

1 cup fresh thinly sliced mushrooms

2 medium tomatoes, diced

1 cup chopped celery

1 ¹/₂ cups fresh bean sprouts

1 ¹/₂ cups Cheddar cheese, shredded

¹/₂ to 1 cup roasted sunflower nuts

¹/₂ teaspoon salt

¹/₂ teaspoon pepper

¹/₂ teaspoon garlic salt

Dressing:

¹/₃ cup garlic vinegar

¹/₃ cup salad oil

³/₄ teaspoon sugar

¹/₂ teaspoon seasoned salt

1. Combine salad ingredients and toss. 2. Combine dressing ingredients and mix well. 3. Pour dressing over salad when ready to serve and toss.

Leslie Nelson Martin
(Mrs. Dennis)

A Berry Delicious Spinach Salad ❧

Beautiful and unique—great for entertaining.

Planning: Can be made ahead, but add dressing just before serving
Preparation Time: 15 minutes

Quantity: 6-8 servings
Baking Time: None

2 bunches fresh spinach, cleaned, dried and torn
1 pint fresh strawberries, cleaned, hulled and halved

Dressing:
¹/₂ cup sugar
2 tablespoons sesame seed
1 tablespoon poppy seed
1¹/₂ teaspoons minced onion
¹/₄ teaspoon Worcestershire sauce
¹/₄ teaspoon paprika
¹/₂ cup vegetable oil
¹/₄ cup cider vinegar

1. Arrange spinach and strawberries on individual serving plates. 2. Place dressing ingredients in blender and blend until thoroughly mixed and thickened. Do not overmix. 3. Drizzle desired amount of dressing over salad and serve immediately. 4. Salad can also be placed in serving bowl and tossed gently with dressing.

Hint: This salad is a must during strawberry season.

Angela Geiger Hamer
Linda Johnston Rust
(Mrs. Larry)

Romaine Salad with Cashews ❧

Planning: None
Preparation Time: 20 minutes

Quantity: 12 servings
Baking Time: None

3 heads romaine lettuce, broken into bite-sized pieces
1 cup salted cashews
¹/₂ cup thinly sliced sweet red onion
¹/₂ cup garbanzo beans, rinsed and drained
¹/₄ cup cider vinegar
¹/₂ cup salad oil
1 tablespoon Dijon mustard
pinch cumin
pinch cardamon (optional)

1. Combine lettuce, cashews, onion and garbanzo beans in large glass salad bowl. 2. In small covered jar, combine vinegar, oil, mustard, cumin, and cardamon; shake well. 3. When ready to serve, pour dressing over salad and toss gently.

Janice Schukei Hahn
(Mrs. William)

Orange-Almond Salad

Outstanding combination of flavors and textures.

Planning: Can be made ahead, but add bacon, almonds and dressing when ready to serve
Preparation Time: 30-45 minutes

Quantity: 4-6 servings
Chilling Time: A few hours

Dressing:
- ¹/₄ cup vegetable oil
- 2 tablespoons sugar
- 2 tablespoons vinegar
- ¹/₄ teaspoon salt
- ¹/₄ teaspoon almond extract

Dressing:
1. Combine oil, sugar, vinegar, salt and almond extract.   2. Mix well and chill.

Salad:
- 6 cups mixed greens (romaine or leaf lettuce)
- 1 11-ounce can mandarin oranges, drained
- 1 cup sliced celery
- 6 slices bacon, fried crisp and crumbled
- ¹/₃ cup slivered almonds, toasted

Salad:
1. Combine greens, oranges, and celery.   2. Just prior to serving, add bacon and almonds.   3. Pour dressing over all and lightly toss.

Ellie Kennedy Everitt
(Mrs. David)
Suzanne Colbert Goodell
(Mrs. James)

Avocado Salad
Serve to special guests.

Planning: Can be made ahead
Preparation Time: 30 minutes

Quantity: 8-10 servings
Chilling Time: 1 hour

Dressing:
1 clove garlic, minced
2 tablespoons onion, grated
2 tablespoons capers, chopped
1 tablespoon chopped parsley
$^1/_2$ teaspoon chopped chives
$^1/_2$ teaspoon sugar
$^1/_2$ cup olive oil
$^1/_4$ cup tarragon vinegar
1 teaspoon salt
$^1/_2$ teaspoon pepper

1. Combine the dressing ingredients and mix well.   **2.** Tear the romaine lettuce leaves and separate the endive. Combine the greens and the avocado in a salad bowl.   **3.** Pour dressing over the greens and toss lightly. Chill for one hour. Toss again before serving.

Salad:
2 heads romaine lettuce
1 head endive lettuce
1 avocado, peeled and thinly
   sliced

Hint: For variation, add sliced fresh mushrooms to the salad.

*Norma Smith Hassman
(Mrs. Dale)*

Mixed Greens and Artichoke Salad ❧

A good salad to serve with a grilled meal.

Planning: Can be made ahead, except for adding dressing
Preparation Time: 15-20 minutes

Quantity: 4 servings
Chilling Time: Until ready to serve.

Dressing:
1/2 cup salad oil
1/4 cup tarragon vinegar
1 teaspoon salad seasoning (salad dressing envelope mix)

Salad:
4 cups torn mixed greens (spinach, leaf, iceberg lettuce)
1 6-ounce jar marinated artichoke hearts, drained and quartered
8 cherry tomatoes, halved
freshly ground pepper
salt
sesame seed

1. In screw-top jar, combine dressing ingredients and shake well. Chill.
2. At serving time, combine salad greens, artichoke hearts and tomatoes. **3.** Shake dressing well again and add enough to coat salad well; toss.
4. Sprinkle salad with pepper, salt and sesame seed.

Connie Stroh Werner
(Mrs. Charles, Jr.)

Herbed Garden Vegetable Salad

Planning: Must be made ahead
Preparation Time: 30-40 minutes

Quantity: 8 servings
Chilling Time: Several hours

3/4 cup vegetable oil
1/3 cup cider vinegar
1 tablespoon parsley flakes
1/2 teaspoon salt
1 1/2 teaspoons basil leaves, crushed
1 teaspoon onion powder
1/2 teaspoon garlic powder
1/4 teaspoon black pepper
6 cups warm cooked potatoes, peeled and sliced
3 cups warm cooked green beans, cut
2 cups warm cooked carrots, peeled and sliced
chives (optional)

1. In a small covered jar, combine oil, vinegar, parsley flakes, salt, basil, onion and garlic powders and black pepper; shake well. **2.** In large bowl, combine warm potatoes, beans and carrots; toss gently. **3.** Pour in enough dressing mix to coat vegetables thoroughly.
4. Cover and chill vegetables several hours, tossing occasionally. **5.** When ready to serve, add more dressing if needed and chill any remaining dressing. **6.** Garnish with chives if desired.

Mary Jo Rymars Piech
(Mrs. Drury)

Asparagus Vinaigrette 🌿

Very attractive—good for a dinner party.

Planning: Must do ahead for better blend of flavors
Preparation Time: 20-30 minutes

Quantity: 8 servings
Baking Time: None

Sauce Vinaigrette:
1/4 cup white wine vinegar
1 teaspoon salt
freshly ground black pepper
1/2 teaspoon tarragon
1/2 teaspoon chervil
sprig parsley, finely minced
1 teaspoon chives, snipped (or 1 teaspoon freeze-dried chives)
3/4 cup salad oil

Sauce Vinaigrette:
1. In a screw-top jar, combine vinegar, salt, pepper, tarragon, chervil, parsley and chives.   2. As soon as the salt had dissolved and the dried herbs have freshened, add the oil and shake. Chill thoroughly.

2 pounds fresh, young asparagus
pimento strips for garnish
Boston or Bibb lettuce for lining salad plates

1. Wash asparagus; trim away ends evenly, making sure to discard any woody or tough parts. Cook until tender, being careful not to overcook.
2. Lay asparagus in flat container and immediately drizzle generously with Sauce Vinaigrette. Refrigerate until serving time.   3. At serving time, drain asparagus and arrange individual servings on lettuce-lined salad plates.
4. Garnish with Mimosa garnish and crisscross two strips of pimento at mid-stalk of each serving.

Mimosa Garnish:
1 egg, hard-boiled
parsley, fresh and finely minced

Mimosa Garnish:
1. Grate the hard-boiled egg into fine particles. Combine with an equal amount of finely minced parsley.

Margie Lahey Skahill
(Mrs. Timothy)

Creamy Raw Vegetable Salad ❧

A favorite and attractive salad to be used anytime.

Planning: Must be made ahead
Preparation Time: 45 minutes

Quantity: 10 servings
Chilling Time: 2 hours

Dressing:
1 cup green onion, chopped
1 cup sour cream
1 cup mayonnaise
2 tablespoons sugar
2 tablespoons vinegar
dash of red hot pepper sauce
dash of Worcestershire sauce
salt to taste

Dressing:
1. Combine dressing ingredients and mix well.   2. Let dressing chill for several hours to blend flavors.

Salad:
1 medium head cauliflower, cut into small flowerets
1 medium bunch of broccoli, cut into bite-size pieces
2 cups frozen peas, uncooked
6 stalks of celery, cut into bite-size pieces
cherry tomatoes, halved

Salad:
1. Mix together cauliflower, broccoli, frozen peas and celery in large bowl. Set aside in refrigerator.   2. Approximately 1 to 2 hours before serving, pour dressing over vegetables. Toss, and refrigerate until ready to serve.   3. Serve in a glass bowl and garnish with cherry tomatoes.

Mary Manning Bracken
(Mrs. Robert)

Dilly Carrots

Planning: Must be made ahead
Preparation Time: Overnight

Quantity: 6-8 servings
Chilling Time: Several hours

1 pound carrots, cut into small sticks or coin shapes
1 cup dill pickle juice (from regular dill pickles, not kosher dills)
1/2 pint sour cream
1 teaspoon dried dill weed
1/4 teaspoon salt
1/8 teaspoon pepper

1. Boil carrots in pickle juice until barely tender. Chill overnight in juice.
2. Next day, drain carrots well. Add sour cream, dill weed, salt and pepper.
3. Chill before serving for several hours.

Mary Strack Kabel
(Mrs. David)

Petite Vegetable Salad
Better than a 3-bean salad.

Planning: Must be made ahead
Preparation Time: 20 minutes

Quantity: 12 servings
Cooking Time: 5 minutes
Standing Time: Overnight

Marinade:
1/2 cup salad oil
1/2 cup sugar
3/4 cup vinegar
1 teaspoon salt
1 teaspoon celery seed

Marinade:
1. Combine marinade ingredients (except for celery seed) and boil for 3 minutes. 2. Cool and add celery seed.

Vegetable Mixture:
1 8-ounce can white shoepeg
  (small kernel) corn, drained
1 8-ounce can tiny peas, drained
1 8-ounce can French-style green
  beans, drained
(Use an 8-ounce can to measure
  the next three ingredients)
1 cup chopped raw carrots
1 cup chopped celery
1/2 cup chopped onion
1 whole green pepper, chopped

Vegetable Mixture:
1. Mix vegetables together. 2. Pour cooled marinade over vegetables.
3. Let stand overnight in refrigerator.

Mary Lutgen Lichty
(Mrs. R. F.)

Calico Corn Salad ❧
Great with barbecued meats or Mexican dishes.

Planning: Must be made ahead
Preparation Time: 20 minutes

Quantity: 8 servings
Chilling Time: Several hours

2 12-ounce cans corn, well
  drained
1/4 cup red onion, chopped
1/3 cup green pepper, chopped
1 4-ounce jar pimento, chopped
  and drained
1/3 cup salad dressing
1/3 cup sour cream
salt and pepper to taste

1. Combine vegetables in medium bowl. 2. In small bowl, mix salad dressing, sour cream, salt and pepper.
3. Blend salad dressing mixture with vegetables. 4. Chill for several hours before serving.

Deborah Prust Adams
(Mrs. David)

Cheesy Cauliflower Salad

Great for summer.

Planning: Keeps well 3 to 4 days

Preparation Time: 20 minutes (easy to prepare with a food processor)

Quantity: 6-8 servings

Chilling Time: Until ready to serve

1 medium head cauliflower, chopped, or in small flowerets
1/2 cup chopped celery
1 green pepper, chopped
1 red onion, sliced and separated into rings
8 (or more) ripe olives, sliced
8 (or more) green olives, drained
small jar red pimento, drained
8-ounces Cheddar cheese, grated

Dressing:
1 8-ounce carton sour cream
1 8-ounce jar creamy Caesar salad dressing
2 tablespoons ripe olive juice (use this juice to rinse out salad dressing container)

1. Combine salad ingredients in a bowl. 2. Mix dressing ingredients and pour over salad. 3. Marinate in refrigerator until ready to serve.

Hint: Chop, slice or dice vegetables according to your preference.

Norma Smith Hassman
(Mrs. Dale)

Green 'n Gold Salad

Unique and pretty.

Planning: Must be made ahead
Preparation Time: 30 minutes

Quantity: 6-8 servings
Chilling Time: 6 hours

Marinade:
1/2 cup mayonnaise
2 tablespoons vinegar
2 tablespoons sugar
4 tablespoons milk

1. Combine marinade ingredients.
2. Combine remaining ingredients and pour marinade over salad ingredients.
3. Put in refrigerator and let flavors mingle six hours or more.   4. Add the bacon just before serving.

Salad:
1/2 pound bacon, fried crisp and
   crumbled
1 1/2 pounds fresh broccoli,
   chopped
1/2 cup dry roasted sunflower
   seeds
1/2 cup golden raisins
3 tablespoons minced onion

Joan Dawson Huhn
(Mrs. Kenneth)

Nutty Pea Salad

You'll love the flavors and crunchiness.

Planning: None
Preparation Time: 20 minutes

Quantity: 10 1/2-cup servings
Chilling Time: Overnight

1 20-ounce package frozen peas
1/4 teaspoon minced onion
1 cup chopped celery
1/2 pound bacon, fried crisp and
   crumbled
1/2 cup sour cream
1/4 cup mayonnaise
1/4 teaspoon seasoned salt
1/2 cup Spanish peanuts
1/2 cup Cheddar cheese, shredded
   (optional)

1. Cook frozen peas according to directions on package and salt to taste; drain.   2. Combine all ingredients with peas except for peanuts and cheddar cheese.   3. Refrigerate overnight.
4. Add peanuts just before serving.
5. If desired, sprinkle Cheddar cheese on top for garnish.

Cheri French O'Connor
(Mrs. Gary)

Pea Pod Salad

Something different for a summer salad.

Planning: Can be made ahead
Preparation Time: 30 minutes

Quantity: 8 servings
Chilling Time: Until ready to serve

3 cups fresh pea pods or 2 6-ounce
    packages frozen pea pods, cut
    into 1" pieces
1 medium head cauliflower, cut
    into flowerets
2 cups celery, diced
1 10-ounce package frozen peas,
    partially thawed and separated
1/2 cup chopped green onions
1 8-ounce can water chestnuts,
    sliced

1. In a large bowl, combine vegetables. 2. Blend all dressing ingredients together. 3. Pour dressing over vegetables and toss. 4. Cover and chill.

Dressing:
1 cup mayonnaise
1 cup sour cream
1 teaspoon garlic powder
1/4 teaspoon salt
1/4 teaspoon pepper
1/2 teaspoon Worcestershire sauce

Hint: Keeps well 3 or 4 days in refrigerator.

Carol Hayes Steckelberg
(Mrs. Randy)

Stuffed Tomatoes

Easy, low calorie and an attractive way to use all those garden tomatoes.

Planning: Can do ahead; stuffing must marinate for 2 hours
Preparation Time: 30 minutes

Quantity: 6 servings
Chilling Time: 2 hours

Stuffing:
1 9-ounce package of frozen Italian green beans, cooked and drained (or use cooked fresh beans)
1 3-ounce can sliced mushrooms, drained (or use fresh mushrooms)
1/3 cup low calorie Italian salad dressing
1/4 cup green onions, sliced
1/4 teaspoon salt

Stuffing:
1. Toss stuffing ingredients together.
2. Refrigerate stuffing ingredients for 2 hours.

Shells:
6 medium tomatoes
pepper
6 lettuce leaves (optional)

Shells:
1. Cut a thin slice from top of each tomato. Scoop out center leaving shell about 1/4" thick. Invert on paper towel to drain. Chill. 2. At serving time season shells with salt and fill with bean mixture. 3. Serve on lettuce leaf, if desired.

Donna Robinson Brown
(Mrs. Gary)

Simply Super Tomatoes ❧

Herby, tangy flavor—use with a summer menu.

Planning: Can make dressing ahead; must marinate tomatoes 1 to 2 hours
Preparation Time: 15 minutes

Quantity: 6 servings
Chilling Time: 1-2 hours

Dressing:
²/₃ cup oil
¹/₄ cup wine vinegar
¹/₄ cup parsley, chopped
¹/₄ cup chopped green onion
   (including tops)
1 garlic clove, minced
1 teaspoon salt
1 teaspoon dill weed
1 teaspoon basil
¹/₄ teaspoon pepper

6 firm, medium tomatoes, peeled
   and sliced ¹/₂" thick

1. In a small bowl or screw-top jar, combine dressing ingredients and mix well.   **2.** Arrange sliced tomatoes in a serving dish. Pour dressing over tomatoes.   **3.** Cover; chill 1 to 2 hours, basting occasionally.

Sue Willett Sawyer
(Mrs. Gary)

Sauerkraut Salad ❧

Planning: Must be made ahead
Preparation Time: 20 minutes

Quantity: 10 servings
Chilling Time: Several hours

1 32-ounce can sauerkraut,
   squeezed dry
³/₄ cup chopped celery
³/₄ cup chopped onion
1 cup green pepper, chopped
1 4-ounce jar sliced pimento,
   drained
1 cup sugar
¹/₃ cup vinegar

Hint: Serve in glass bowl.

1. Combine vegetables in large bowl.
2. Melt sugar with vinegar over low heat.   **3.** Pour dressing over vegetables and mix well.   **4.** Chill for several hours or overnight.

Tricia McArthur Elmer
(Mrs. Clark)

Springtime New Potato-Bean Salad

Planning: Requires food processor
Preparation Time: 45 minutes

Quantity: 6 servings
Cooking Time: 25 minutes

Dressing:
4 egg yolks, at room temperature
$1/3$ cup red wine vinegar
1 teaspoon Dijon mustard
$1/2$ teaspoon salt
freshly ground pepper
1 cup plus 2 tablespoons salad oil

Salad:
1$1/2$ pound small new potatoes
3 teaspoons salt
$1/2$ pound fresh green beans
$1/2$ cup walnuts, chopped
$1/4$ cup minced onion
$1/4$ cup parsley, chopped
freshly ground pepper
Boston lettuce leaves

Dressing:
1. In food processor, combine egg yolks, vinegar, mustard, salt and pepper.
2. Cover and process until well mixed. With motor running drizzle oil through the feed tube in a thin stream. Process just until all oil is added.

Salad:
1. Cook whole unpeeled potatoes in boiling water with cover with 1 teaspoon salt until fork-tender. Drain and let cool to room temperature.   2. Trim ends from beans and cut in half crosswise. Cook beans in boiling water with remaining salt just until crisp tender, about 8 minutes.   3. In large bowl, combine cooled potatoes, cut into $1/2$" slices, beans, walnuts, onions, parsley, dressing, and pepper to taste. Toss well.   4. Arrange lettuce leaves on serving platter; top with salad. Serve at room temperature.

Diana Lichty Hansen
(Mrs. Milton)

Greek Potato Salad

Planning: None
Preparation Time: 5-20 minutes

Quantity: 10-12 servings
Boiling Time: 20-30 minutes

5 pounds of potatoes, washed and
    scrubbed
³/₄ cup olive oil
juice of ¹/₂ to 1 lemon
¹/₂ cup minced onions
3 tablespoons parsley, minced
2 teaspoon oregano
salt and pepper to taste
parsley sprigs
lemon slices

1. Boil potatoes until tender. Cool, peel, and dice. 2. Whisk olive oil and juice of ¹/₂ lemon together until creamy, in a small bowl. Add minced onions and let marinate for 10 to 15 minutes.
3. Sprinkle potatoes with parsley and oregano. 4. Pour marinated mixture over potatoes and toss. Add more lemon juice, salt and pepper to taste. 5. Garnish with parsley sprigs and lemon slices.

Karen Karman Gartelos
(Mrs. Peter)

Glazed Fruit Salad
Serve this at your next party.

Planning: Must be made ahead
Preparation Time: 15 minutes

Quantity: 12-16 servings
Chilling Time: Overnight

2 eggs, beaten
3 cups light brown sugar
1 cup evaporated milk
1 tablespoon white vinegar
1 tablespoon cornstarch
24 cups fruit, any combination or
    simply oranges and bananas
¹/₂ cup peanuts, chopped
    (optional)

1. Place beaten eggs in sauce pan and add sugar, milk, vinegar and cornstarch. 2. Heat until thick. 3. Transfer into bowl and refrigerate overnight. 4. Prepare fresh fruit just before serving and spoon cold sauce over fruit. 5. Pour into a large glass bowl and, if desired, sprinkle with peanuts.

Nancy Allbee Fox
(Mrs. James)

Fresh Fruit Kabobs

Makes an attractive addition to brunch, a luncheon, or a buffet table.

Planning: Can be made ahead
Preparation Time: 1 hour

Quantity: Several servings
Chilling Time: Until ready to serve

Dressing:
1 7-ounce jar marshmallow creme
1 8-ounce carton whipping cream, whipped
1 teaspoon orange rind, grated
¼ teaspoon ginger
½ teaspoon cinnamon

Possible Fruits to Use:
pineapple chunks
watermelon chunks or balls
cantaloupe chunks or balls
honey dew melon chunks or balls
banana slices, dipped in lemon juice
grapes
strawberries
Monterey Jack cheese, cubed

1. For dressing, combine marshmallow creme and whipped cream until smooth. Add orange rind and spices; stir and refrigerate until served. **2.** For the kabobs, use whatever combination of fruits you like and place on skewer in order of colors, using cheese cubes every third piece. **3.** Arrange skewers in a tall glass bowl or on a serving plate. Serve with dressing in a small bowl.

Hint: Try this dressing with pound cake, apple cake or pie.

Barb Stoen Dowd
(Mrs. Don)

Million Dollar Salad

The added lemon sauce is outstanding.

Planning: Must be made ahead
Preparation Time: 30 minutes

Quantity: 8 servings
Chilling Time: Overnight

1 fresh medium pineapple, cut
    into chunks and drained or 1
    2-pound can pineapple chunks,
    drained
4 cups miniature marshmallows
1 cup slivered almonds, lightly
    toasted
1 cup sour cream
¹/₂ cup mayonnaise
1 1-pound can dark pitted
    cherries, well drained

1. Combine first 5 ingredients in large bowl. Refrigerate overnight. **2.** Just before serving, fold in cherries. Serve with dressing on the side.

Dressing:
1 cup pineapple juice
6 tablespoons sugar
5 tablespoons lemon juice
3 large egg yolks, lightly beaten
1 tablespoon lemon peel, grated

Dressing:
1. Combine all ingredients except lemon peel in top double boiler. Cook over gently, boiling water, stirring frequently, until thickened, about 15 minutes. **2.** Remove from heat and stir in lemon peel. **3.** Cool completely before serving. It will thicken more as it cools.

Linda Johnston Rust
(Mrs. Larry)

Strawberry Frozen Fruit Salad ❧

The strawberries and cream cheese make this delightful.

Planning: Must be made ahead
Preparation Time: 10 minutes

Quantity: 12-16 servings
Freezing Time: 6-8 hours

1 8-ounce package cream cheese
³/₄ cup sugar
1 20-ounce can crushed pineapple, drained
1 10-ounce package frozen strawberries with juice, partially thawed
1 12-ounce container frozen dessert topping
3 bananas, halved and sliced
walnuts, chopped (optional)
fresh strawberries (optional)

1. Soften cream cheese with fork. Add sugar and mix.   2. Add pineapple, strawberries, and frozen topping. Mix well. Stir in bananas.   3. Put in 9" x 13" pan and freeze 6 to 8 hours.
4. Cut in squares. If desired, garnish with some chopped walnuts and/or a fresh strawberry.

Sandy Smith Ritland
(Mrs. George)

Party Cranberry Salad

Good for Thanksgiving dinner with turkey.

Planning: Must be made ahead; needs a 10-cup mold
Preparation Time: 45 minutes

Quantity: 12-16 servings
Chilling Time: Several hours

1 pound fresh cranberries, ground
2 cups sugar
1 tablespoon unflavored gelatin
¹/₄ cup cold water
1 cup miniature marshmallows
¹/₂ cup pecans, chopped
1 cup white grapes, sliced
1 cup whipping cream

1. Add the sugar to the ground cranberries. Let stand for several hours.
2. Pour off the juice from the cranberries and bring to a boil. Add the gelatin, dissolved in the ¹/₄ cup cold water, to the cranberry juice. Add the ground cranberries, marshmallows, nuts and grapes. Let the mixture cool until it begins to thicken.   3. Whip the cream and add to the slightly thickened gelatin mix and put in a mold.   4. Chill several hours until firm.

Parkey Harris Copeland
(Mrs. Hugh)

Eggnog Mold with Raspberry Sauce
An exciting addition to a festive meal.

Planning: Can do ahead; recipe can be cut in half
Preparation Time: 1 hour

Quantity: 12 servings
Chilling Time: 2-3 hours

5 cups dairy eggnog
¹/₃ cup sugar
3 envelopes (about 3 tablespoons) unflavored gelatin
6 tablespoons cold water
¹/₂ teaspoon ground nutmeg
2 cups whipping cream

1. Heat 1 cup eggnog to scalding. Stir in sugar. Set aside. **2.** Sprinkle gelatin over cold water to soften. **3.** Stir softened gelatin into hot eggnog mixture. **4.** Heat and stir until gelatin is dissolved. **5.** Pour into large bowl; stir in remaining eggnog and nutmeg. Chill until slightly thickened. **6.** Whip cream until very thick. Fold into thickened eggnog. **7.** Spoon into 8-cup mold. Chill until set. **8.** To serve, invert mold onto serving platter. Drizzle sauce over, reserving extra to pass.

Raspberry Sauce:
2 10-ounce packages frozen raspberries, thawed
2 tablespoons cornstarch
2 tablespoons brandy

Raspberry Sauce:
1. Prepare raspberry sauce by draining raspberries into measuring cup (about 1¹/₂ cups). Reserve juice. **2.** Blend juice and cornstarch in small saucepan until smooth. Heat to boiling, stirring constantly. **3.** Boil and stir until thickened and clear. **4.** Stir in raspberries and brandy and cool.

Cynthia Staley Kenyon
(Mrs. James)

Iowa Corn Relish

Planning: Sterilize pint jars
Preparation Time: 2 hours

Quantity: 16 pints
Cooking Time: One hour

12 ears sweet corn, cut off cob
2 red peppers, diced
4 green peppers, diced
1 quart onions, chopped
1 quart nearly ripe cucumbers, peeled and diced
1 quart ripe tomatoes, peeled and chopped
1 quart vinegar
3 cups sugar
1/2 cup salt
2 teaspoons turmeric
5 teaspoons mustard seed

1. Put all ingredients into a large container and bring to a boil; stir occasionally to prevent burning. 2. Boil for one hour. 3. Pour relish into sterilized jars and seal.

Deborah Vonnahme Pedersen
(Mrs. Robert)

Green Pepper Jelly

Planning: Sterilized jars
Preparation Time: 20 minutes

Quantity: Eight 1-cup jars
Cooking Time: 5 minutes

3 very large green peppers
1 1/2 cups cider vinegar
6 1/2 cups sugar
1 tablespoon cayenne pepper
1/2 teaspoon salt
1 6-ounce bottle fruit pectin
green food coloring
paraffin wax

1. Cut green peppers into small pieces and blend in blender with 1/2 cup vinegar 2. Combine pepper mixture with remaining vinegar, sugar, cayenne pepper and salt in saucepan. 3. Boil for 5 minutes. 4. Cool 2 minutes and add fruit pectin and food coloring.
5. Pour into jars and seal with wax.

Hint: Leave out cayenne pepper and blend 5 jalapeno peppers with the green peppers. Then add red food coloring instead of green. Can be served over cream cheese using rich butter crackers. May be used instead of mint jelly.

Sharon Gossman Fereday
(Mrs. Thomas)

Wine-Cranberry Sauce for Ham ❧

Planning: None
Preparation Time: 10 minutes

Quantity: 1½ cups sauce
Cooking Time: 5 minutes for sauce;
30 minutes with ham

1 cup brown sugar
1 16-ounce can whole cranberries
½ cup burgundy wine
2 teaspoons dry mustard

1. Stir together all the ingredients.
2. Simmer uncovered for 5 minutes.
3. Pour ½ of the mixture over ham the last 30 minutes of baking.   4. Reserve ½ of the mixture to put on the table to serve as a sauce with the ham.

Hint: An easy and tasty condiment for canned or smoked ham.

Marsha Kohler Fisher
(Mrs. Michael)

Spaghetti Sauce 🐖

Planning: None
Preparation Time: 20 minutes

Quantity: 10-12 servings
Cooking Time: 2½ hours

1 16-ounce can tomatoes
2 8-ounce cans tomato sauce
1 13-ounce can tomato paste
1 cup chopped onion
2 pounds ground beef
2 eggs
3 or 4 pounds Italian sausage
salt and pepper

1. Combine tomatoes, tomato sauce, tomato paste and ½ cup chopped onion in large pot.   2. Fill each can ¼ to ½ full of water and add to sauce.
3. Start heating and stir occasionally.
4. Combine ½ cup chopped onion, ground beef and eggs and form meatballs. Brown and add to sauce.   5. Cut sausage into 1" pieces and brown and add to sauce. Season with salt and pepper.   6. Reduce heat, cover and simmer gently for two hours. Stir occasionally. Sauce will reduce and thicken. Serve on spaghetti.

Eileen Madigan Bolster
(Mrs. William)

Smokey Barbecue Sauce ❧

Planning: 2 weeks in advance
Preparation Time: 10 minutes

Quantity: 1 quart
Baking Time: None

2 cups ketchup
8 tablespoons brown sugar
4 tablespoons Worcestershire
　　sauce
4 tablespoons vinegar
4 teaspoons chili powder
4 teaspoons liquid smoke
2 teaspoons dry mustard
2 teaspoons onion salt
2 teaspoons garlic salt

1. Combine all ingredients in a 1-quart jar. **2.** Shake well to combine.

Gina Swaim Greene
(Mrs. Paul)

Chinese Barbecue Sauce ❧

Planning: None
Preparation Time: 10 minutes

Quantity: Approximately 3 cups or
　　enough for large amount of ribs or
　　2 chickens
Marinating Time: 1 hour or
　　overnight

5 cloves of garlic
5 tablespoons brown sugar
1 cup hoisin sauce
1 cup soy sauce
1 cup cooking sherry

1. Peel garlic, smash with heavy knife and chop. **2.** Stir all ingredients together. **3.** Let meat marinate an hour at room temperature or overnight in refrigerator. **4.** Store extra marinade in refrigerator.

Hint: Buy hoisin sauce in oriental market or specialty shop. Sauce may be used on country style pork ribs or quartered chickens.

Anna Griffith Randall
(Mrs. Ross)

EGGS, CHEESE & PASTA

EGGS, CHEESE & PASTA

Shrimp and Crabmeat Scrambled Eggs

Planning: Cannot be made ahead
Preparation Time: 30 minutes

Quantity: 6 servings
Cooking Time: 20 minutes

7 ounces cooked shrimp
7¹/₂ ounces cooked crabmeat
3 tablespoons dry sherry
6 tablespoons butter
2 tablespoons flour
³/₄ cup milk
1 tablespoon chives, chopped
12 eggs
1 teaspoon seasoned salt
¹/₈ teaspoon pepper
4 drops red hot pepper sauce
chives, chopped

1. In medium bowl mix shrimp, crabmeat and sherry, set aside. 2. Melt 2 tablespoons butter in medium saucepan. Remove from heat; stir in flour until smooth. 3. Gradually stir in milk. Bring to boil, stirring constantly. 4. Reduce heat; simmer 1 minute. Stir in the chives and shrimp/crabmeat mixture. Set aside. 5. In large bowl combine eggs, salt, pepper and red hot pepper sauce. Beat until well combined. 6. In large skillet, heat remaining 4 tablespoons butter until bubbly. Pour in egg mixture, cook over low heat. 7. When bottom of egg begins to set, stir with a spatula until partially cooked. Stir in seafood mixture. Cook until eggs are done. Sprinkle with chopped chives.

Diana Lichty Hansen
(Mrs. Milton)

Egg Casserole

Planning: Can prepare ahead
Preparation Time: 1 hour

Quantity: 10 servings
Baking Time: 45 minutes, 350°

White Sauce:
¹/₂ cup butter
¹/₂ cup flour
4 cups milk
¹/₄ teaspoon basil
¹/₄ teaspoon thyme
¹/₄ teaspoon marjoram
salt to taste
pepper to taste
2 pounds Cheddar cheese, grated

White Sauce
1. Over medium heat, melt butter and stir in flour. Cook 2 to 3 minutes.
2. Add milk and cook, stirring constantly until sauce thickens and boils.
3. Add seasonings and cheese and cook, stirring constantly, until cheese melts.

Assembly:
3 dozen hard-boiled eggs, sliced
1 pound bacon, cooked crisp and crumbled
2 tablespoons chopped parsley

Assembly:
1. Layer egg slices, bacon, and sauce in a greased 3-quart casserole. Sprinkle parsley on top. **2.** Bake 45 minutes at 350°.

Hint: Serve for brunch with a sweet roll or danish and fresh fruit.

Jane Rife Field
(Mrs. Hugh)

Ham-Broccoli-Egg Casserole

Planning: Prepare 1 day ahead
Preparation Time: 45 minutes

Quantity: 10 servings
Cooking Time: 55-60 minutes, 325°

12 slices bread, crusts trimmed and cubed
1 10-ounch package frozen broccoli, chopped and cooked crisp tender (a comparable amount of fresh broccoli, chopped and crisp cooked can be used)
2 cups cooked ham, cubed
3 cups Cheddar cheese, shredded
1 tablespoon onion, minced
3¹/₂ cups milk
6 eggs, slightly beaten
¹/₄ teaspoon dry mustard

1. Remove crusts and dice the bread into ¹/₂″ cubes. **2.** Layer bread, broccoli, ham, cheese and onion in a greased 3-quart casserole. **3.** Repeat layering. **4.** Mix milk, eggs and dry mustard together and pour over all.
5. Refrigerate several hours or overnight. **6.** Bake at 325° for 55 to 60 minutes.

Jane Rife Field
(Mrs. Hugh)

120

Midwest Enchiladas

Planning: Prepare 1 day ahead
Preparation Time: 30 minutes

Quantity: 8 servings
Cooking Time: 48-53 minutes

12 ounces or 2 cups cooked ham, ground
1/2 cup sliced green onions
1/2 cup chopped green peppers
2 1/2 cups Cheddar cheese, shredded
8 7" flour tortillas
4 eggs, beaten
2 cups light cream or milk
1 tablespoon all-purpose flour
1/4 teaspoon salt
1/4 teaspoon garlic powder
3 drops red hot pepper sauce

1. Combine in bowl ground ham, onions and green pepper. 2. Place 1/3 cup of the mixture and 3 tablespoons shredded cheese at one end of each tortilla. 3. Roll up. 4. Arrange tortillas, seam side down in a greased 12" x 8" baking dish. 5. Combine eggs, cream, flour, salt, garlic powder, and hot pepper sauce. 6. Pour over tortillas. 7. Cover and refrigerate several hours or overnight. 8. Bake uncovered, in 350° oven for 45 to 50 minutes or until set. 9. Sprinkle with remaining cheese. 10. Bake 3 minutes more or until cheese is melted. 11. Let stand 10 minutes.

Hint: Great for late breakfast or brunch. Serve with fresh fruit for a new twist for breakfast.

Marty McNutt Port
(Mrs. Dale)

Quick Cheese Casserole

Planning: Can prepare ahead of time
Preparation Time: 15 minutes

Quantity: 8 servings
Baking Time: 1 hour, 350°

6 ounces processed American cheese
2 ounces sharp Cheddar cheese
6 tablespoons butter
2 1/2 tablespoons flour
4 eggs, well-beaten
1 6-ounce can green chilies, chopped
3 drops hot red pepper sauce

1. Cube cheeses and butter and mix together. 2. Add other ingredients to cheese mixture and bake. Bake in a greased 8 1/2" x 11" pan at 350° for 1 hour.

Hint: Good for brunch with fresh fruit, muffins and/or sweet rolls.

Patricia Callahan Berry
(Mrs. Earl)

Never-Fail Cheese Soufflé ⊌

Planning: Prepare 1 day ahead
Preparation Time: 20 minutes

Quantity: 6-8 servings
Baking Time: 1 hour, 350°

8 slices day-old bread
1/4 cup butter
1 5-ounce jar Old English
   cheese spread
4 eggs, slightly beaten
2 cups warm milk
1/8 teaspoon salt

1. Remove crusts and dice the bread into 1/2" cubes. Set aside.   **2.** Melt butter and cheese in double boiler. **3.** Remove melted cheese mixture from heat and add slightly beaten eggs. Stir well.   **4.** Add salt and warm milk. **5.** Put bread cubes into greased 2-quart casserole.   **6.** Pour sauce over and stir lightly.   **7.** Refrigerate several hours or overnight.   **8.** Bake uncovered at 350° for 1 hour, with casserole set in a 9" x 13" pan of warm water.

Cynthia Staley Kenyon
(Mrs. James)

Easy Clam Alfredo ⊌

Planning: Sauce can be made ahead
Preparation Time: 5 minutes

Quantity: 3-4 servings
Cooking Time: 30 minutes

1 12-ounce package vermicelli
2 6 1/2-ounce cans minced clams
1/4 cup Parmesan cheese, grated
1/4 cup Romano cheese, grated
3/4 cup milk
2 tablespoons cornstarch
1/4 teaspoon garlic powder
1 teaspoon dried parsley
3 tablespoons butter
salt
pepper

1. Drain and reserve clam liquid. **2.** Mix all other ingredients (except vermicelli) and stir over low heat until thick. (Stir often, if using a microwave.)   **3.** Add clam liquid and continue stirring until blended.   **4.** Keep hot over low heat while cooking vermicelli.   **5.** Cook vermicelli according to package directions.   **6.** Pour sauce over pasta and serve on large platter.

Hint: Serve with spinach salad and white wine.

Rae Murphy Freet
(Mrs. Dennis)

Shrimp Tetrazzini

Planning: May be prepared ahead
Preparation Time: 25 minutes

Quantity: 6-8 servings
Baking Time: 8 minutes for individual casseroles, 15 minutes for 9" x 13" casserole, 375°

1/2 cup butter
1 cup thinly sliced green onions (including some tops)
5 tablespoons flour
2 1/2 cups chicken broth (canned or fresh)
1/2 cup clam juice
1/2 cup dry white wine
1/2 cup whipping cream
1/2 cup fresh Parmesan cheese, grated
2 whole cloves garlic
1/2 pound mushrooms, sliced
salted water
8 ounces noodles (spaghetti or vermicelli)
4 cups shrimp, shelled, cooked and deveined
salt

1. Melt 1/4 cup of butter in 2-quart saucepan, add onion and cook, stirring until soft. 2. Mix in flour and gradually blend in chicken broth, clam juice, wine and cream. Cook stirring for about 3 minutes after sauce begins to simmer. 3. Stir in 1/4 cup of the cheese. Set sauce aside. 4. Melt remaining butter in saucepan, add garlic, mushrooms and cook quickly until lightly browned. Discard garlic. 5. In 4 or 6 quart pot boil a quantity of salted water, add noodles. Cook until they are tender to bite, but not soft. Drain. 6. Combine sauce, mushrooms, noodles and shrimp (save a few shrimp for garnish) and season with salt to taste. Pour into a 9" x 13" casserole or 6 to 8 individual casseroles. Top with reserved shrimp and sprinkle with remaining cheese. 7. Bake uncovered at 375° until bubbling. Broil top until lightly browned.

Tricia McArthur Elmer
(Mrs. Clark)

Shrimp Fettucini Primavera

Easy, elegant dish for entertaining…also a family favorite.

Planning: None
Preparation Time: 20 minutes

Quantity: 6 servings
Cooking Time: 1 hour

1 12-ounce package fettucini
   noodles
2 green onions, sliced
¹/₂ pound fresh mushrooms, sliced
3 tablespoons butter
¹/₄ cup chopped parsley
1 pound shrimp, cooked
4 cups broccoli flowerets, cooked
   and drained
1¹/₂ cups whipping cream
2 tablespoons butter
¹/₂ teaspoon salt
²/₃ cup fresh Parmesan cheese,
   grated
pepper

1. Cook fettucini according to package directions. Drain. **2.** Meanwhile sauté onions and mushrooms in 3 tablespoons butter. **3.** Add parsley, shrimp and broccoli. Stir and cook until warmed through. **4.** In another small pan, heat cream, the 2 tablespoons of butter and salt. **5.** Stir the vegetable mixture into the drained noodles. Add cream mixture, Parmesan and pepper to taste. Serve immediately.

Sally Brees Young
(Mrs. Jeff)

Fettucini Verde ❧

Planning: Uses a wok or electric
   skillet, cannot be made ahead
Preparation Time: 30 minutes

Quantity: 6-8 servings
Cooking Time: 20 minutes

6 tablespoons butter, cut into
   chunks
1 cup chopped green onions
   and tops
2 cloves garlic, minced
1 cup whipping cream
3 to 4 cups (8 ounces) hot, cooked
   fettucini noodles, drained
1 cup Parmesan cheese
salt
pepper
nutmeg

1. Melt butter in medium hot wok or electric skillet. **2.** Add onion and garlic and stir-fry until onion is transparent. **3.** Add cream and cooked noodles. Stir over high heat until cream just begins to boil. **4.** Sprinkle with Parmesan cheese. Toss and mix until noodles are well coated and heated through. **5.** Add salt, pepper and nutmeg to taste.

Shirley Crandell Mast
(Mrs. Kenneth)

Spaghetti Primavera

A must when garden vegetables are ready.

Planning: None
Preparation Time: 45 minutes

Quantity: 6-8 servings
Cooking Time: 15 minutes

1 pound spaghetti
2 tablespoons butter or oil
1 1/2 cups coarsely chopped
   broccoli
1 1/2 cup snow peas
1 cup sliced zucchini
1 cup baby peas
6 stalks asparagus, sliced
1 tablespoon olive oil
2 medium tomatoes, chopped
3 teaspoons garlic, minced
1/4 cup parsley, chopped
salt and pepper
1/4 cup olive oil
1/3 cup pine nuts
10 mushrooms, sliced
1 cup whipping cream
1/2 cup Parmesan cheese
1/3 cup butter
1/3 cup fresh basil, chopped or
2 1/2 teaspoons dried basil

1. Cook spaghetti with oil in rapidly boiling water until barely tender. Drain.   **2.** Blanch broccoli, snow peas, zucchini, baby peas and asparagus in boiling water 3 to 4 minutes. Rinse in cold water and set aside.   **3.** In medium skillet heat 1 tablespoon olive oil. Add tomatoes, garlic, parsley, salt and pepper to taste. Sauté 2 to 3 minutes. Set aside and keep warm.   **4.** Heat small amount of olive oil in large skillet and brown pine nuts. Add remaining oil, mushrooms and blanched vegetables. Simmer a few minutes.   **5.** Add spaghetti, cream, Parmesan, butter and basil. Mix gently with fork. Top with sautéed tomatoes and serve immediately.

Susan Willett Sawyer
(Mrs. Gary)

Upside-Down Ravioli

Planning: Can be made ahead and refrigerated; bake slightly longer then

Preparation Time: 35 minutes

Quantity: 10-12 servings
Baking Time: 45 minutes, 350°

1 10-ounce package frozen chopped spinach
1 pound ground beef
1 medium onion, chopped
1 clove garlic, minced
1 tablespoon oil
1 16-ounce jar spaghetti sauce with mushrooms
1 8-ounce can tomato sauce
1/2 teaspoon salt
1/8 teaspoon pepper
2 cups cooked skroodles, drained, (corkscrew shaped pasta noodles)
1 cup Cheddar cheese, shredded
1/2 cup bread crumbs (1 slice bread)
2 eggs, well beaten

1. Cook spinach according to package directions. Drain and reserve liquids. Add water to make 1 cup. Set aside. 2. Sauté beef, onion and garlic in oil until lightly browned. Drain. 3. Add spinach liquid, spaghetti sauce, tomato sauce, salt and pepper. Simmer uncovered 10 minutes. 4. Combine spinach, skroodles, cheese, crumbs and eggs. Pour into 9" x 13" baking dish. Top with meat sauce. 5. Bake for 45 minutes at 350.°

Hint: Serve with crisp salad, French bread, and wine.

Jane Schneider Overbeeke
(Mrs. John)

ENTREES

ENTREES

Beef

Chicken

Fish and Seafood

Lamb and Veal

Individual Beef Wellingtons
Impressive for company.

Planning: None
Preparation Time: 1 hour

Quantity: 8 servings
Baking Time: 12 minutes for rare, 15 minutes for medium rare, 17 minutes for medium, 450°

8 5-ounce filets of beef or beef tenderloin
vegetable oil
salt and pepper
1 pound ground sirloin
¹/₈ teaspoon garlic salt
1 tablespoon snipped parsley
8 frozen pastry shells, thawed

1. Place filets in freezer for twenty minutes.   2. Brush with vegetable oil. Sprinkle with salt and pepper.   3. In hot skillet, brown filets for five minutes on each side.   4. While browning, combine ground sirloin, garlic salt, parsley and dash pepper. Divide into 8 portions.   5. After filets are browned, place a rounded portion of the ground sirloin on each filet. Refrigerate on paper towels.   6. Roll each pastry shell into approximately a 9" x 5" rectangle. Place a filet, ground sirloin side down, on each rectangle. Fold over sides and ends of pastry and pinch or pat to seal. Place seamed side down in shallow baking pan and refrigerate.   7. Bake at 450°,according to desired doneness.

Cheri French O'Connor
(Mrs. Gary)

Cognac Steak a la Flambé

Planning: None
Preparation Time: 25 minutes

Quantity: 4 servings
Cooking Time: 20 minutes

3 tablespoons butter
4 small beef filet mignons, 1 1/2"
   to 2" thick
salt and pepper
1 ounce cognac
1/2 cup whipping cream

1. Melt butter in heavy skillet. Season steaks with salt and pepper and cook over medium heat about 10 minutes on each side.   2. Pour cognac over steaks and ignite. Immediately spoon juices and flaming cognac over steaks. Remove to a heated platter.   3. Stir cream into pan juices. Pour sauce over steaks and serve at once.

Janice Merfeld Yagla
(Mrs. James)

Teriyaki Steak
Also great using chicken.

Planning: Allow for marinating
Preparation Time: 15 minutes

Quantity: 6-8 servings
Broiling Time: 10 minutes

1 1/3 cups cider vinegar
1 1/4 cups tomato puree
1 cup pineapple juice
1 cup soy sauce
1 cup brown sugar, firmly packed
1/3 cup molasses
1/4 teaspoon ground ginger
1/4 teaspoon garlic powder
6 to 8 sirloin or tenderloin steaks,
   1" thick

1. Combine all ingredients, except steaks, in saucepan, and mix thoroughly.   2. Bring sauce to a boil, stirring to prevent sticking. Taste sauce. If too bitter, add a little more brown sugar; if too sweet, add more pineapple juice.   3. Cool and store in refrigerator.   4. Marinate steaks in sauce for 24 hours; drain well.   5. Broil meat, approximately 5 minutes per side, and remove to serving platter.   6. Heat remaining sauce and pour over steaks if desired. Extra sauce may also be used for dipping.

Linda Johnston Rust
(Mrs. Larry)

Charlie's Peppered Sirloin

Planning: Can be made ahead and baked just before serving
Preparation Time: 30 minutes

Quantity: 8 servings
Cooking Time: 10 minutes
Baking Time: 30 minutes, 350°

2 pounds boneless beef sirloin
2 tablespoons olive oil
4 tablespoons butter
1 teaspoon salt
1/2 teaspoon pepper
dash cumin
dash sage
1 pound fresh mushrooms, quartered
2 cloves garlic, chopped
1 medium onion, cut into 8 wedges
2 green peppers, slice
2 tomatoes, cut into 8 wedges
1/2 cup soy sauce
2 teaspoons vinegar
1 6-ounce can tomato paste

1. Slice beef into ¼ " strips and sauté in 1 tablespoon olive oil and 2 tablespoons butter.   **2.** Place in 2-quart casserole. Sprinkle with salt, pepper, cumin and sage. Toss to mix.   **3.** Sauté mushrooms in remaining 2 tablespoons butter and 1 tablespoon olive oil for 2 minutes; add to meat. Add tomatoes to meat.   **4.** Stir garlic, onion and green peppers into drippings and sauté 2 minutes. Add to meat.   **5.** Combine soy sauce, vinegar and tomato paste in same skillet and heat, stirring constantly until mixture bubbles. Pour over meat and toss lightly.   **6.** Bake 30 minutes at 350°.

Joanne Fuessle Manternach (Mrs. Daniel)

Oriental Pepper Steak
Quick and very authentic tasting.

Planning: Requires wok or skillet.
Preparation Time: 45 minutes

Quantity: 6-8 servings
Cooking Time: 15-20 minutes

1 to 2 pounds round steak (frozen slightly)
oil
1 onion, thinly sliced
$^1/2$ teaspoon fresh garlic, minced
2 green peppers, thinly sliced
1 4-ounce can mushrooms, sliced and drained, or 4 ounces fresh
1 8-ounce can water chestnuts, sliced
1 tablespoon cornstarch
$^1/2$ cup water
2 tablespoons soy sauce
1 tablespoon sugar
$^3/4$ teaspoon salt
$^1/2$ teaspoon pepper

1. Slice the round steak in thin strips about 2″ to 3″ long. It is easier to slice thin when slightly frozen. **2.** Brown the meat in a small amount of oil in skillet or wok. Remove meat to plate. **3.** In meat juices quick-fry onions, garlic, and green peppers; add mushrooms and water chestnuts. **4.** Dissolve cornstarch in water, soy sauce and sugar and add to onions and green peppers. Add spices. **5.** Cook quickly until thick and clear. Add meat and cook only to reheat meat. Season to taste.

Susan Nejdl Junaid
(Mrs. Raja)

Salvatore Beef
Serve with pasta for a treat.

Planning: None
Preparation Time: 20 minutes

Quantity: 4 servings
Baking Time: 1$^1/2$-2 hours, 325°

1 (1$^1/2$ to 2 pounds) round steak
1 pound Italian sausage
$^1/2$ cup green onions, sliced
$^1/2$ cup mushrooms, sliced
$^1/2$ teaspoon tarragon leaves
1 15$^1/2$-ounce can Italian tomato sauce

1. Trim fat off steak. Spread sausage over steak. Sprinkle with onions, mushrooms, and tarragon. **2.** Roll up steak. Secure with skewers. Place in a baking dish. Pour $^1/3$ can of sauce over meat. **3.** Cover and bake 1$^1/2$ to 2 hours at 325°. **4.** Heat remaining $^2/3$ can sauce. **5.** Slice meat when done. Garnish with heated sauce.

Jeri Mixdorf Jenner
(Mrs. Billy)

German Sauerbraten

Planning: Must be prepared a day ahead
Preparation Time: 1 hour

Quantity: 8 servings
Cooking Time: 3-4 hours

5 to 6 pound beef rump or top round roast
flour
oil
1 16-ounce jar spiced whole crab apples
1 cup wine vinegar
1 medium onion, sliced
1 bay leaf
6 whole cloves
1 cube beef bouillon
1/4 teaspoon pepper
1/2 cup raisins
3 tablespoons brown sugar
2/3 cup gingersnap cookies, crumbled

1. Flour roast and brown in small amount of oil before marinating.
2. Drain crab apples and combine crab apple liquid with vinegar, onion, bay leaf, cloves, bouillon and pepper. Bring mixture to boil and simmer 10 minutes. Cool to room temperature.   3. Pour marinade over meat. Cover tightly and refrigerate 24 hours, turning occasionally. 4. Cook meat slowly with marinade in large, tightly covered pot for 3 to 4 hours, or until fork tender.   5. Remove meat to hot platter.   6. Add water, if needed, to make 2 cups of liquid.
7. Add raisins, brown sugar and gingersnaps crumbs.   8. Heat and stir until thickened.   9. Slice meat and pour gravy over. Garnish with crab apples.

Hint: Serve with German Moselle wine.

Loretta Davidson Ercius
(Mrs. Bernard)

Beef Brisket ❧

Planning: Needs to marinate
   overnight
Preparation Time: 15 minutes

Quantity: 10-12 servings
Baking Time: 1 hour per pound plus
   1 hour at 275°

fresh beef brisket
2 ounces liquid smoke
1 tablespoon celery salt
1 teaspoon garlic salt
1 tablespoon onion salt
Worcestershire sauce
salt and pepper
¹/₂ cup barbecue sauce

1. Place meat in a flat glass dish approximately the same size as meat.   **2.** Mix liquid smoke, celery, garlic, and onion salts. Pour over meat and marinate overnight in refrigerator.   **3.** When ready to bake sprinkle both sides of meat with Worcestershire sauce, salt and pepper. Cover with foil and bake.   **4.** After baking 1 hour per pound at 275,° uncover meat and baste with barbecue sauce. Bake 1 hour more uncovered.

Gini Naber Langlas
(Mrs. David)

Calico Burgers
Hamburger for company.

Planning: Patties can be made up to
   ¹/₂ hour ahead
Preparation Time: 30-45 minutes

Quantity: 4 servings
Grilling Time: 15 minutes

¹/₂ cup rice, cooked
¹/₄ cup chopped green pepper
¹/₄ cup chopped onion
1 tablespoon parsley, snipped
1 teaspoon salt
¹/₄ teaspoon garlic salt
¹/₈ teaspoon pepper
1 ¹/₂ pounds ground beef

1. Combine rice, green pepper, onion, parsley and seasonings.   **2.** Add ground beef and mix well.   **3.** Shape into four oval patties, 1″ thick.   **4.** Grill over hot coals for 15 minutes, turning once.
5. Serve patties with sauce and garnish with a skewer of green olives or pickle.

Sauce:
¹/₄ cup ketchup
2 tablespoons chili sauce
1 teaspoon Worcestershire sauce
¹/₂ teaspoon beef flavored gravy
   base (envelope mix)
¹/₄ teaspoon basil, dried
²/₃ cup water

Sauce:
1. Mix all ingredients.   **2.** Spoon over patties.

Mary Ludlow Alfrey
(Mrs. Gary)

Enchilada Casserole

Planning: Can be partially made a day ahead or frozen, 9" x 13" baking dish

Preparation Time: 1½ hours

Quantity: 8 enchiladas

Baking Time: 20-25 minutes, 350°

1½ pounds ground beef
salt and pepper to taste
1 8-ounce can kidney or pinto beans
1 1½-ounce package taco seasoning mix
1¼ cup water
cooking oil
8 large flour tortillas
1 cup grated medium cheddar cheese
1 10-ounce can enchilada sauce
1 4-ounce can green chilies
1 cup sour cream
1 cup grated Monterey Jack cheese
4 or 5 black olives, sliced

1. Brown ground beef in skillet. Season with salt and pepper to taste. Drain grease. 2. Rinse and drain beans. 3. Add taco seasoning mix and water to browned ground beef. Mix until blended. 4. Add beans to ground beef mixture and simmer uncovered for 15 minutes. 5. In another skillet, heat cooking oil until hot. Cook tortillas, one at a time, until soft and limp, about 5 to 10 seconds on each side. Drain on paper toweling. 6. Spoon ⅓ cup meat mixture in center of tortilla. Sprinkle with small amount of cheddar cheese. Roll up and place seam side down into greased 9" x 13" baking dish. 7. Add enchilada sauce and small amount of green chilies to taste to remaining meat mixture. Spoon over tortillas. (Recipe may be prepared ahead or frozen to this point.) 8. Cover and bake in 350° oven for 20 minutes. Uncover, spread sour cream over tortillas. Sprinkle Monterey Jack cheese over all. Add black olives. 9. Return to oven to heat sour cream and melt cheese, about 5 minutes.

Ellie Kennedy Everitt
(Mrs. David)

Veal a la Louisiana

Planning: Can be made several hours ahead
Preparation Time: 1 hour

Quantity: 4 servings
Cooking Time: 20-25 minutes

4 3-ounce slices boneless veal
salt
white pepper
flour
2 tablespoons vegetable oil
1/2 pound mushrooms, sliced
2 cups heavy cream
1/4 cup Madeira wine
1/4 cup butter, cut into 12 pieces
4 ounces cooked crabmeat
8 jumbo shrimp, peeled, deveined and cooked

1. Pound veal to 1/4" thickness.
2. Season with salt and pepper.
3. Dredge lightly with flour, shaking off excess. 4. Heat oil in large skillet over medium heat. 5. Add veal and brown 45 seconds on each side. 6. Transfer veal to platter and keep warm. 7. Add mushrooms to oil and sauté 5 minutes. 8. Add cream, Maderia and reduce until thickened, about 15 minutes. 9. Season with salt and pepper. 10. Stir in butter, 1 piece at a time. 11. Add crabmeat, shrimp and heat about 1 minute. 12. Pour over veal.

Terri Dennis Walker
(Mrs. John)

Veal Casserole Supreme

Planning: Must be made ahead
Preparation Time: 20 minutes

Quantity: 8 servings
Chilling Time: Overnight
Cooking Time: 45-60 minutes, 350°

2 pounds veal cutlet, cut in cubes
1/4 cup butter
1 cup chopped onion
1 medium clove garlic, minced
1/4 teaspoon oregano
2 11 1/2- ounce cans mushroom soup
2 cups canned tomatoes, cut up
4 cups cooked noodles
1 cup sour cream
2 tablespoons chopped parsley

1. Brown veal in butter. Remove.
2. Sauté onion and garlic. Add oregano. Add veal. 3. Blend soup, tomatoes and noodles. 4. Combine mixture with cutlets. Cover and refrigerate overnight. 5. Uncover, and bake 350° for 45 to 60 minutes. 6. Add 1 cup sour cream. Sprinkle with parsley and serve.

Margie Lahey Skahill
(Mrs. Timothy)

Roast Leg of Lamb

Planning: None
Preparation Time: 20-30 minutes

Quantity: 8-10 servings
Baking Time: 30 minutes at 400°,
3-4 hours, 350°

1 leg of lamb, 7 to 8 pounds
3 to 4 cloves garlic, cut in halves
   lengthwise
juice of 1 lemon
3 to 4 tablespoons butter, melted
salt and pepper to taste
1 teaspoon oregano
1 to 2 cups boiling water

1. Preheat oven to 400.° Rinse lamb well and pat dry. Make 6 to 8 slits in meat with a sharp knife. Insert garlic slivers all around lamb.   2. Place lamb in roasting pan. Squeeze lemon juice all over lamb. Rub the lamb thoroughly with lemon juice and butter.   3. Sprinkle with salt, pepper, and oregano on all sides. Allow lemon, butter and seasoning drippings to remain in pan.   4. If using meat thermometer, place in fleshiest part of lamb.   6. Place lamb in 400° oven for 30 minutes. Remove from oven and reduce heat to 350.°   7. Add water to juices in pan and return to oven for 3 to 4 hours or until meat thermometer reads 170° to 180.°

Karen Karman Gartelos
(Mrs. Peter)

Chicken a la Suisse

Elegant party dish.

Planning: Can be prepared early in day; refrigerate and warm in oven 15 minutes prior to serving
Preparation Time: 1 1/2 hours

Quantity: 6 servings
Cooking Time: 45 minutes

6 whole medium chicken breasts, skinned and boned
8 ounces Swiss cheese slices
8 ounces sliced cooked ham
3 tablespoons flour
1 teaspoon paprika
6 tablespoons butter
1/2 cup dry white wine
1 chicken flavored bouillon cube
1 tablespoon cornstarch
1 cup whipping cream
minced cooked ham and parsley sprig for garnish

1. Spread chicken breasts flat; cut cheese and ham slices to fit on top; fold breasts over filling; fasten edges with toothpicks, enclosing filling well.
2. On waxed paper, mix flour and paprika; use to coat chicken. 3. In large skillet over medium heat, in hot butter, cook chicken breasts until browned on all sides. 4. Add white wine and chicken bouillon cube. Reduce heat to low, cover and simmer 30 minutes, or until tender. 5. Remove chicken to warm platter; remove toothpicks; keep chicken warm. 6. In cup, with fork, blend cornstarch and whipping cream until smooth. Gradually stir cornstarch mixture into liquid in skillet. Cook, stirring constantly, until mixture is thickened. 7. Spoon sauce over chicken. Sprinkle with minced ham; garnish with parsley sprigs.

Diana Lichty Hansen
(Mrs. Milton)

Crab-Stuffed Chicken

Planning: Can be prepared ahead
Preparation Time: 30 minutes

Quantity: 8 servings
Baking Time: 1 hour, 350°

4 large chicken breasts, halved,
  skinned and boned
4 tablespoons butter
¹/₄ cup flour
³/₄ milk
³/₄ cup chicken broth
¹/₃ cup dry white wine
¹/₄ cup chopped onion
1 7¹/₂-ounce can crab meat,
  drained and flaked
1 3-ounce can chopped
  mushrooms, drained
¹/₂ cup coarsely crumbled saltine
  crackers (10 crackers)
2 tablespoons snipped parsley
¹/₂ teaspoon salt
dash pepper
1 cup Swiss cheese, grated
¹/₂ teaspoon paprika

1. Place one chicken piece, boned side up, between two pieces of waxed paper. Working from center out, pound chicken lightly with meat mallet to make cutlet about ¹/₈″ thick. Repeat with remaining chicken. 2. In saucepan, melt the 3 tablespoons butter and blend in the flour. Add milk, chicken broth and wine all at once. Cook and stir until mixture thickens and bubbles. Set aside. 3. In skillet, cook onion in remaining 1 tablespoon butter until tender, but not brown. 4. Stir in crab, mushrooms, cracker crumbs, parsley, salt and pepper. 5. Stir in 2 tablespoons of the sauce. 6. Top each chicken piece with about ¹/₂ cup crab mixture. Fold sides in and roll up. Pour remaining sauce over all. 7. Bake covered at 350° for 1 hour, or until chicken is tender. 8. Uncover and sprinkle with cheese and paprika. Bake two minutes longer or until cheese melts. Watch carefully!

Margie Lahey Skahill
(Mrs. Timothy)

Chicken with Braised Garlic and Rosemary

Planning: None
Preparation Time: 30 minutes

Quantity: 6 servings
Baking Time: 45 minutes, 425°

18 cloves garlic
6 tablespoons butter
1 1/2 chickens, quartered, or breast
  pieces
2 teaspoons dried rosemary,
  crumbled
salt and pepper to taste
1/2 cup dry white wine
1 cup chicken stock
3 tablespoons fresh lemon juice
watercress for garnish

1. Separate garlic cloves (do not peel) and drop into small saucepan of boiling water. Simmer 2 to 3 minutes. Drain well, slip off skins and set garlic aside. **2.** Preheat over to 425°. Melt butter in shallow roasting pan to hold chicken in single layer. **3.** Roll chicken in butter and arrange in pan skin side down. Sprinkle with rosemary, salt and pepper. Roast 15 minutes. **4.** Turn chicken over and scatter all but 7 garlic buds over top. Baste with butter during roasting until chicken is golden, about 30 minutes. **5.** Transfer chicken to serving platter. Reserve about 7 cloves of garnish and sprinkle remainder over top. **6.** Pour off fat from roasting pan. Add wine to pan and bring to boil over medium high heat, stirring in reserved garlic cloves and scraping up any browned bits. When most of wine has evaporated, add chicken stock and lemon juice and boil rapidly until sauce thickens slightly. **7.** Season with salt and pepper to taste. **8.** Pour sauce over chicken and garnish with watercress. Serve immediately, including some sauce, garlic cloves and watercress with each portion of chicken.

Joan Anderson Hollen
(Mrs. Michael)

Chicken Breasts Lombardy

Planning: Can be prepared ahead, up to baking in oven
Preparation Time: 30-45 minutes

Quantity: 8-10 servings
Baking Time: 10-12 minutes, 450°
Broiling Time: 1-2 minutes

6 whole chicken breasts, halved and boned
$^1/_2$ cup flour
1 cup butter, melted
1 $^1/_2$ cup fresh mushrooms, sliced
$^1/_2$ teaspoon salt
$^1/_8$ teaspoon pepper
$^3/_4$ cup Marsala wine
$^1/_2$ cup chicken stock
$^1/_2$ cup fontina or mozzarella cheese, shredded
$^1/_2$ cup grated Parmesan cheese

1. Pound chicken to $^1/_8$" thickness.
2. Dredge chicken in flour and sauté in $^1/_2$ cup butter 3 to 4 minutes per side.
3. Place chicken in greased 9" x 13" baking dish overlapping edges. Sprinkle with salt and pepper.   4. Sauté mushrooms in remaining butter and sprinkle over chicken.   5. Stir wine and chicken stock into drippings in skillet. Simmer 10 minutes.   6. Stir in $^1/_2$ teaspoon salt and $^1/_8$ teaspoon pepper.
7. Spoon about $^1/_3$ of the sauce evenly over the chicken. Reserve remainder of sauce.   8. Bake 10 to 12 minutes at 450° or until brown.   9. Combine cheeses and sprinkle over chicken.
10. Place under broiler 1 to 2 minutes until lightly browned. Serve with reserved sauce.

Jane Walker Christensen
(Mrs. Samuel)

Chicken Wellington
Nice company dish.

Planning: Can be prepared ahead
Preparation Time: 1 hour

Quantity: 4 servings
Baking Time: 18-20 minutes, 375°

2 chicken breasts, halved, boned and skinned
1 3-ounce package cream cheese, softened
1 4-ounce can mushrooms, drained
2 tablespoons chopped green onion
$^{1}/_{4}$ teaspoon salt
$^{1}/_{8}$ teaspoon pepper
2 tablespoons butter
1 10-ounce can refrigerated crescent rolls
1 egg, slightly beaten

1. Place one chicken breast half between two pieces of plastic wrap. Using a rolling pin, flatten to $^{1}/_{8}$" thickness. Peel off wrap and flatten remaining breast halves. **2.** Combine cream cheese, mushrooms, onion, salt and pepper. Place two tablespoons of mixture in center of each chicken piece. Starting with the small end, roll up and secure with toothpicks. **3.** Melt butter in skillet over medium heat. Sauté chicken rolls, turning occasionally, six minutes or until opaque. Set aside. **4.** Separate dough into four rectangles. Seal perforations and roll into 6" x 7" rectangles. **5.** Remove toothpicks from chicken and place each roll on center of dough. Wrap around chicken and seal edges. **6.** Place seam-side down on ungreased cookie sheet. Brush dough with egg. Bake 18 to 20 minutes.

Sauce:
3 tablespoons butter
1 tablespoon green onion, chopped
2$^{1}/_{2}$ tablespoons flour
1$^{1}/_{4}$ cups milk
$^{1}/_{4}$ cup white wine
$^{1}/_{2}$ teaspoon salt
1 2-ounce can mushrooms, drained

Sauce:
1. Melt butter. Sauté onion until tender. **2.** Blend in flour. Gradually add milk. Stir in wine. Cook until thickened, stirring constantly. **3.** Add salt and mushrooms. **4.** Serve over chicken rolls.

Hint: Puffed pastry sheets may be substituted for crescent roll dough. A half cup chopped or sliced fresh mushrooms may be substituted for each 2 ounces of canned mushrooms called for in recipe.

Susan Walker Crouse
(Mrs. James)

Walnut-Stuffed Chicken Breasts

Planning: Shortened preparation time if breasts are purchased already boned
Preparation Time: 45 minutes

Quantity: 6 servings
Cooking Time: 20-30 minutes

6 whole chicken breasts, halved
1 cup Cheddar cheese, shredded
1/2 cup walnuts, chopped
1/2 cup fresh bread crumbs
2 tablespoons minced onion
1/4 teaspoon salt
1/8 teaspoon pepper
1/2 cup flour
3 tablespoons butter
1 1/4 cups chicken broth
3/4 cup white wine
2 tablespoons chopped parsley
parsley for garnish

1. Bone and skin chicken breast halves. Place each between two sheets of waxed paper. With a mallet or rolling pin pound each to 1/4" thickness.
2. In a small bowl, combine cheese, walnuts, bread crumbs, onion, salt and pepper. Spoon 1 1/2 tablespoons filling in center of each chicken breast; spread filling to 1/2" of edge. From narrow end, roll each jelly roll style; fasten with a toothpick.   **3.** Roll chicken in flour; let stand 10 minutes.   **4.** Melt butter in large skillet. Add chicken and sauté until lightly brown on all sides. Pour in chicken broth and wine; cover and cook over low heat for 20 minutes.
5. Remove chicken to warm platter; keep warm, remove toothpicks.
6. Increase heat to high and stir sauce until slightly thickened. Add parsley and pour sauce over chicken. Garnish with more parsley.

Mary Ehm Strattan
(Mrs. Charles)

Chicken Almond Casserole

Excellent casserole for a large group.

Planning: Stew chicken the day before and reserve broth; casserole may be frozen

Preparation Time: 1 1/2 hours

Quantity: 14-16 servings

Baking Time: 1 hour, 150° or shorter time if divided

1 3 to 4 pound chicken, stewed, skinned, boned and cubed

chicken broth, add water to make 9 cups

2 cups uncooked rice

1 pound bulk sausage or diced ham*

2 large onions, chopped

1 large bunch celery, chopped

2 green peppers, chopped

2 8-ounce cans sliced water chestnuts, drained

1 small jar pimento, drained, optional

1 10³/₄-ounce can cream of mushroom soup

3 4-ounce packages dry noodle soup mix

2 2³/₄-ounce packages almonds, slivered

1. In large saucepan, stew chicken in water for 1 hour, or until chicken is done and tender. Remove chicken to cool and reserve broth. **2.** Bring broth to boil. Add rice and continue boiling 9 minutes. Set aside. **3.** Brown sausage in skillet and remove with slotted spoon. In sausage drippings, sauté onions, celery and peppers. Stir in water chestnuts and pimento and remove from heat. **4.** Stir mushroom soup into rice mixture. **5.** In one large or several small casseroles, layer rice, dry noodle soup mix, sausage, chicken and vegetables. Sprinkle slivered almonds on top. Bake, covered, 1 hour for large casserole, shorter time for smaller casseroles, at 350.°

Hint: Can also be divided into 3 or 4 smaller casseroles; serve one and freeze other for use later. *If using ham, melt 1/2 cup butter in skillet and sauté. If necessary, add more butter to skillet when sautéing vegetables.

Donna Cerwinske Sheldon
(Mrs. Robert)

Orange Chicken

Planning: None
Preparation Time: 2 hours

Quantity: 4 servings
Cooking Time: 10 minutes
Baking Time: 1 hour, 10
  minutes, 350°

1/3 cup flour
1 teaspoon salt
1/4 teaspoon poultry seasonings
1/4 teaspoon paprika
3 1/2 pound fryer, cut up
oil
3/4 cup pineapple juice
1/4 cup orange gelatin (1/2 3-ounce package)

1. In paper bag, combine flour, salt, poultry seasoning and paprika. Shake chicken in bag, a few pieces at a time, and brown in oil. **2.** Arrange chicken in 9" x 13" baking dish and bake 30 minutes at 350° **3.** Bring pineapple juice to a boil and dissolve orange gelatin in it. Pour over chicken. Bake an additional 40 minutes, or until meat is golden and tender, basting every 10 to 15 minutes.

Terri Dennis Walker
(Mrs. John)

Hot Mexican Chicken Casserole
Good for a crowd.

Planning: Can be made a day ahead; can be frozen
Preparation Time: 30 minutes

Quantity: 12 servings
Cooking Time: 1 hour, 350°

3 10 3/4-ounce cans of mushroom soup
1 cup milk
1 envelope taco seasoning
3 tablespoons celery flakes
3 tablespoons instant dry onion
1 4-ounce can green chili peppers
1 package corn tortillas (any size)
5 whole chicken breasts, cooked 1/2 hour
4 cups cheese, grated (combination of Cheddar, Monterey Jack and mozzarella)

1. Combine soup, milk, taco seasoning, celery flakes and onions. **2.** Drain and remove seeds from chilies. Chop or dice. **3.** Cut corn tortillas into 1" squares. **4.** Cut chicken breasts into bite-size pieces. **5.** Combine grated cheeses to total 4 cups. **6.** Layer the following three times each: chicken, tortillas, chilies, soup mix, cheese. Makes one 9" x 12" and one 8" x 8" baking dishes. **7.** Bake uncovered at 350° for 1 hour.

Barb Alt Dodd
(Mrs. Bill)

Chicken Lasagne Florentine

Planning: Chicken can be cooked, deboned, and refrigerated a day ahead
Preparation Time: 20-30 minutes

Quantity: 10 servings
Baking Time: 45 minutes, 375°

1/2 cup butter
1/2 cup flour
1/2 teaspoon salt
1/2 teaspoon dried basil
3 cups chicken broth, defatted
2 1/2 cups chicken, cooked and diced
2 cups cream-style cottage cheese
1 egg, slightly beaten
1/2 pound lasagne noodles
1 10-ounce package frozen chopped spinach, cooked and drained
1/4 pound mozzarella cheese, thin sliced
1/4 cup Parmesan cheese, grated

1. Melt butter in large saucepan. Blend in flour, salt and basil. 2. Stir in chicken broth left from boiling chicken. Cook, stirring constantly, until mixture thickens and comes to a boil. 3. Remove from heat, add chicken. 4. Mix cottage cheese with beaten egg. 5. Cook and drain noodles. 6. Lightly grease 9" x 13" baking dish. 7. Place 1/3 of the chicken mixture on bottom of dish. Top with half of noodles, half of cottage cheese mixture, half of spinach and half of mozzarella. Repeat, ending with last 1/3 of chicken mixture and the Parmesan cheese. 8. Bake 45 minutes at 375.° Remove from oven and let stand a few minutes before cutting into squares.

Hint: A citrus salad such as grapefruit and mandarin orange, or an aspic, goes well with this recipe.

Mary Jean Adams Clark
(Mrs. Craig)

Cajun Chicken Pie

Planning: Can be made ahead; can be frozen
Preparation Time: 1 hour

Quantity: 6 servings
Cooking Time: 1 hour, 15 minutes
Baking Time: 30-40 minutes, 375°

Filling:
1 3½ to 4 pounds chicken
4 cups water
⅓ cup butter
¼ cup flour
1 cup chopped onion
2 teaspoons garlic, minced
⅓ cup chopped green pepper
3 tablespoons minced parsley
2 tablespoons chopped celery
½ cup chopped green onion, including tops
1 teaspoon salt
¾ teaspoon black pepper
⅛ teaspoon cayenne
¼ cup whipping cream
2 tablespoons brandy
1 crust recipe, below

Crust:
2½ cup flour
1 teaspoon salt
½ cup butter
½ cup ice water

Filling:
1. Place chicken in a pot with water and bring to boil. Cover and reduce heat. Simmer 45 minutes to 1 hour. Remove chicken and cool. Remove chicken bones and cube meat. Set aside. **2.** In large skillet, melt butter over low heat. Gradually add the flour and stir until light golden roux forms. Add vegetables and continue cooking until they are soft. **3.** Add salt, pepper, cayenne, cream and brandy. Cook 5 minutes longer over low heat. Stir in chicken and cook 5 more minutes. **4.** Fill crust. Roll out top crust, place over filling and seal edges of top and bottom crust together. With a sharp knife slit top crust in four places to allow steam to escape. Bake 30 to 40 minutes in 375° oven or until crust is golden brown.

Crust:
1. Sift flour and salt in large mixing bowl. **2.** Cut in butter until it is evenly distributed. Add ice water and mix. **3.** Roll pastry into a ball, wrap and chill for 30 minutes or overnight. **4.** Divide dough into ⅓ and ⅔'s. On a floured board roll out larger portion of dough to fit 9″ pie pan.

Marilyn Workman DeKoster
(Mrs. Jim)

Shrimp and Scallops with Vermouth and Grapes

Planning: Allowing more time if you make your own fish stock
Preparation Time: 1 hour

Quantity: 4 servings
Cooking Time: 1 hour

¹/₂ cup whipping cream
¹/₂ cup dry vermouth
ground black pepper
3 tablespoons butter
³/₄ pound shrimp, shelled and deveined
³/₄ pound bay scallops
fish veloute, recipe below
³/₄ cup seedless green grapes

1. Heat ¹/₄ cup cream, ¹/₄ cup vermouth and pepper in large skillet. Cook over medium heat until mixture is reduced to one tablespoon. **2.** Whisk in butter. When hot, add shrimp. Cook and stir just until shrimp turn opaque. **3.** Add scallops. Cook, shaking pan, 3 to 5 minutes until scallops are opaque. **4.** Remove from heat. Transfer shrimp/scallops to warm serving platter with a slotted spoon and keep warm. **5.** Add remaining vermouth to pan. Cook over high heat until liquid is almost evaporated. **6.** Stir in fish veloute and remaining cream. Taste and adjust seasoning. Add grapes, toss to heat. Grind pepper over sauce. Cook 30 seconds. **7.** Pour sauce over fish and serve immediately.

Fish Veloute:
¹/₄ cup butter
¹/₄ cup flour
2²/₃ cup fish stock or clam broth

Fish Veloute:
1. Melt butter in medium saucepan.
2. Stir in flour. Cook and stir two minutes. **3.** Gradually whisk in fish stock or clam broth. Whisk until smooth. Heat to boil. **4.** Reduce heat, simmer 20 minutes, whisking often. Makes 2 cups.

Hint: Serve with rice and steamed fresh green vegetables.

Patti Corkery Sulentic
(Mrs. Richard)

Seafood Supreme ❧

Nice for a luncheon or a light, formal dinner.

Planning: May be prepared ahead and refrigerated before baking
Preparation Time: 20 minutes

Quantity: 6-8 servings
Baking Time: 30 minutes, 350°

1 7½-ounce can small shrimp, drained
1 7½-ounce can crab meat, flaked, drained
1 cup chopped green pepper
1 cup chopped celery
1 cup chopped onion
1 teaspoon Worcestershire sauce
1 cup herb-seasoned stuffing cubes, crumbed and buttered

1. Combine all ingredients except crumbs and place in 2-quart casserole or 6 to 8 individual shells. **2.** Sprinkle buttered crumbs on top. Bake 30 minutes for casserole or 20 minutes for individual shells in 350° oven.

Pamela Pronty Correll
(Mrs. David)

Super Shrimp Supper

Good after-theater/after-symphony supper.

Planning: Fresh shrimp preferred
Preparation Time: 1 hour, 30 minutes

Quantity: 12 servings
Baking Time: 30-35 minutes, 350°

1½ pounds shrimp, shelled, deveined and cooked
2 cups thinly sliced celery
1 cup thinly sliced green pepper
1 cup thinly sliced onion
¼ cup butter
¼ cup pimento, chopped
2 cups sour cream
1 cup light cream
2 tablespoons lemon juice
2 teaspoons salt
1 to 2 teaspoons white pepper
4 cups cooked rice
2 4-ounce cans sliced mushrooms, drained
½ cup dry bread crumbs
2 tablespoons melted butter

1. Thaw shrimp, if using frozen. **2.** Sauté celery, green pepper and onion in ¼ cup butter until partially cooked. Combine shrimp, vegetables and pimento and set aside. **3.** Stir together the sour cream, light cream, lemon juice and seasonings. Combine ¾ cup of this mixture, rice and mushrooms and spread evenly in well-greased 9" x 13" baking dish. **4.** Place shrimp on top of rice mixture. Pour remaining cream mixture over shrimp. **5.** Combine bread crumbs and melted butter and sprinkle over top. Bake for 30 to 35 minutes at 350°

Gayle Price Denkinger
(Mrs. Donald)

Shrimp Creole

Planning: Fresh shrimp preferred
Preparation Time: 15 minutes

Quantity: 4 servings
Cooking Time: 1 hour

3 onions, chopped
1 bell pepper, chopped
¹/₄ cup butter
1 4-ounce can of mushroom
  pieces, drained
1 16-ounce can of pear-shaped
  tomatoes
1 to 2 teaspoons Italian seasoning
¹/₂ teaspoon salt
2 cups shrimp, shelled and
  deveined
1 6-ounce can tomato paste (only
  if sauce needs thickening)
2 cups cooked rice

1. Sauté onions and pepper in butter.
Add mushrooms and cut up tomatoes.
Season with Italian seasoning and
salt.   2. Simmer mixture for 30 minutes. Add shrimp and cook 15 minutes
longer over low heat.   3. Serve over
cooked rice.

*Mary Margaret Brinkman Halverson
(Mrs. Jeffery)*

Zeis Scalloped Oysters
A holiday must.

Planning: None
Preparation Time: 10 minutes

Quantity: 8-10 servings
Baking Time: 45 minutes to 1 hour,
  350°

8 ounces soda crackers (¹/₂ of 1
  pound box)
1 to 1¹/₂ pints fresh oysters,
  drained; rinsed and picked
  over. Reserve juice.
pepper
¹/₄ to ¹/₂ cup butter
1 pint half and half

1. Crush crackers coarsely (do it in the
package) and sprinkle layer on bottom
of 2 to 3-quart casserole. (Save enough
crushed crackers for layering.)
2. Place layer of oysters on top, sprinkle
pepper, and dot with several small
chunks of butter.   3. Repeat layering,
topping with crushed crackers.
4. Combine juice from oysters and half
and half and pour over casserole until
liquid just shows after being soaked
up.   5. Bake, uncovered, 45 minutes to
one hour at 350° until puffy and
browned.

*Peg Zeis McGarvey
(Mrs. Thomas)*

Seafood Casserole ❧

Wonderful for a bridal or bridge luncheon.

Planning: Can be made ahead
Preparation Time: 15 minutes

Quantity: 6 servings
Baking Time: 20 minutes, 350°

3/4 pound seafood (any
  combination of crabmeat,
  lobster, cooked shrimp or
  scallops; can be canned meat;
  best to use 1/3 crabmeat)
3 slices soft bread, cubed
1/2 cup milk
4 hard-boiled eggs, finely diced
1 teaspoon onion
1 teaspoon Worcestershire sauce
1 cup mayonnaise
buttered crumbs for topping

1. Combine all ingredients.   2. Place in buttered casserole or individual shell casseroles or ramekins.   3. Bake at 350° for 20 minutes.

Margie Lahey Skahill
(Mrs. Timothy)

Bacon-Stuffed Flounder Rolls 🐷

Planning: None
Preparation Time: 30 minutes

Quantity: 4 servings
Baking Time: 30 minutes, 375°

3 slices bacon
butter, melted
1 6-ounce package San
  Francisco-style stuffing mix
1/4 cup onion, finely chopped
2 tablespoons parsley, snipped
8 flounder fillets or other white
  fish fillets, about 1 1/4 pounds
1 7/8-ounce package bearnaise
  sauce mix or your own from
  scratch

1. Grease eight 2 1/2" muffin cups and set aside.   2. Cook bacon until crisp and reserve drippings. Crumble the bacon and set aside.   3. Measure drippings and add enough melted butter to equal 1/4 cup.   4. Prepare stuffing mix according to package directions, using drippings mixture instead of butter. Stir in bacon, onion and parsley.   5. Wrap one fish fillet inside each muffin cup, pressing it against sides. Spoon about 1/3 cup stuffing mixture into center of each roll. Brush with additional butter.
6. Bake for 30 minutes at 375.° Meanwhile, prepare bearnaise sauce. Serve over fish.

Hint: Cod or sole fillets are good alternatives for the fish in this recipe.

Margie Lahey Skahill
(Mrs. Timothy)

Fishmarket Catfish with Dill Sauce

Worth the effort to catch your own fish.

Planning: Use fresh fish
Preparation Time: 30 minutes

Quantity: 4-6 servings
Cooking Time: 25 minutes

2 pounds catfish fillets
flour, as needed
2 eggs, beaten
3/4 cup vegetable oil
2 cubes beef bouillon
2 1/2 cups boiling water
2 parsley sprigs
1/4 cup butter
6 tablespoons flour
1/4 cup butter
1 tablespoon lemon juice
1/2 teaspoon dill, chopped

Garnish:
lemon wedges
parsley

1. Dust catfish fillets with flour and dip into eggs. Heat oil until very hot. Add fish and sauté until golden on both sides, 7 to 10 minutes. Remove to heated platter. 2. To prepare demi-glace, dissolve bouillon in boiling water and add parsley. Simmer 10 minutes. Remove parsley and return to boil.
3. Melt first butter in separate pan and stir in flour to make thick paste. Add this mixture to boiling bouillon. Stir until glace has reached a medium consistency. 4. Heat second butter and lemon juice. Add dill and blend in 1/4 cup of demi-glace sauce. Cook, stirring until heated through and blended.
5. Spoon dill sauce over fillets. Garnish with lemon wedges and parsley.

Patricia Spraggins Welton
(Mrs. Michael)

PORK SPECIALTIES

PORK SPECIALTIES

Pork Chops

Black Forest Pork Chops	160
Garnished Sauerkraut	162
Grilled Iowa Chop Dijonaise	158
Iowa Chops with Apples	161
Pork Chop Rhubarb Casserole	161
Pork Chops with Honey Curry Sauce	159

Pork Roasts

Fruited Pork Roast	163
Pork Crown Roast with Wild Rice Stuffing	165
Pork Loin Roast with Orange Glaze Cups	164
Pork Roast with Tangy Sauce	166

Pork Tenderloin

Chinese Pork	163
Pork Tenderloin Towers	166

Boneless Pork

Pork Kabobs	167
Pork 'n Cider	172

Ham

Glazed Ham Loaf Ring with Mustard Sauce	168
Ham and Breast of Chicken en Croute	167

Ground Pork and Sausage

Ground Pork Quiche	172
Pork Burger King	170
Stuffed Cabbage Rolls	169
Torta Rustica	170

The tale of an Iowa pig...

The tale of a pig from the time it is a squeal to when it is a meal is indeed one of Iowa's finest farm to market stories.

Here in the corn state, pork producers raise 25 percent of the United State's hog population. The production of pork is a very important segment of our state's economy.

Major concerns of these producers center around herd health, housing facilities and their costs, feed expenses, the weather, market fluctuations and farrowing numbers. In short, hog farmers in Iowa need a lot of "pig sense" to succeed.

The pig? His job is to take an average of 2.5 pounds of feed and convert this to one pound of gain (meat). Average daily gain on some pigs has exceeded 3.5 pounds. Now that's efficiency!

The consumer? She does her part every time she chooses lean, meaty, 98 percent digestible pork products to feed her family. Pork's low cholesterol, low calories and high nutritive value make it a natural for all occasions.

That's why Iowa pork producers urge consumers to pick pork... it always tastes good and always is in good taste.

A few particulars about pork...

Today's pork is bred leaner to yield a higher percentage of body-building protein. Pork is "nutrient dense" which refers to the high amount of nutrients delivered per calorie contained.

3 1/2-ounce serving of cooked lean pork provides 28 grams of protein, 13 grams of fat, and only 240 calories. So "lean on pork" for many delicious, nutritious meals.

Pork is a principal dietary source of thiamine (three times as much as any other food source), and other B vitamins which are essential to food utilization, appetite, healthy nerves, skin and oral health.

The iron in pork is Heme iron, a more easily absorbed form of food iron. It combines with the amino acids of the complete protein in vital formation of red blood and prevention of anemia.

Other prominent minerals include zinc, phosphorus, and magnesium.

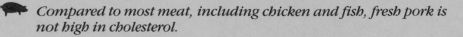

 Compared to most meat, including chicken and fish, fresh pork is not high in cholesterol.

 Buy fresh pink cuts of pork with some marbling (flecks of fat). Refrigerate or freeze immediately.

 When buying pork one serving equals:
¹/₄ to ¹/₃ pound boneless meat such as tenderloin
¹/₃ to ¹/₂ pound meat with little bone such as chops
³/₄ to 1 pound meat with much bone such as spareribs

 Fresh pork can be refrigerated for two days, smoked pork for one to two weeks. Store canned hams according to directions.

 Freeze ground pork one to three months; other fresh pork three to six months; and most smoked pork one to two months.

 Thaw pork: (1) in refrigerator in original wrappings; (2) during cooking (increase cooking time ¹/₃ to ¹/₂ longer); or (3) in microwave according to manufacturer's directions.

 Today's leaner, meatier and more tender pork calls for changes in cooking methods. All fresh pork roasts should be cooked to internal temperature of 170 degrees for most tender, juicy, and flavorful meat. Oven temperature should be 325 degrees. This low temperature reduces amount of shrinkage and meat cooks uniformly.

 To roast: Place meat fat side up on rack in roasting pan with meat thermometer.

 To broil: Chops or loin should be one to one and a half inches thick. Broil three to five inches from heat. Season after broiling.

 To pan broil: Do not add fat or water or cover. Pour liquid off as it accumulates. Season after cooking.

 To pan fry: Use a small amount of fat. Do not cover. Season as meat cooks.

 To braise: Season meat, add liquid, cover and cook at low temperature until done.

 Ham labels give all the facts. Ham can be fresh, cured, cured and smoked, or canned. Cured ham has been processed with pickle cure which acts as a preservative and adds flavor.

 Canned hams can be cured, smoked or unsmoked. Some are specifically flavored and some glazed. Some are shelf stable and some must be refrigerated.

Hams labeled fully cooked can be eaten without further cooking. To serve hot, heat ham in 325 degree oven to internal temperature of 140 degrees. Hams labeled "cook before eating" should be cooked to an internal temperature of 160 degrees.

 Create an endless variety of palate pleasers using cooked ham. Stir cubed ham into Danish or Hawaiian-style frozen vegetables. Use ham to boost the flavor of canned pork and beans; or add zest to macaroni and cheese or egg dishes. Grill ham slices or rotissiere canned and boneless hams. Use ham in kabobs.

Seasoning tricks:
- *Citrus fruits, tart apples or cherries are all go-togethers for fresh pork.*
- *Herb combinations like poultry seasonings and herb salts are tasty.*
- *Try sage, thyme, rosemary, marjoram, prepared mustard and tarragon.*
- *A good rule of thumb with dried herbs is to use 1/4 teaspoon per four servings.*

Garnishes:
- *Try parsley, mint or celery leaves.*
- *Pickled or preserved fruits are colorful and tasty.*
- *Kumquats, peaches, apples and pears are good additions.*

Pork favorites include: pork loin, rib or butterfly chops, smoked chops, blade steaks, country-style ribs, back ribs and spareribs. Also, Boston shoulder roasts, loin roast, rib roast, tenderloin, smoked ham, smoked ham slices, kabobs, ground pork, Canadian-style bacon, sausage, rolled log of pork and crown roast.

An "Iowa Chop" is a 1 1/4 inch thick loin chop.

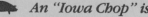

Grilled Iowa Chop Dijonaise

Planning: Herb butter can be made ahead

Preparation Time: 25 minutes

Quantity: 4-6 servings

Grilling Time: About 20 minutes

2 tablespoons Dijon mustard
1 teaspoon dry mustard
1 teaspoon salt
1/2 teaspoon pepper, freshly ground
4 to 6 Iowa Chops
3 tablespoons butter, softened

1. Make a paste of the mustards, salt, and pepper and 2 tablespoons butter. Rub into chops.   **2.** Grill chops over a very hot charcoal fire for 4 to 6 minutes on each side.   **3.** Place each chop on a square of foil and brush with a little butter. Wrap each chop and return packets to grill for 10 minutes.   **4.** Brush chops with herb butter and serve.

Herb Butter:
2 tablespoons butter, softened
1 tablespoon parsley, finely chopped
1 tablespoon chives, finely chopped
1/2 teaspoon lemon juice
salt and pepper

Herb Butter:
1. Combine all ingredients.   **2.** Brush on pork chops.

Liz Cooper Yagla
(Mrs. Gene)

Pork Chops with Honey Curry Sauce

Planning: Use Iowa Chops; let sauce stand 2 hours
Preparation Time: 15 minutes

Quantity: 6 servings
Marinating Time: 3-6 hours or overnight
Broiling Time: 30 minutes

3 slices bacon, diced
1 cup onion, finely chopped
2 cloves garlic, minced
$1/2$ cup soy sauce
$1/3$ cup lemon juice
2 tablespoons honey
1 tablespoon curry powder
2 teaspoons chili powder
salt
2 tablespoons light rum (optional)
6 pork loin chops, cut $1 1/4''$ thick

1. Cook bacon in frying pan over low heat until lightly browned. Add onion and garlic; cook just until onion is tender. Add soy sauce, lemon juice, honey, curry powder, chili powder and salt. Mix and simmer 2 to 3 minutes. Stir in rum. 2. Cover, let stand 2 hours to let flavors blend or store in refrigerator until ready to use. 3. Arrange pork chops in shallow dish, pour sauce over chops and marinate 3 to 6 hours or overnight. 4. Drain chops and save sauce. 5. To broil, place chops on rack in broiler pan. Place in broiler so top of meat is 4'' from heat. Broil 12 to 15 minutes on first side, turn and broil 10 to 15 minutes on second side. Brush chops frequently with marinade while broiling. 6. Heat remaining sauce and serve with chops.

Hint: May also be cooked on outdoor grill.

Marty McNutt Port
(Mrs. Dale)

Black Forest Pork Chops 🐖

A special company recipe.

Planning: Use Iowa Chops
Preparation Time: 1 hour

Quantity: 4 servings
Cooking Time: 1¼ hours

2 tablespoons oil
4 pork loin chops, cut 1½" thick
salt and pepper
1 ounce heated kirsch
¼ cup beef stock
1 17-ounce can pitted dark sweet
  cherries
¼ teaspoon nutmeg
¼ teaspoon cloves
¼ teaspoon marjoram
½ teaspoon lemon rind, grated
2 tablespoons lemon juice
2 tablespoons cornstarch
½ cup toasted walnuts, chopped

1. Heat oil in skillet over medium heat; add chops and cook until brown on both sides. Season with salt and pepper. **2.** Drain fat from pan and flambé chops with heated kirsch. **3.** Pour in stock, cover and simmer over low heat for one hour. **4.** Separate syrup from cherries; reserve both. Add seasonings and lemon rind to syrup. Stir lemon juice and cornstarch together and slowly add to syrup mixture. Cook over low heat until sauce is thick and glossy. **5.** After chops have cooked 45 minutes, pour syrup mixture into pan with chops. **6.** Just before serving, add reserved cherries and walnuts and cook over low heat until warmed through.

Carol Hayes Steckelberg
(Mrs. Randy)

Iowa Chops with Apples

Planning: None
Preparation Time: 35 minutes

Quantity: 4-6 servings
Baking Time: 30-35 minutes, 350°

4 Iowa Chops
1 tablespoon oil
1 teaspoon salt
1 cup brown sugar
²/₃ cup brandy
¹/₂ cup apple cider
2 tart apples
1 tablespoon butter
¹/₄ cup dry white wine
2 tablespoons candied ginger,
    chopped (optional)

1. Heat oil in ovenproof skillet and quickly brown chops on both sides. Season with salt.   **2.** Combine brown sugar, brandy, and cider in saucepan and heat until well blended (about 3 minutes).   **3.** Spoon sauce over chops and bake, uncovered, 30 minutes.   **4.** Cut apples into thick rings.   **5.** Melt butter in small skillet. Add wine.   **6.** Sauté apples until tender.   **7.** Arrange chops and apples on a serving platter. Sprinkle with candied ginger.

Hint: Serve sauce over rice or chops.

Liz Cooper Yagla
(Mrs. Gene)

Pork Chop Rhubarb Casserole

A must at rhubarb time.

Planning: None
Preparation Time: 30 minutes

Quantity: 6 servings
Baking Time: 50 minutes, 350°

6 pork loin or rib chops, cut
    ³/₄" to 1" thick
¹/₂ to 1 teaspoon salt
¹/₈ teaspoon pepper
2 cups soft bread crumbs
¹/₄ teaspoon salt
¹/₂ cup brown sugar
¹/₂ cup sugar
3 tablespoons flour
¹/₂ teaspoon cinnamon
6 cups sliced rhubarb

1. Brown chops in frying pan. Pour off drippings and save ¹/₄ cup. Season chops with salt and pepper.   **2.** Combine crumbs, ¹/₄ cup drippings and ¹/₄ teaspoon salt.   **3.** Mix together sugars, flour and cinnamon. Add to rhubarb. **4.** Place half of crumbs in bottom of a 2 to 3-quart casserole or baking dish. Spoon half of rhubarb over crumbs and arrange chops on rhubarb. Place remaining rhubarb on chops.   **5.** Cover tightly and bake at 350° for 40 minutes.   **6.** Remove cover and top with remaining crumbs. Bake 10 minutes longer.

Bev Greiner Rutten
(Mrs. Russ)

Garnished Sauerkraut

Planning: Use smoked pork chops
Preparation Time: 1 hour

Quantity: 6-8 servings
Cooking Time: 45 minutes

12 slices bacon, cut up
1 1/2 cups chopped onion
1 27-ounce and 1 14-ounce can
   sauerkraut, drained
3 medium carrots, bias-sliced
1 1/2 tablespoons brown sugar
8 to 10 juniper berries (optional)
9 whole black peppercorns
3 whole cloves
1 1/2 bay leaves
1 large sprig parsley
1 1/4 cups chicken broth
3/4 cup dry white wine
4 potatoes, peeled and quartered,
   or in smaller pieces
4 smoked pork chops
4 knockwurst, smoked
   knockwurst or bratwurst, or
   mixture of all three

1. In large skillet, cook bacon and onion. Drain off most of fat. **2.** Stir the sauerkraut, carrots and brown sugar into skillet. **3.** Loosely tie juniper berries, peppercorns, cloves, bay leaves and parsley into cheese cloth bag. Bury in center of kraut. **4.** Add broth and wine. Bring to boiling and reduce heat. Simmer covered for 10 minutes.
5. Add potatoes, pushing them into kraut. Simmer covered for 15 minutes.
6. Top with the meats. (Diagonally score knockwurst, bratwurst and brown first if you prefer.) Simmer covered for 20 minutes if precooked and 40 minutes if uncooked. Discard herb bag.
7. Take smoked pork chops off bone and cut into large pieces. Cut knockwurst in half. **8.** Arrange kraut and potatoes on platter. Top with meats.

Linda Lichty Anderson
(Mrs. Robert)

Chinese Pork

Planning: Marinate tenderloin several hours or overnight
Preparation Time: 20 minutes

Quantity: 4-6 servings
Cooking Time: 1 hour

1/2 cup soy sauce
2 tablespoons honey
1/2 teaspoon cinnamon
2 cloves garlic, crushed
2 green onions, cut in half
1 teaspoon ginger
2 12-ounce whole pork tenderloins
1/2 pound bacon
1/2 cup maple syrup

1. Combine first six ingredients.
2. Add tenderloin, stirring to coat completely. Cover and marinate at room temperature for several hours or refrigerate overnight.   3. Drain pork and overlap ends to form one long piece.
4. Starting at one end, wrap bacon around pork, overlapping edges. Secure with toothpicks.   5. Cook over moderate heat on grill. Baste with maple syrup. Cook until 170° on meat thermometer, approximately 1 hour.

*Linda Johnston Rust
(Mrs. Larry)*

Fruited Pork Roast

A wonderful combination.

Planning: None
Preparation Time: 20 minutes

Quantity: 8-12 servings
Baking Time: 2 1/2-4 hours, 325°

1 12-ounce package mixed dried fruits
1 3" cinnamon stick
1/2 lemon, sliced
2 cups apple juice
2 tablespoons orange juice
2 tablespoons honey
1 4 to 6 pound fresh pork shoulder, boned and rolled, or boneless loin
salt and pepper to taste

1. Cook dried fruits as directed on package, adding cinnamon and lemon to water. Add apple juice, orange juice and honey to cooked fruit.   2. Heat oven to 325.° Place seasoned pork on a rack in shallow roasting pan.   3. Pour fruit mixture over pork. Bake uncovered 35 to 40 minutes per pound, or until meat thermometer registers 170.° Baste pork frequently with pan drippings.

*Dee Reinhart Vandeventer
(Mrs. David)*

Pork Loin Roast with Orange Glaze Cups

Very impressive.

Planning: None
Preparation Time: 1 hour

Quantity: 8 servings
Baking Time: 3 hours, 325°

1 center cut pork loin roast, about
   5¹/₂ pounds
1 teaspoon salt
¹/₂ teaspoon pepper

1. Preheat oven to 325° 2. Place meat, fat side up, on a rack in a roasting pan. Sprinkle with salt and pepper. Insert meat thermometer so the bulb reaches the thickest part of the meat. Roast 3 hours or until meat thermometer reaches 170°

Glaze:
1 cup orange juice
2¹/₂ teaspoons cornstarch
1 teaspoon grated orange rind
¹/₂ teaspoon ground ginger
¹/₂ teaspoon ground mace
fresh parsley

Glaze:
1. Combine orange juice, cornstarch, rind, ginger and mace in small saucepan. Cook, stirring constantly, until thickened. 2. Brush glaze on meat during the last 30 minutes of roasting. 3. To serve, place roast on platter. Garnish with parsley and orange cups. Pass remaining glaze.

Orange Cups:
4 oranges
1 13¹/₂-ounce can pineapple
   chunks, drained (or use fresh
   pineapple)
2 tablespoons Grand Marnier

Orange Cups:
1. Cut oranges in half and scoop out pulp and dice. 2. Drain off juice and combine pulp and pineapple. Add liquor. Chill. 3. Spoon fruit into orange shells.

Ruth Lutz Buck
(Mrs. David)

Pork Crown Roast
with Wild Rice Stuffing

Planning: Rice can be made a day
  ahead
Preparation Time: 30 minutes

Quantity: 10 servings
Roasting Time: 10 minutes at 400°,
  4 to 5 hours (30 minutes per
  pound) at 325°

1 crown roast of pork (8 to 10
  pounds)
2 6-ounce packages wild rice mix
$^1/_2$ cup chopped onion
$^1/_3$ cup chopped celery
1 clove garlic, finely chopped
$^1/_4$ cup butter
$^1/_2$ cup pine nuts
1 8-ounce package dried apricots,
  finely chopped
4 to 5 tablespoons preserved
  ginger, finely chopped
$^1/_2$ teaspoon ground allspice
1 large can whole apricots,
  (optional garnish)

1. Place meat on rack in large shallow roasting pan. 2. Cook rice according to package directions. 3. Sauté onion, celery, and garlic in butter until tender. 4. Combine sautéed vegetables, rice, pine nuts, apricots, ginger, and allspice. Mix well. 5. Spoon lightly into center of roast. Spoon any extra stuffing into buttered shallow baking dish which will be baked during last 30 minutes of roasting. 6. Cover ends of bones and top of stuffing with foil. 7. Roast for 10 minutes in preheated 400° oven. 8. Reduce oven to 325° and roast about 4 hours until meat thermometer registers 185° in thickest part.

Hint: For color, garnish serving platter with parsley and put whole apricots on rib ends.

Susan Walker Crouse
(Mrs. James)

Pork Roast with Tangy Sauce

Delicious sweet and sour sauce.

Planning: Sauce may be prepared ahead and reheated
Preparation Time: 15 minutes

Quantity: 12 servings
Baking time: 2 hours, 325°

^{1}/$_2$ **teaspoon salt**
^{1}/$_2$ **teaspoon garlic salt**
^{1}/$_2$ **teaspoon chili powder**
1 4-pound boneless pork loin roast, rolled and tied

1. In small bowl combine salt, garlic salt and chili powder. Rub on roast.
2. Place roast, fat side up, on rack in shallow roasting pan. Roast 2 hours, or until meat thermometer reads 185°, in 325° oven.   **3.** Approximately 15 minutes before roast is done, brush with some sauce. When roast is done, remove from oven and let rest 10 minutes before carving.   **4.** Mix ^{1}/$_2$ cup pan drippings with remaining sauce. Reheat sauce and serve with roast.

Tangy Sauce:
1 cup apple jelly
1 cup ketchup
2 tablespoons vinegar
2 teaspoons chili powder

Tangy Sauce:
1. In medium saucepan, combine sauce ingredients and bring to boil.   **2.** Reduce heat and simmer, uncovered, 2 minutes. Set aside.

Diana Lichty Hansen
(Mrs. Milton)

Pork Tenderloin Towers

Planning: None
Preparation Time: 15 minutes

Quantity: 6 servings
Baking time: 1 hour, 15 minutes, 350°

6 ^{1}/$_2$" slices pork tenderloin or boneless loin chop
1 teaspoon salt
^{1}/$_2$ teaspoon pepper
6 thin slices onion
6 slices tomato
6 slices American cheese
6 slices bacon

1. Season tenderloin slices with salt and pepper.   **2.** Place in greased 9" x 13" baking dish.   **3.** Top each slice with onion, then tomato, then cheese, and then bacon. Spear with a toothpick to hold in place.   **4.** Bake covered at 350° for 1 hour.   **5.** Uncover, and bake 15 minutes more for the bacon to brown.

Marty Gillam Clark
(Mrs. Mark)

Pork Kabobs

Planning: Must be made ahead
Preparation Time: 1 hour

Quantity: 4 servings
Chilling Time: Overnight
Grilling Time: Depends on heat of coals

1 ¹/₂ **pounds pork, trimmed and cut into 1″ cubes**
1 **12-ounce can beer**
¹/₂ **cup orange marmalade**
¹/₄ **cup sugar**
¹/₂ **cup soy sauce**
1 **clove garlic, minced**
16 **large mushrooms**
8 **pearl onions, peeled and blanched**
1 **large green pepper, cut into eighths**

1. Place pork in deep bowl. Combine beer, marmalade, sugar, soy sauce and garlic thoroughly and pour over pork. Refrigerate overnight, stirring several times.   2. One hour before cooking, add vegetables to marinade.   3. String pork and vegetables on skewers. Cook over medium hot charcoal fire, basting frequently with marinade.

Linda Johnston Rust
(Mrs. Larry)

Ham and Breast of Chicken En Croute

Planning: Use deboned chicken breasts
Preparation Time: 30 minutes

Quantity: 4 servings
Baking Time: 25 minutes, 400°

2 **frozen 9″ pie shells**
2 **chicken breasts, boned and skinned**
1 **tablespoon butter**
¹/₄ **teaspoon thyme**
1 **4 to 5-ounce Brie, Gruyere or Camembert cheese**
4 **slices boiled ham**
1 **egg**

1. Thaw pie shells.   2. Split each chicken breast in half. Rinse and drain chicken.   3. In 1 tablespoon butter, sauté chicken on both sides in covered pan, until golden. Sprinkle with thyme.   4. Cut cheese into thin slices.   5. Remove pie shells from pans and cut in half. Cut a diamond-shaped hole in center of each half. Place a slice of ham, cheese and half of chicken breast on each. Fold pastry over and pinch edges together.   6. Place seam side down on ungreased cookie sheet. Beat egg slightly and brush on pastry.
7. Bake 25 minutes at 400° or until golden.

Cathy Ercius Enstrom
(Mrs. Kenneth)

Glazed Ham Loaf Ring with Mustard Sauce

Planning: Begin mustard sauce the night before; requires a 5½-cup ring mold
Preparation Time: 45 minutes

Quantity: 6-8 servings
Baking Time: 1 hour 30 minutes, 350°

Mustard Sauce:
2 tablespoons dry mustard
¼ cup vinegar
1 egg beaten
⅓ cup sugar
dash of salt
mayonnaise

Mustard Sauce:
1. In a jar, mix mustard and vinegar. Cover and let stand overnight.   2. In top of double boiler, stir egg, sugar and salt into mustard and vinegar mixture. Cook over hot, not boiling, water until thickened slightly. Cool.   3. To serve, combine equal quantities of cooled mustard mixture and mayonnaise. Mix and drizzle over loaf or serve separately.

Loaf:
1½ pounds ground ham
1¼ pound ground fresh pork
1½ cup soft bread crumbs
1½ cups onion, finely chopped
2 eggs, beaten
½ cup milk

Loaf:
1. Thoroughly combine meats, bread crumbs, onion, eggs and milk. Press into a lightly oiled 5½-cup ring mold.
2. Invert on shallow baking pan, remove mold. Bake 1½ hours at 350,° basting with glaze 3 or 4 times during baking.   3. Serve with mustard sauce.

Glaze:
½ cup brown sugar
1 tablespoon prepared mustard
2 tablespoon vinegar
1 tablespoon water

Glaze:
1. Combine all ingredients thoroughly.   2. Use as directed above.

Hint: A nice buffet dish. Serve with twice-baked or scalloped potatoes.

Mary K. Boucher Brixius
(Mrs. William)

Stuffed Cabbage Rolls

Planning: Can be prepared ahead and frozen without sauce
Preparation Time: 1 1/2 hours

Quantity: 6 servings
Cooking Time: 1 1/2 hours

1 medium head cabbage
1/2 cup long grain rice
1 1/2 cups milk
1/2 pound ground round
1/2 pound ground pork
1 egg, slightly beaten
1 1/2 teaspoon salt
1/4 teaspoon pepper
2 tablespoons butter
3 tablespoons brown sugar
1 1/2 cups beef broth
2 1/2 tablespoons flour
1 1/2 cups light cream

1. Separate cabbage leaves, trimming off the thick part. Place in boiling water and cook for 5 minutes. Drain well.
2. Bring 1 cup water to boil. Add rice; simmer until all water is absorbed.
3. Add 1 1/2 cups milk; simmer until rice is tender, stirring occasionally. (Approximately 20 minutes.)   4. Mix rice, ground round, ground pork, egg, salt and pepper.   5. Place 2 tablespoons stuffing on each cabbage leaf. Fold leaf over stuffing and secure with toothpick.   6. Brown rolls in heated butter on both sides. Place in a heavy kettle.
7. Sprinkle with brown sugar, add beef broth. Cover and bring to boil.
8. Simmer slowly for 1 hour, basting occasionally. Remove from pan, and keep warm.   9. Mix flour into 1/2 cup of light cream, stirring until smooth.
10. Stir into kettle drippings; bring to boil. Add remainder of light cream and simmer for 5 minutes. 11. Season with salt and pepper to taste. Pour sauce over cabbage rolls.

Linda Lichty Anderson
(Mrs. Robert)

Pork Burger King

Planning: Make ahead to the grilling point; patties may be frozen
Preparation Time: 20 minutes

Quantity: 8 servings
Cooking Time: 20 minutes

Patties:
2 pounds ground pork
1 cup soft bread crumbs
1/3 cup finely chopped green onion
1 6-ounce can water chestnuts, drained and chopped
1 egg
2 tablespoons dry cooking sherry
1 small clove garlic, crushed
1/8 teaspoon ginger

Patties:
1. Combine pork with next 7 ingredients. Mix well.   2. Shape into 8 equal-sized patties. Cover and place in refrigerator. Chill.

Sauce: (may be made in microwave)
1/2 cup crushed pineapple, drained
1/3 cup ketchup
2 tablespoons vinegar
2 tablespoons orange marmalade
1 tablespoon prepared mustard

Sauce:
1. Combine sauce ingredients. Heat until marmalade melts.

Sandwiches:
8 large hamburger buns
1 8-ounce can bean sprouts, rinsed and drained, or 1 cup fresh alfalfa sprouts

Sandwiches:
1. Broil or grill patties until done. Spoon sauce over during the last few minutes.   2. Place on warmed or toasted bun halves.   3. Spoon any remaining sauce over patties.   4. Cover with sprouts and top with bun.

Marty McNutt Port
(Mrs. Dale)

Torta Rustica

Planning: Can be made several hours ahead
Preparation Time: 2 hours

Quantity: 10-12 servings
Baking Time: 40-45 minutes, 375°

Sour Cream Pastry:
3 cups flour
1 teaspoon salt
1/4 teaspoon sugar

Sour Cream Pastry:
1. Combine dry ingredients.   2. Cut in butter and shortening until the mixture forms pea-sized balls.   3. Beat sour cream with cold water.   4. Mixing

Continued...

12 tablespoons unsalted butter
¹/₂ cup vegetable shortening,
  chilled
¹/₄ cup sour cream
¹/₄ cup ice water (more if needed)

lightly with a fork, drizzle in sour cream mixture until the dough forms a ball.
5. Divide pastry in half and pat into 2 rectangles.   6. Wrap in waxed paper and refrigerate about 1 hour.

Torta Filling:
1 10-ounce package frozen
  chopped spinach
¹/₂ pound spicy bulk Italian
  sausage
1 6-ounce carton ricotta cheese
³/₄ cup Parmesan cheese, freshly
  grated
1 ¹/₄ cups pitted ripe olives,
  coarsely chopped
3 eggs, slightly beaten
¹/₂ teaspoon salt

Torta Filling:
1. Thaw spinach and squeeze dry.
2. Sauté sausage until crumbly and drain on paper towels.   3. Combine spinach with drained sausage and sauté 2 minutes more.   4. Blend together ricotta, Parmesan, olives, beaten eggs, salt and cooled spinach-sausage mixture. 5. Prepare to assemble.

Assembly:
1 recipe sour cream pastry
1 egg, slightly beaten
1 tablespoon water

Assembly:
1. Roll out first half of pastry into a 10" x 14" rectangle. Pastry can be rolled into a circle, oval, or square as well.
2. Transfer to a baking sheet.   3. Beat egg with 1 tablespoon water to make an egg wash and brush over pastry.
4. Spoon filling over pastry leaving 1" all around.   5. Roll out second half of pastry the same size as the bottom.
6. Lay the top loosely over the filling.
7. Roll bottom edges up over the top edges and press together with a fork.
8. Brush top with egg wash.   9. Form decorations with excess pastry and place on top.   10. Cut 4 or 5 slits for steam vent.   11. Refrigerate the torta for 30 minutes or longer before baking.   12. Bake at 475° for 40 to 50 minutes or until golden brown.
13. Allow torta to sit 30 minutes before cutting.

Hint: This dish can be served as a light entree with a green salad for luncheon or supper. It can also be cut into bite-size squares and served as an appetizer.

Nancy Allbee Fox
(Mrs. James)

Ground Pork Quiche

A new way to serve a real man quiche.

Planning: None
Preparation Time: 30 minutes

Quantity: 6 servings
Baking Time: 40-50 minutes, 350°

1 9″ pie shell
1 pound ground pork, 75 to 80% lean
³/₄ cup milk
1 3-ounce package cream cheese
¹/₃ cup chopped onion
1 tablespoon butter
4 eggs
1 cup Cheddar cheese, shredded
¹/₂ teaspoon Worcestershire sauce
1 tablespoon flour
¹/₂ teaspoon salt
2 ounces pimento, chopped
¹/₈ teaspoon fresh ground pepper
dash nutmeg

1. Bake pie crust at 350° for 10 minutes.   **2.** Brown ground pork, drain well.   **3.** Heat milk in a small saucepan, add cream cheese and stir until melted.   **4.** Sauté onions in butter until soft.   **5.** In a large bowl beat eggs. Gradually beat in milk mixture until smooth.   **6.** Add onions, cheese, Worcestershire sauce, flour, salt, pimento, pepper and nutmeg.   **7.** Layer ground pork in baked crust. Pour egg mixture on top.   **8.** Bake at 350° for 40 to 50 minutes until custard is set.   **9.** Cool 5 to 10 minutes. Slice into wedges to serve.

Mary Kadera McNutt
(Mrs. Paul)

Pork 'n Cider

A good autumn dish.

Planning: None
Preparation Time: 20 minutes

Quantity: 4 servings
Cooking Time: 1 hour

1 pound boneless pork, cut into bite-size strips
1 tablespoon cooking oil
1 cup apple cider
¹/₄ cup chopped onion
4 teaspoons cornstarch
1 tablespoon brown sugar
¹/₂ teaspoon salt
¹/₄ teaspoon ground cinnamon
2 tablespoons vinegar
1 medium apple, cored and coarsely chopped
2 cups cooked rice, hot

1. In Dutch oven or large saucepan brown pork strips in oil. Drain off fat.   **2.** Add first ¹/₂ cup cider and onions. Bring to a boil. Reduce heat, cover, and simmer 40 minutes or until meat is tender.   **3.** Combine cornstarch, brown sugar, salt, and cinnamon. Add remaining ¹/₂ cup apple cider and vinegar.   **4.** Add mixture to pork. Add apple. Cook and stir until mixture is thickened and bubbly. Cook and stir 2 minutes more.   **5.** Serve over hot rice.

Black Hawk County Extension Office

VEGETABLES

VEGETABLES

Iowa Corn Pudding

Easy and unique topping.

Planning: Can be made ahead and
  baked later
Preparation Time: 15 minutes

Quantity: 6 servings
Baking Time: 1-1¼ hours, 325°

1 16-ounce can cream-style corn
1 cup medium-fine dry bread
  crumbs
1 cup milk
1 teaspoon salt
¼ teaspoon pepper
4 ounces sliced Cheddar cheese,
  cut in 1½" squares
3 slices bacon, cut in 1½" lengths

1. Combine cream-style corn, bread
crumbs, milk, salt and pepper, mix well.
Pour mixture into a greased 10" x 6" x
2" baking dish. **2.** Arrange pieces of
cheese and bacon alternately across the
top in checkerboard fashion. **3.** Bake
pudding at 325° for about 1 to 1¼
hours or until done.

Jeri Mixdorf Jenner
(Mrs. Billy)

Unique Corn Bake

Sweet and delicious cornbread taste.

Planning: None
Preparation Time: 10 minutes

Quantity: 12 or more servings
Baking Time: 30-35 minutes, 350°

1 17-ounce can cream corn
1 17-ounce can whole kernel corn,
  drained
2 eggs
½ cup butter, cut in pieces
1 cup sour cream
1 8½-ounce box corn muffin mix

1. Mix ingredients together and put in
greased 9" x 13" pan. **2.** Bake at 350°
for 30 to 35 minutes.

Marty Parrish Halupnik
(Mrs. Dale)

Broccoli-Cheddar Timbales

Perfect party dish—serve hot or cold.

Planning: Can be made ahead and baked later

Preparation Time: 20 minutes

Quantity: 8 servings

Baking Time: 35-40 minutes, 325°

¾ **pound (3 cups) fresh broccoli chopped**

¼ **cup chopped green onion**

2 **tablespoons butter**

1½ **cups liquid nonfat dry milk**

4 **eggs**

1 **cup plain bread crumbs (or use half plain and half seasoned)**

1¼ **cups sharp Cheddar cheese, shredded**

¾ **teaspoon salt**

¼ **teaspoon white pepper**

1. Cook broccoli slightly (crisp-tender); drain. 2. Sauté the chopped onion in the 2 tablespoons butter. Remove from heat and toss with broccoli. 3. Beat milk and eggs in medium bowl. Stir in broccoli mixture, bread crumbs, cheese, salt and pepper. 4. Spoon into eight buttered custard cups (or it will fill 12-cup cupcake pan). 5. Place cups in pan with enough water to reach ⅔ of the way up the sides of cups. 6. Bake at 325° for 35 to 40 minutes or until knife inserted near center comes out clean. 7. Unmold and serve hot or cold.

Hint: If serving hot, place each timbale onto a butter-sautéed tomato slice. If serving cold, place on cold tomato slice or lettuce liner.

Janice Merfeld Yagla
(Mrs. James)

Layered Broccoli-Wild Rice Casserole

Beautiful dish for company or buffet.

Planning: None
Preparation Time: 3 hours

Quantity: 6 servings
Baking Time: 30 minutes, 350°

2 tablespoons butter
4 tablespoons finely chopped onion
2 tablespoons flour
$1/2$ teaspoon salt
1 cup milk
$1/2$ cup sour cream
4 cups cooked wild rice (1 cup uncooked)
6 broccoli stalks, cut in half, lengthwise, cutting through the flowerets
1 cup Monterey Jack cheese, grated
$1/2$ cup pecans, chopped

1. Melt butter and sauté onion in butter, stirring until onion begins to soften slightly. Sprinkle in the flour and salt, stirring and cooking over low heat until mixture is smooth. **2.** Slowly stir in the milk, stirring until sauce thickens slightly. Fold in sour cream. **3.** Blend mixture into cooked wild rice.
4. Steam broccoli until just barely tender. Rinse under cold water to retain green color. **5.** Layer half of wild rice mixture in the bottom of a lightly buttered 7" x 11" glass casserole dish.
6. Alternating the flowerets toward the sides of the casserole, place the broccoli, cut-side down, on top of the rice.
7. Spoon the remaining rice down the center of the broccoli. **8.** Sprinkle the cheese over the center of the rice; sprinkle chopped pecans overall.
9. Bake covered 20 minutes at 350.° Uncover and bake 10 minutes or until cheese bubbles.

Carol Hayes Steckelberg
(Mrs. Randy)

177

Broccoli-Carrot Bake

This combination is interesting—good for a luncheon.

Planning: This recipe needs a 3-quart greased baking dish.
Preparation Time: 30-40 minutes

Quantity: 6-9 servings
Baking Time: 50-60 minutes

2 tablespoons butter
$^{1}/_{2}$ pound fresh broccoli, broken into flowerets, stems cut into $^{1}/_{2}''$ pieces
2 tablespoons soy sauce
1 $^{1}/_{2}$ teaspoons fresh garlic, minced
1 teaspoon celery seed
$^{1}/_{2}$ teaspoon dill weed
salt and pepper
$^{1}/_{2}$ pound carrots, peeled and diced
1 small onion, diced
7 eggs
1 $^{1}/_{4}$ cups milk
1 pound Monterey Jack cheese, shredded

1. Melt butter in skillet. 2. Add broccoli stems and sauté briefly. 3. Add soy sauce, garlic, celery seed, dill weed, salt and pepper. Cook over low heat about 5 minutes, stirring occasionally. 4. Add carrots, onion, and broccoli flowerets. Cover and cool until tender, about 10 minutes, stirring occasionally. 5. Beat eggs and milk in large bowl. Add cheese and vegetables. 6. Put in greased 3-quart baking dish. Place in large shallow pan and add boiling water to depth of 1 inch. 7. Bake at 350° for 50 to 60 minutes or until knife inserted into center comes out clean.

Linda Johnston Rust
(Mrs. Larry)

Carrot-Zucchini Casserole

Planning: None
Preparation Time: 20 minutes

Quantity: 10-12 servings
Baking Time: 30-50 minutes, 325°

5 medium zucchini
8 medium carrots, peeled
$^{1}/_{4}$ cup chopped green pepper
3 tablespoons pimento, chopped
$^{1}/_{4}$ cup butter
3 tablespoons fresh lemon juice
1 teaspoon salt
$^{1}/_{2}$ teaspoon chervil
parsley flakes

1. Slice zucchini in $^{3}/_{4}''$ lengths. 2. Cut carrots into thin, diagonal slices. 3. Place both in 2 quart casserole. 4. Top with green pepper and pimento. 5. In pan, melt butter; add lemon juice, salt and chervil. 6. Pour this mixture over vegetables. 7. Sprinkle with parsley. 8. Cover casserole and bake at 325° for 30 minutes for extra crisp vegetables or 50 minutes for tender vegetables.

Kate Della Maria Weidner
(Mrs. Steven)

Carrots au Gratin

Excellent cheese flavor.

Planning: Can be made ahead and baked later

Preparation Time: 40 minutes

Quantity: 8 servings

Baking Time: 15-20 minutes, 350°

3 tablespoons butter
$1/3$ cup chopped onion
3 tablespoons flour
1 teaspoon salt
$1/8$ teaspoon pepper
$1 1/2$ cups milk
1 cup American cheese, grated
$1 1/2$ pounds (4 cups) carrots, cooked, sliced and drained
1 tablespoon dried parsley flakes or fresh parsley, snipped

1. In large saucepan over low heat, melt the 3 tablespoons butter. Add onion; cook only until tender.   2. Stir in flour, salt and pepper; remove from heat.
3. Add milk gradually, stirring until smooth. Return to medium heat and cook until bubbly and thickened, stirring constantly.   4. Add cheese, stirring until melted; remove from heat. Stir in carrots and parsley.   5. Spread mixture in greased 10" x $6 1/2$" x 2" ($1 1/2$ quart) baking dish.

Topping:
2 cups corn flakes or $1/2$ cup packaged corn flake crumbs
1 tablespoon butter, melted

Topping:
1. If using corn flakes, measure; crush into fine crumbs. Combine and mix corn flake crumbs with the butter.
2. Sprinkle the crumb topping evenly over top of casserole.   3. Bake 15 to 20 minutes at 350°   4. Let stand 3 to 5 minutes before serving.

Patti Welch Holm
(Mrs. Richard)

Cauliflower Pie

Wedge-shaped servings add an impressive touch.

Planning: Can be made ahead and baked later

Preparation Time: 30 minutes

Quantity: 6-8 servings

Baking Time: 20 minutes, 375°

½ cup bread crumbs
2 tablespoons flour
¾ cup sharp Cheddar cheese, shredded
1 medium head cauliflower
1 cup sour cream
2 eggs
¾ teaspoon salt
¼ teaspoon white pepper

1. Blend the bread crumbs, flour and ½ cup of the cheese. Put half of his mixture into well buttered 9" pie pan (or use a shallow baking dish). 2. Cut cauliflower into flowerets and cook until tender. Place cooked cauliflower evenly in pan. 3. Beat sour cream, eggs, salt and pepper. Pour over cauliflower. 4. Add the remaining ¼ cup Cheddar cheese to the leftover crumb mixture. Sprinkle this mixture over top of sour cream mixture. 5. Bake 20 minutes at 375°.

Carol Hayes Steckelberg
(Mrs. Randy)

Ratatouille

Planning: None

Preparation Time: 40 minutes

Quantity: 6-8 servings

Cooking Time: 30 minutes

3 slices bacon, cut in 1" pieces
¼ cup oil
1 medium onion, sliced
1 clove garlic, minced
2½ pounds russet potatoes, peeled and cut in ¾" cubes
½ pound green beans, snapped
3 medium zucchini, thickly sliced
2 large tomatoes, wedged
2 tablespoons minced parsley
1½ teaspoons salt
½ teaspoon sweet basil
¼ teaspoon ground pepper

1. In large saucepan, fry bacon. Remove bacon and reserve grease. 2. Add oil to grease. Sauté onion and garlic.
3. Add potatoes and green beans. Cover and simmer 15 minutes.
4. Add zucchini, tomatoes, bacon and seasonings. 5. Cover and simmer about 10 minutes. Stir gently from time to time. Cook until vegetables are tender.

Cynthia Staley Kenyon
(Mrs. James)

Hearty Iowa Beans

A meal in itself...full of exciting flavors.

Planning: None
Preparation Time: 20 minutes

Quantity: 8 servings
Baking Time: 1 hour, 15 minutes, 375°

½ pound bacon, diced
2 pounds ground pork or beef
2 cups chopped onion
1 cup chopped celery
2 beef bouillon cubes
⅔ cup boiling water
1½ cloves garlic, minced
1½ cups ketchup
3 tablespoons prepared mustard
1½ teaspoons pepper
2 29-ounce cans molasses-style beans

1. In Dutch oven or roasting pan fry bacon until crisp; set aside. Drain fat.
2. Cook and stir ground pork, onion and celery until meat is brown and vegetables are tender. Spoon off excess fat.
3. Dissolve bouillon cubes in boiling water. Stir water and remaining ingredients into meat.   **4.** Cover and bake 1 hour and 15 minutes or until bubbly.
5. Garnish with bacon.

Juliann Ward Rounds
(Mrs. Douglas)

Far East Green Beans

Sour cream topping makes it interesting.

Planning: Serve in a 1½ quart bowl
Preparation Time: 1 hour

Quantity: 6 servings
Cooking Time: 30 minutes

2 10-ounce packages frozen cut green beans or 2 pounds fresh green beans, cut in 1″ pieces
1 8½-ounce can water chestnuts
½ cup onion, minced
2 tablespoons butter
1 teaspoon sugar
1 teaspoon seasoned salt
dash pepper
1 teaspoon cider vinegar
1 cup sour cream

1. Cook green beans according to package directions.   **2.** Drain and thinly slice water chestnuts; add to green beans and heat through.   **3.** Sauté onion in butter until transparent; add sugar, salt, pepper, vinegar and sour cream. Heat through, but do not boil.
4. At serving time, drain beans and pour them into serving bowl. Top with sour cream mixture and serve.

Gayle Price Denkinger
(Mrs. Donald)

Celery Almondine

Planning: None
Preparation Time: 30 minutes

Quantity: 6-8 servings
Cooking Time: 25 minutes
Baking Time: 35 minutes, 350°

1 large bunch pascal celery
¼ cup butter
¼ cup flour
½ teaspoon salt
dash pepper
3 green onions, chopped
1 2-ounce jar sliced pimento, drained
1 cup chicken broth
1 cup half and half
1 cup Swiss cheese, grated
¾ cup almonds, slivered
1 tablespoon butter

1. Cut celery diagonally into 1" pieces. **2.** Cook covered in ½ cup boiling salted water for 5 minutes; drain. Rinse with cold water. Drain. **3.** Melt ¼ cup butter; blend in flour, salt and pepper. **4.** Add green onions, pimento, broth, half and half, and ½ cup of the grated cheese. **5.** Cook, stirring constantly, until sauce is thickened. **6.** In skillet, toast almonds in 1 tablespoon butter. **7.** Mix half of the almonds with the celery and place in 9" x 13" casserole dish. **8.** Top with sauce and remaining ½ cup cheese. **9.** Sprinkle with remaining almonds. **10.** Bake for 35 minutes at 350°

Tricia McArthur Elmer
(Mrs. Clark)

Sweet Tomato Kraut

Surprisingly good—try it with bratwurst.

Planning: Can be made ahead and baked later
Preparation Time: 10 minutes

Quantity: 8 servings
Baking Time: 1 hour, 350°

4 slices bacon
1 medium onion, chopped
1 29-ounce can sauerkraut
1 20-ounce can tomatoes, well drained and cut into small pieces
1 cup brown sugar

1. Cut bacon in small pieces and fry with onion till golden and bacon is very crisp. (If desired, fry additional bacon to add as topping to casserole.) **2.** Mix bacon and onion mixture with remaining ingredients. Bake at 350° for 1 hour in a 2-quart casserole; uncover the last 15 minutes.

Diana Lichty Hansen
(Mrs. Milton)

Garden Vegetable Parmigiana

Healthy, different, and amazingly good.

Planning: Can be prepared ahead and baked later

Preparation Time: 25 minutes

Quantity: 6-8 servings

Baking Time: 20 minutes, 350°

1 eggplant, peeled and sliced ¼" thick
1 egg, beaten
prepared bread crumbs
2 tablespoons olive oil
2 medium zucchini, sliced
2 green peppers, cut in strips
1 or 2 large onions, sliced
2 tomatoes, sliced
¾ pound mozzarella cheese, grated
½ teaspoon salt
⅛ teaspoon pepper
½ teaspoon oregano
¼ teaspoon tarragon
6 tablespoons grated Parmesan cheese

1. Dip eggplant slices in egg, then in bread crumbs. Heat oil in skillet and sauté eggplant. 2. Place eggplant in bottom of greased 9" x 13" glass baking dish. 3. Layer other vegetables, mozzarella cheese, seasonings, and Parmesan cheese. 4. Bake 20 minutes at 350° or until cheese is melted.

Hint: This dish can be used as a meatless main dish or with hamburgers, steak or roast.

Kate Della Maria Weidner
(Mrs. Steven)

Winter Vegetable Medley 🐖
Great taste and good for you!

Planning: None
Preparation Time: 20 minutes

Quantity: 10-12 servings
Baking Time: 1¹/₂ hours, 350°

Vegetables:
1 8-ounce package frozen pea pods
1 8-ounce package fresh mushrooms
¹/₂ cup chopped onion
³/₄ cup chopped green pepper
1 cup diced celery
1¹/₂ cups thinly sliced raw carrots
7-ounce can water chestnuts, drained and sliced
1 16-ounce can french-cut green beans, drained
2 cups canned whole tomatoes, chopped
¹/₂ head fresh cauliflower, separated to flowerets

Vegetables:
1. Toss all the vegetables together.
2. Put into a 9" x 13" pan.

Sauce:
6 tablespoons butter
6 tablespoons sugar
4 tablespoons quick-cooking tapioca
2 teaspoons salt
1 teaspoon pepper
2 tablespoons real bacon bits
¹/₂ teaspoon oregano
¹/₈ teaspoon basil

Sauce:
1. Melt the butter.   2. Blend with the sugar, tapioca, salt, pepper, bacon bits, oregano and basil.   3. Pour sauce over the vegetables and mix.   4. Bake covered for 1¹/₂ hours at 350.°

Marsha Kohler Fisher
(Mrs. Michael)

Gratin of Leeks

Planning: Can be made ahead; use individual casserole dishes
Preparation Time: 1 1/2 to 2 hours

Quantity: 10-12 servings
Baking Time: 40 minutes, 350°

10 to 11 large leeks
4 slices bacon, cut into 1/2" pieces, blanched 20 seconds
1 cup water
salt
pepper, freshly ground
1/2 teaspoon thyme
2 tablespoons butter
2 tablespoons flour
1 1/2 cups milk
1 cup heavy cream
2 tablespoons Swiss cheese, grated
1 tablespoon Parmesan cheese

1. Trim tops and roots from leeks; wash leeks well and drain. 2. Cut leeks in 2" pieces and quarter them. 3. Cook blanched bacon in a saucepan until nicely browned. 4. Add leeks, water, salt, pepper and thyme and cover tightly. 5. Cook for 20 to 25 minutes until leeks are tender and water has evaporated. 6. Melt butter in a saucepan and stir in flour until smooth. 7. Add milk, whisking constantly until sauce boils. Cook for 5 minutes. 8. Stir in cream and Swiss cheese, and fold in leeks. 9. Transfer leeks to a shallow baking dish and sprinkle with Parmesan cheese. 10. Bake about 40 minutes at 350° until golden brown. Let stand 20 minutes before serving.

Hint: Leeks, members of the onion family, have a uniquely mild sweet flavor all their own. In Europe leeks are frequently used, not only because of their pleasant flavor, but because they are plentiful and inexpensive. Leeks are becoming increasingly popular in the United States but are sometimes difficult to find and relatively expensive.

To clean a leek, lay it on a cutting board and cut in half the long way, leaving the root end intact. Fan out leaves and rinse under cold water to remove dirt and sand. Then cut off root and tough green tops. Pat dry before using.

Dee Reinhart Vandeventer
(Mrs. David)

Scalloped Mushrooms

For mushroom lovers, this is the best.

Planning: Must stand in refrigerator overnight
Preparation Time: 30 minutes

Quantity: 6-10 servings
Baking Time: 30 minutes, 350°

2 pounds fresh mushrooms, sliced
3 tablespoons butter
3 tablespoons flour
dash of paprika
juice of ¹/₂ lemon (1 tablespoon)
1 egg yolk
1 cup cream

1. Briefly sauté mushrooms in 3 tablespoons butter. Add flour and simmer 10 minutes. **2.** Combine paprika, lemon juice, egg yolk and cream; add to mushrooms. **3.** Place mushroom mixture in a 9" x 13" baking pan. Sprinkle topping on. Let stand in refrigerator overnight. **4.** Bake at 350° for 30 minutes. Do not brown top too much.

Topping:
¹/₂ large package rich, round butter crackers, crushed
¹/₄ pound butter, softened

Topping:
1. Combine crushed crackers and the butter. **2.** Sprinkle topping on mushroom mixture before refrigeration.

Hint: If a creamier scalloped effect is desired, bake in a casserole dish.

Norma Smith Hassman
(Mrs. Dale)

Potato Parmesan Sticks

Crispy sticks—fun to eat.

Planning: Prepare up to 3 hours ahead and refrigerate until ready to bake
Preparation Time: 20 minutes

Quantity: 6 servings
Baking Time: 30-35 minutes, 400°

2 pounds Idaho baking potatoes
¹/₂ cup butter, melted
³/₄ cup fine dry bread crumbs
³/₄ cup grated Parmesan cheese
³/₄ teaspoon salt
¹/₄ teaspoon garlic powder
¹/₄ teaspoon black pepper

1. Peel potatoes; cut lengthwise into quarters. Cut each quarter into 3 strips. **2.** Roll in melted butter, then in mixture of bread crumbs, cheese, salt, garlic powder and pepper. **3.** Place in a single layer in a shallow baking dish or cookie sheet. **4.** Pour any remaining butter over potatoes. (optional) **5.** Bake at 400° for 30 to 35 minutes or until potatoes are tender.

Cathy Ercius Enstrom
(Mrs. Kenneth)

Gourmet Potatoes
Easy elegance.

Planning: Must cool potatoes first
Preparation Time: 45 minutes

Quantity: 8 servings
Baking Time: 30 minutes, 350°

6 medium red potatoes
2 cups Cheddar cheese, shredded
1/4 cup butter
1 1/2 cups sour cream
1/4 cup chopped onion
1 teaspoon salt
1/4 teaspoon pepper
paprika

1. Cook potatoes in skins until just tender. Chill. 2. Peel potatoes. Shred coarsely with grater or food processor. 3. In saucepan over low heat, combine cheese and 1/4 cup butter. Stir until almost melted. Remove from heat. 4. Blend in sour cream, onion, salt, and pepper. 5. Fold in potatoes and turn into a greased casserole. Sprinkle with paprika. Bake covered, for 30 minutes at 350.°

Marie Shipman Spears
(Mrs. Jon)

Sweet Potatoes in Orange Cups

Planning: None
Preparation Time: 30 minutes

Quantity: 8 servings
Baking Time: 20 minutes, 350°

4 medium oranges
8 medium sweet potatoes, cooked
   and peeled
1/3 cup butter
1/3 cup brown sugar
1/2 cup orange juice
rind of 1 orange, grated
1/2 teaspoon salt
1/2 cup pecans, broken
1/4 cup dry sherry
1/2 cup tiny marshmallows

1. Cut oranges in half; extract juice and remove pulp. 2. Scallop or cut in "w" shape the edges of orange shells. 3. Mash potatoes until smooth and fluffy. 4. Add butter, brown sugar, orange juice, rind and salt. 5. Beat until well blended. 6. Add nuts and sherry. 7. Fill orange shells with potato mixture. 8. Dot with marshmallows. 9. Bake for 20 minutes at 350.°

Hint: Surround your roast pork with these.

Kate Della Maria Weidner
(Mrs. Steven)

Brandied Apple Wild Rice ❧

Planning: None
Preparation Time: 45 minutes

Quantity: 6 servings
Cooking Time: 25 minutes

1 tablespoon brandy (do not
    substitute other liquors)
1 tablespoon honey
1 medium apple, diced
2¹/₂ cups water
1 tablespoon butter
1 6-ounce package long grain and
    wild rice
¹/₄ cup walnuts, coarsely chopped

1. Combine brandy and honey in medium bowl, stirring until well
blended.   2. Add apple, tossing to coat.
Let stand, covered, stirring occasionally
while rice is cooking.   3. Combine
water, butter and contents of rice and
seasoning packet in medium saucepan.
Bring to boil; reduce heat; cover tightly
and simmer until all liquid is absorbed,
about 25 minutes.   4. Stir apple mixture and walnuts into rice. Let stand
covered 2 to 3 minutes. Serve
immediately.

Janet Rohlf Holden
(Mrs. L. Sam)

Wild Rice with Wine ❧

Planning: Can be prepared ahead,
    can be frozen before baking
Preparation Time: 40 minutes

Quantity: 8-10 servings
Cooking Time: 30 minutes
Baking Time: 50-70 minutes, 325°

1 cup wild rice, rinsed and
    drained
¹/₂ cup brown rice
2 cups chicken broth
1 cup dry white wine
¹/₂ cup chopped celery
¹/₄ chopped onion
¹/₂ pound fresh mushrooms, sliced
¹/₄ cup butter
1 8-ounce can water chestnuts,
    sliced
³/₄ teaspoon salt
¹/₄ teaspoon pepper
2 ounces sliced almonds

1. Combine rice, chicken broth and
wine in saucepan. Bring to boil; reduce
heat. Simmer, covered, for 30 minutes.
Do not drain.   2. Sauté celery, onion
and mushrooms in butter until just tender.   3. Add water chestnuts, salt and
pepper and stir into rice.   4. Place in 2-
quart casserole and bake, covered, for
45 minutes to 60 minutes at 325°
5. Sprinkle with almonds and bake
uncovered for 5 to 10 minutes longer.

Dorothy Hostetter Plager
(Mrs. Vernon)

DESSERTS

DESSERTS

Grandma's Frosted Creams
Make them large like Grandma did.

Planning: Must be made ahead
Preparation Time: 30 minutes

Quantity: 4 dozen
Chilling Time: 3 hours or overnight
Baking Time: 10-15 minutes, 350°

1 cup butter
1 cup sugar
1 cup sorghum
2 eggs
1 tablespoon soda, dissolved in
   2 tablespoons warm water
1 teaspoon ginger
1 teaspoon cloves
5 cups flour (approximately)
1 cup cold water

1. Cream butter and sugar. Add sorghum, eggs, and soda. Beat well.
2. Sift together dry ingredients.
3. Add dry ingredients alternately with cold water. 4. Stir in additional flour one tablespoon at a time until dough is the consistency of rolled cookie dough.
5. Chill for at least 3 hours—overnight if possible. 6. Roll out on floured cloth to $^1/_4$ to $^1/_2$ inch thickness. Cut desired shapes. 7. Bake for 10 to 15 minutes at 350° or until golden brown.

Browned Butter Frosting:
4 tablespoons butter
6 tablespoons milk
$^1/_2$ cup brown sugar
powdered sugar, sifted
2 teaspoons vanilla

Browned Butter Frosting:
1. Brown butter. 2. Add milk and brown sugar. Stir and cook 3 minutes. Cool slightly. 3. Add enough sifted powdered sugar to thicken as desired.
4. Add vanilla.

Hint: This frosting recipe makes 3 to 4 cups.

*Junean Goschke Witham
(Mrs. Dick)*

Lemonade Cookies

Planning: Can freeze
Preparation Time: 15 minutes

Quantity: 6 dozen
Baking Time: 8 minutes, 400°

1 cup butter
1 cup sugar
2 eggs
3 cups flour
1 teaspoon baking soda
1 6-ounce can frozen lemonade
  concentrate, thawed

1. Cream butter and sugar.   2. Add eggs one at a time, beating well after each addition.   3. Combine flour and baking soda.   4. Add dry ingredients alternately with 1/2 cup of the lemonade concentrate.   5. Drop by teaspoonsful 2" apart on ungreased cookie sheet. 6. Bake about 8 minutes.   7. Remove from oven and brush lightly with remaining concentrate and sprinkle with sugar.

Hint: You can use a lemon glaze for a stronger lemon flavor.

Diana Lichty Hansen
(Mrs. Milton)

Chocolate Cherry Cookies

Planning: Can be made ahead and
  frozen
Preparation Time: 1 hour

Quantity: 3 dozen
Baking Time: 10 minutes, 350°

1/2 cup butter
1 cup sugar
1 egg
1/2 teaspoon vanilla
1 1/2 cups flour
1/2 cup cocoa
1/4 teaspoon salt
1/4 teaspoon baking powder
1/4 teaspoon baking soda
1 6-ounce package chocolate
  chips, melted
1/2 cup sweetened condensed milk
1 10-ounce jar maraschino
  cherries, drained with 1/4 cup
  juice reserved

1. Cream butter, sugar, egg and vanilla until light and fluffy.   2. Add dry ingredients and mix.   3. Roll cookie dough into small balls and make a thumbprint.   4. Place a cherry in the depression.   5. Combine melted chocolate chips, sweetened condensed milk and 1/4 cup reserved cherry juice.   6. Spoon about 1/2 teaspoon sauce over cherry.   7. Bake on ungreased baking sheet 10 minutes at 350°.

Joan Dawson Huhn
(Mrs. Kenneth)

Holiday Fruit Cookies
A must for any holiday party.

Planning: Must chill 3 hours or overnight; dough can be frozen
Preparation Time: 1-1½ hours

Quantity: 8-10 dozen
Baking Time: 15 minutes, 350°

1 cup unsalted butter
1½ cups brown sugar
2 eggs
2½ cups (save ½ cup to flour fruit) flour
1 teaspoon cinnamon
dash salt
1 teaspoon soda
2 pounds dates, chopped
½ pound candied cherries, chopped
½ pound walnuts, chopped
½ pound pecans, chopped
½ pound candied pineapple, chopped

1. Cream butter and sugar and add eggs one at a time beating well after each egg.   2. Add dry ingredients and stir to mix.   3. Flour candied fruit and nuts and stir into cookie dough.   4. Chill three hours or overnight.   5. Drop and bake on cookie sheet for 15 minutes at 350°

Jane Rife Field
(Mrs. Hugh)

Christmas Strawberry Coconut Balls ❧
Great on holiday cookie tray.

Planning: Can be frozen
Preparation Time: 30 minutes

Quantity: 3-4 dozen
Chilling Time: 30 minutes

1 14-ounce can sweetened condensed milk
3 3-ounce packages red jello
16 ounces grated coconut
1 teaspoon almond flavoring
few drops of food coloring
plastic strawberry tops (found in cake decorating store)

1. Mix sweetened condensed milk, 2 packages red jello (strawberry, raspberry, etc.), coconut, almond flavoring and food coloring.   2. Chill ½ hour.   3. Roll into the shape of a strawberry and roll each in the 3rd package of dry jello.   4. Place the green strawberry tops on top of the strawberries.

Susan Walker Crouse
(Mrs. James)

Lemon Cheese Bars ✤

Quick and easy, but rich.

Planning: None
Preparation Time: 15-20 minutes

Quantity: 2 dozen
Baking Time: 40 minutes, 350°

1 18-ounce package lemon cake
  mix
¹/₃ cup butter
2 eggs
1 16-ounce can lemon frosting (or
  2 cups if you make your own)
1 8-ounce package cream cheese
¹/₂ cup chopped nuts
1 tablespoon powdered sugar

1. Combine cake mix, butter and 1 egg until crumbly. 2. Press into a 9" x 13" pan. 3. Mix frosting, cream cheese and 1 egg until fluffy. Fold in the nuts. Spread over the crust. 4. Bake for 40 minutes at 350.° Do not overbake. 5. Cool and sprinkle with powdered sugar.

Kris Garetson McIntee
(Mrs. Tom)

Rhubarb Bars

Planning: Can be made ahead
  and frozen
Preparation Time: 1 hour

Quantity: 3 dozen
Baking Time: Crust—10 to 15
  minutes, 350°; filling—25 to 30
  minutes, 350°

Crust:
2 cups flour
2 sticks unsalted butter, cut into
  small pieces
10 tablespoons powdered sugar
³/₄ teaspoon salt

Filling:
3 cups sugar
²/₃ cup flour
1¹/₂ teaspoons baking powder
6 eggs, beaten
1 teaspoon salt
4 cups rhubarb, cut into small
  pieces

Crust:
1. Combine the crust ingredients with your hands or pastry blender until crumbly. 2. Pat into a jelly roll pan and bake 10 to 15 minutes at 350° or until lightly browned.

Filling:
1. Combine flour, sugar and baking powder. 2. Stir in remaining ingredients. 3. Pour over hot crust and continue baking 25 to 35 minutes or until top is lightly browned.

Jane Rife Field
(Mrs. Hugh)

Peanut-Marshmallow Squares

The kids will love this nutritious snack.

Planning: None
Preparation Time: 45 minutes

Quantity: 2 dozen squares
Baking Time: 15-19 minutes, 350°

1/2 cup butter
1 1/2 cups flour
2/3 cup brown sugar
1/2 teaspoon baking powder
1/2 teaspoon salt
1/4 teaspoon baking soda
2 egg yolks
1 teaspoon vanilla
3 cups miniature marshmallows

1. Cut butter into flour, brown sugar, baking powder, salt and baking soda.
2. Beat egg yolks with vanilla and add to the dry ingredients. 3. Press into 9" x 13" pan and bake at 350° for 13 to 15 minutes. 4. Remove from oven and top with marshmallows. Bake 2 to 4 minutes. Cool.

Topping:
2/3 cup light corn syrup
1/4 cup butter
2 teaspoons vanilla
1 12-ounce jar peanut butter
2 cups crisp rice cereal
2 cups salted peanuts

Topping:
1. Cook corn syrup, butter, vanilla and peanut butter slowly until well combined. Add cereal and peanuts.
2. Spread over crust. Cut into bars.

Pat Ley Burroughs
(Mrs. Richard)

Chocolate Bars

Just like candy.

Planning: None
Preparation Time: 5 minutes

Quantity: 2 dozen
Baking Time: 25 minutes, 350°

1 cup butter
1 cup brown sugar
1 cup white sugar
1 egg yolk
1 cup flour
8 to 10 1 1/2-ounce chocolate candy bars

1. Cream together butter, sugars and egg yolk. Add flour. 2. Pat into a greased 8" x 11" baking dish. Bake 25 minutes at 350° 3. Remove from oven and top with chocolate bars.

Gloria Brunskill Paulsen
(Mrs. Tom)

The Ultimate Chocolate Bar
The name says it all!

Planning: Must do ahead
Preparation Time: 45 minutes

Quantity: 36 bars
Baking Time: 35 minutes, 350°

Base:
1/2 cup butter
1 1-ounce square unsweetened
   chocolate
1 cup flour
1 cup sugar
1/2 cup nuts, chopped
1 teaspoon baking powder
1 teaspoon vanilla
2 eggs

Base:
1. Preheat oven to 350.° Grease and lightly flour 9" x 13" pan.   2. In large saucepan melt butter and chocolate over low heat.   3. Lightly spoon flour into measuring cup, level off, stir in remaining base ingredients. Mix well.
4. Spread in prepared pan.

Filling:
2 3-ounce packages cream cheese,
   softened
1/4 cup butter, softened
1/2 cup sugar
2 tablespoons flour
1 egg
1/2 teaspoon vanilla

Filling:
1. In small bowl, combine all filling ingredients. Beat one minute at medium speed until smooth and fluffy.
2. Spread over chocolate mixture.
3. Bake at 350° for 25 to 35 minutes or until toothpick inserted in center comes out clean.

Frosting:
2 cups miniature marshmallows
1/3 cup butter
2 1-ounce squares unsweetened
   chocolate
1/3 cup milk
2 ounces cream cheese
4 cups powdered sugar
1 teaspoon vanilla

Frosting:
1. Sprinkle with marshmallows and bake 2 minutes longer.   2. In large saucepan melt 1/3 cup butter, 2-ounces chocolate, milk, and cream cheese over low heat. Remove from heat.   3. Add powdered sugar and vanilla. Blend well.   4. Immediately pour over marshmallow and swirl together.
5. Chill until firm. Cut into bars. Store in refrigerator.

Sue Willett Sawyer
(Mrs. Gary)
Diana Lichty Hansen
(Mrs. Milton)

Chocolate Peppermint Brownies

Peppermint flavor adds a special touch to these brownies.

Planning: None
Preparation Time: 35 minutes

Quantity: 48 squares
Baking Time: 25-30 minutes, 350°
Chilling Time: Until ready to serve

Brownies:
4 squares unsweetened chocolate
1 cup butter
4 eggs
2 cups sugar
1/4 teaspoon peppermint extract
1 teaspoon vanilla
1 cup flour
1 12-ounce package semi-sweet
    chocolate chips

Brownies:
1. Melt chocolate and butter in small pan. 2. In a large bowl beat the eggs until thick. Add sugar gradually. Stir in the chocolate mixture, peppermint and vanilla. Mix well. 3. Stir in the flour and add the chocolate chips. 4. Pour into 9" x 13" pan and bake at 350° for 25 to 30 minutes. Cool.

Frosting:
4 tablespoons butter, softened
2 cups powdered sugar
2 tablespoons milk
1 teaspoon peppermint extract
2 tablespoons butter
2 squares unsweetened chocolate

Frosting:
1. Cream together butter and powdered sugar. 2. Add milk and peppermint extract. Spread over cooled brownies. 3. Melt chocolate and butter. Drizzle over frosting. 4. Refrigerate brownies.

Kathy Walden Schreiner
(Mrs. Mark)

Chocolate Leaves

For special dessert decorating.

Planning: Uses fig leaves
Preparation Time: 30 minutes

Quantity; 10 to 12 leaves
Freezing Time: 15 minutes

8 ounces semi-sweet chocolate
1 tablespoon vegetable shortening
10 to 12 fig tree leaves (or any
    stable waxy leaf)

1. Melt chocolate and shortening in top of double boiler. 2. Using spoon, generously coat underside of leaves with chocolate mixture and freeze until firm. 3. Peel leaf from chocolate, starting at stem. 4. Garnish desserts.

Peg Zeis McGarvey
(Mrs. Thomas)

Creme de Menthe Squares

Great for a holiday gift.

Planning: Can be done ahead and frozen
Preparation Time: 45 minutes-1 hour

Quantity: 96 small squares
Baking Time: None

1 1/4 cups butter
1/2 cup unsweetened cocoa powder
3 1/2 cups sifted powdered sugar
1 egg, beaten
1 teaspoon vanilla
2 cups graham cracker crumbs
1/3 cup green creme de menthe (syrup can be used)
1 1/2 cups semi-sweet chocolate chips

1. In saucepan, combine 1/2 cup butter and cocoa powder. Heat and stir until well blended.   2. Remove from heat and add 1/2 cup of the powdered sugar, egg and vanilla.   3. Stir in graham cracker crumbs. Mix well.   4. Press into bottom of ungreased 9" x 13" pan.

Middle Layer:
1. Melt another 1/2 cup butter.   2. In small mixer bowl combine melted butter and creme de menthe.   3. At low speed, beat in the remaining 3 cups powdered sugar until smooth.
4. Spread over the chocolate layer.
5. Chill.

Top Layer:
1. Melt the remaining 1/4 cup butter and the chocolate chips.   2. Spread over mint layer. Chill slightly.   3. Cut in small squares. Store in refrigerator.

Hint: Wrap squares individually in plastic wrap and fill clear glass jars. Decorate with holiday ribbons.

Carol Hayes Steckelberg
(Mrs. Randy)
Cathie Pederson Miehe
(Mrs. Fred Jr.)

Chocolate Cream Cheese Cupcakes

A yummy surprise filling.

Planning: None
Preparation Time: 20 minutes

Quantity: 15 cupcakes
Baking Time: 15-20 minutes, 350°

Filling:
1 8-ounce package cream cheese,
    softened
1 egg
¹/₃ cup sugar
¹/₈ teaspoon salt
1 12-ounce package
    mini-chocolate chips

Filling:
1. Combine softened cream cheese, egg, sugar and salt; mix well. 2. Blend in chocolate chips and set aside.

Cake:
1¹/₂ cups flour
1 cup sugar
¹/₄ cup cocoa
1 teaspoon baking soda
¹/₂ teaspoon salt
1 cup water
¹/₂ cup cooking oil
1 teaspoon vanilla
1 tablespoon vinegar

Cake:
1. Sift together flour, sugar, cocoa, baking soda and salt. 2. Stir in water, oil, vanilla and vinegar. 3. Fill paper lined cupcake pans ¹/₃ full of batter. 4. Top with 1¹/₂ teaspoons cheese mixture. 5. Bake at 350° for 15 to 20 minutes. 6. Remove from cupcake pans immediately.

Hint: Can also use mini cupcake pans.

Several League Members

Twinkie Cake
A delicious chocolate version.

Planning: None
Preparation Time: 30 minutes

Quantity: 24 servings
Cooking Time: 30 minutes, 325°

Cake:
1/2 cup butter, softened
2 cups sugar
2 eggs
1 teaspoon vanilla
1/2 cup cocoa
1/2 cup milk
1 cup cold water
2 cups flour
1 teaspoon soda

Cake:
1. Combine butter, sugar, eggs, vanilla and cocoa. Beat in milk and water. Add flour and soda.   2. Pour into greased and floured 13 1/2" x 10" x 1" pan.
3. Bake at 325° for 30 minutes.
4. Cool and remove from pan.
5. Cut cooled cake in half lengthwise with a taut thread.

Filling:
5 tablespoons flour
1 cup milk
1 cup sugar
1/2 teaspoon salt
1/2 cup butter
1/2 cup vegetable shortening
1 teaspoon vanilla

Filling:
1. Mix flour and milk in a saucepan.
2. Cook until thick. Cool.   3. Cream sugar, salt, butter, shortening and vanilla.   4. Add cooled mixture and beat until the consistency of whipped cream.   5. Spread filling between the cake halves.

Frosting:
3 tablespoons butter
2 tablespoons cocoa
1 1/2 cup powdered sugar
2 tablespoons warm milk
1 teaspoon vanilla

Frosting:
1. Melt butter and cocoa in saucepan.
2. Add powdered sugar, warm milk and vanilla.   3. Beat until creamy and spread over the cake.

Barb Burnham Paxson
(Mrs. Richard)

German Apple Cake

Planning: Can be prepared ahead
Preparation Time: 30-40 minutes

Quantity: 12 servings
Baking Time: 45-60 minutes, 350°

2 eggs
2 cups sugar
1 teaspoon baking soda
1 teaspoon vanilla
4 cups fresh apples, thinly sliced
2 cups sifted flour
2 teaspoons cinnamon
1/2 teaspoon salt
1 cup salad oil
1/2 cup to 1 cup walnuts, chopped

1. Mix all ingredients together with a spoon. Batter will be very stiff.
2. Spread into a greased and floured 13" x 9" pan. **3.** Bake 45 to 60 minutes at 350°.

Icing:
2 3-ounce packaged cream cheese, softened
3 tablespoons butter, melted
1 1/2 cups powdered sugar
1 teaspoon vanilla

Icing:
1. Mix the icing ingredients together. Beat until smooth. **2.** Spread icing on cake.

Carolyn Cole Evans
(Mrs. Kevin)

Sour Cream Pound Cake

Planning: May be frozen
Preparation Time: 1 hour

Quantity: 12-15 servings
Baking Time: 1 hour, 350°

3 cups flour
1/4 teaspoon baking soda
6 eggs, separated
1/2 teaspoon salt
1 cup butter
2 3/4 cups sugar
1 teaspoon vanilla
1 8-ounce carton sour cream

1. Grease and flour a 10" tube pan.
2. Sift flour and baking soda three times. **3.** Add salt to egg whites and beat until soft peaks form. **4.** Cream butter and sugar; add vanilla. **5.** Add one egg yolk at a time, beating well after each addition. **6.** Add flour and soda mixture alternately with sour cream.
7. Fold in beaten egg whites. **8.** Bake 1 hour at 350° **9.** Top with fresh fruit or fruit sauce.

Linda Hexom Lott
(Mrs. Charles)

Grandma Mae's Whipped Cream Cake

Planning: Best served same day
Preparation Time: 15 minutes

Quantity: 8-10 servings
Baking Time: 25-30 minutes, 350°

Cake:
1 cup whipping cream
2 eggs
1 cup sugar
1 teaspoon vanilla
1 1/2 cups sifted cake flour
1/4 teaspoon salt
2 teaspoons baking powder

Cake:
1. Whip cream until it holds its shape.
2. Beat eggs until thick and lemon colored.   3. Add eggs to whipped cream. Beat until light as foam.   4. Add sugar and beat well.   5. Add vanilla.   6. Sift dry ingredients together three times. Fold into cream mixture.   7. Bake cake batter in two 8" greased and floured cake pans at 350° for 25 to 30 minutes.

Icing:
3 cups whipping cream
3/4 cup powdered sugar, sifted
1 teaspoon vanilla

Icing:
1. Whip cream until it holds its shape.
2. Add powdered sugar and vanilla and beat until icing consistency.

Filling:
1 to 2 cups fresh fruit such as
    sliced bananas, strawberries,
    raspberries

Filling:
1. To assemble cooked cake, place fruit layer (either single fruit or any combination) between cake layers. Spread icing over entire cake.

Karen Karman Gartelos
(Mrs. Peter)

Popcorn Cake ❧

Great for cake walks, children's birthdays, holiday gifts.

Planning: Can be made ahead
Preparation Time: 20 minutes

Quantity: 10 servings
Baking Time: None

1/2 cup butter
1 16-ounce bag marshmallows
1/4 cup peanut butter
4 quarts popped popcorn
1 cup dry roasted peanuts
1 10-ounce package chocolate
   candy-coated peanuts

1. Melt butter, marshmallows, and peanut butter in large pan until completely melted. Cook one more minute.
2. Pour over popped corn and peanuts; mix in the chocolate candy. 3. Pour into a buttered angel food cake pan and turn out on foil covered cardboard cake plate when it is ready.

Hint: At Christmas decorate with candy canes and foil-wrapped chocolates. Place a plain bow in center.

Susan Walker Crouse
(Mrs. James)

Hazelnut Cheesecake

Planning: Can be made 3 to 4 days
   ahead
Preparation Time: 20-30 minutes
   ahead

Quantity: 12-16 servings
Baking Time: 1 hour 40 minutes,
   300°

Crumb Crust:
1 cup graham cracker crumbs
1/4 cup sugar
4 tablespoons butter

Crumb Crust:
1. Blend ingredients together for crust. 2. Press mixture evenly into buttered bottom of 9" springform pan.

Cheesecake:
1 cup hazelnuts (filberts), toasted
   and finely chopped
4 8-ounce packages cream cheese,
   softened
1 1/2 cups sugar
1 teaspoon vanilla
4 eggs
1/4 cup whipping cream, whipped

Cheesecake:
1. Toast nuts on cookie sheet in 400° oven for 10 minutes stirring occasionally. Rub warm nuts in clean towel to remove skins. Sift to separate skins before chopping. 2. Beat cream cheese, sugar, vanilla, eggs and cream in large bowl until smooth. 3. Stir in hazelnuts. Pour into prepared pan. 4. Bake at 300° for 1 hour and 40 minutes. Turn off heat; let cake cool in oven, with door ajar, for 1 hour. Remove from oven.

Several League Members

205

Chocolate Cheesecake

Planning: Can be frozen
Preparation Time: 30 minutes

Quantity: 6-8 servings
Baking Time: 1 hour, 375°
Chilling Time: Overnight

Crust:
1 8¹/₂-ounce package chocolate wafers or 1³/₄ cup graham cracker crumbs with ¹/₄ cup sugar added.
6 tablespoons butter, melted

Crust:
1. Crush wafers and mix with butter.
2. Press into a 9" springform pan.

Filling:
1 12-ounce package chocolate chips
3 8-ounce packages cream cheese, softened
1 cup sugar
1 tablespoon Kahlua or vanilla extract
3 eggs
1 8-ounce carton sour cream

Garnish:
chocolate curls
whipped cream, whipped

Filling:
1. Melt chocolate chips, set aside.
2. In large bowl, with mixer at medium speed, beat cream cheese, sugar and Kahlua until smooth.   3. Beat in melted chocolate chips.   4. Add eggs, one at a time, beating well after each addition.   5. Add sour cream, beat until smooth.   6. Pour into crumb crust.   7. Bake 1 hour at 375.°
8. Remove to wire rack to cool completely. Cover with foil and refrigerate overnight before serving.   9. To serve, carefully remove side of pan and garnish with chocolate curls or whipped cream.

Jane Schnieder Overbeeke
(Mrs. John)
Tricia Staley Early

Valentine Tarts

Planning: Can be done 6 to 8 hours ahead; needs 6 heart-shaped molds
Preparation Time: 2 hours

Quantity: 6 heart-shaped molds
Chilling Time: 30-60 minutes
Baking Time: 20-25 minutes, 350°

Crust:
¼ cup sugar
3 cups unbleached flour, sifted
1 teaspoon salt
⅓ cup vegetable shortening, chilled
¾ cup unsalted butter, cold
ice water

Crust:
1. Combine sugar, flour, and salt in a chilled bowl. 2. Cut in shortening and butter until mixture resembles coarse meal. 3. Add water until mixture can be formed into a ball. 4. Chill 30 to 60 minutes wrapped in wax paper.
5. Roll out dough on floured surface to ⅛" thick and cut into six equal pieces. 6. Grease backs of six oven proof heart-shaped molds and fit dough into molds. Trim excess with a sharp knife. 7. Press bottoms gently in several places, place on baking sheet, and bake at 350° for 25 to 30 minutes or until golden brown. 8. Cool, carefully remove shells from molds and place on platter and fill.

Filling:
2-ounces semi-sweet chocolate
2 3-ounce packages cream cheese, softened
1 cup powdered sugar
⅓ cup whipping cream
1 tablespoon orange liqueur
½ teaspoon vanilla
2 pints fresh strawberries, washed and hulled
½ cup seedless raspberry jam, melted

Filling:
1. Melt chocolate over very low heat and while warm, gently spread over bottoms of cooled shells, and allow to set. 2. Beat cream cheese and powdered sugar until smooth and creamy. Add whipping cream, orange liqueur and vanilla. 3. Spoon over chocolate and chill 30 minutes. 4. Combine strawberries and jam, tossing berries gently to coat. 5. Arrange over filling, cover carefully and refrigerate. Serve within 6 to 8 hours.

Jane Rife Field
(Mrs. Hugh)

Red Flame Seedless Grape Tart

Exquisite.

Planning: Must chill minimum
2 hours
Preparation Time: 1 hour

Quantity: 12-16 servings
Chilling Time: 3 hours

11" or 12" baked tart shell, cooled
1 14-ounce can sweetened
  condensed milk
1/2 cup sour cream
1/4 cup lemon juice, fresh
1/2 teaspoon grated lemon peel
4 to 5 cups Red Flame seedless
  grapes
1 8-ounce jar red currant jelly
2 tablespoons orange liqueur
1/4 teaspoon ground cinnamon

1. Mix milk, sour cream, lemon juice
and peel in medium bowl until
blended. 2. Spread in tart shell and
refrigerate until filling is firm, about 1
hour. 3. Arrange grapes over filling,
standing cut halves partly on edge and
overlapping in rings, starting from the
outside. 4. Heat jelly, liqueur and
cinnamon over low heat in small
saucepan until melted. 5. Cool
slightly; brush over grapes. 6. Chill,
covered, two hours or overnight.

Marjorie Van Hoesen Butler
(Mrs. Wallace)

Meringue Pie

A light dessert.

Planning: None
Preparation Time: 20 minutes

Quantity: One 9" pie
Baking Time: 20 minutes, 350°

4 egg whites
1/2 teaspoon baking powder
1 cup sugar
20 round rich butter crackers
1/2 cup pecans, chopped
1 teaspoon vanilla
1 cup whipping cream, whipped
unsweetened chocolate shavings

1. Beat egg whites and baking powder
until stiff peaks form. Slowly beat in 1
cup sugar. 2. Crush crackers by hand
and stir into egg white mixture.
3. Fold in pecans and vanilla. 4. Place
in ungreased, metal pie plate. 5. Bake
at 350° for 20 minutes. 6. Cool and
top with whipped cream and chocolate
shavings.

Susie Kaldor Heaton
(Mrs. Robert)

Tin Roof Mousse Pie
Very rich.

Planning: Can be made a day before
Preparation Time: 30 minutes

Quantity: 6 servings
Chilling Time: At least 2 hours

Cookie Crust:
1¹/₂ cups cream-filled chocolate cookies, crumbled
4 to 6 tablespoons butter, melted

Cookie Crust:
1. Butter 9" pie plate.   2. Stir crumbled cookies and butter together and press into pie plate. Reserve some crumbs for topping. Chill.

Filling:
¹/₂ cup butter, softened
³/₄ cup sugar
2 squares unsweetened chocolate
2 eggs
2 cups frozen whipped topping
¹/₃ cup peanut butter chips
¹/₃ cup chocolate chips

Filling:
1. Cream butter and sugar.   2. Melt and add the unsweetened chocolate.
3. Add eggs, one at a time, and beat for 5 minutes.   4. Fold in whipped topping, peanut butter chips and chocolate chips.   5. Pour into cookie crust. Chill 2 hours.

Topping:
1 cup whipping cream
1 tablespoon powdered sugar
Spanish peanuts
cookie crumbs

Topping:
1. Whip together the powdered sugar and whipping cream until firm.
2. Pour over dessert and garnish with peanuts and cookie crumbs.

Terry Rosenberg Poe
(Mrs. Stan)

French Lemon Pie

Planning: Can prepare ahead
Preparation Time: 5 minutes

Quantity: 7 servings
Baking Time: 50 minutes, 350°

4 eggs
1 cup light corn syrup
1 teaspoon lemon peel, grated
¹/₃ cup lemon juice
2 tablespoons butter, melted
1 cup sugar
2 tablespoons flour
1 9" pastry shell, unbaked
sweetened whipped cream

1. In medium bowl beat eggs well.
2. Add corn syrup, lemon peel, lemon juice and melted butter.   3. Combine sugar and flour; stir into egg mixture.
4. Pour into unbaked pastry shell.
5. Bake for 50 minutes at 350°.
6. Chill.   7. Serve with whipped cream.

Diana Lichty Hansen
(Mrs. Milton)

Angel Pie
An elegant end to any meal.

Planning: None
Preparation Time: 30 minutes

Quantity: One 10″ pie
Baking Time: 1 hour, 275°

Crust:
4 egg whites
1 cup sugar
¼ teaspoon cream of tartar
½ teaspoon vanilla

Crust:
1. Beat egg whites until very stiff gradually adding sugar, cream of tartar and vanilla.   2. Spread in lightly greased 10″ pie pan.   3. Bake at 275° for 1 hour.

Filling:
4 egg yolks
½ cup sugar
juice of 1 large lemon
¼ teaspoon grated lemon peel
1 cup whipped cream topping

Filling:
1. Cook egg yolks, sugar, lemon juice, and peel in double boiler until thick.
2. Cool.   3. Spread over crust and top with whipped cream.

Leslie Nelson Martin
(Mrs. Dennis)

Sour Cream Apple Pie

Planning: None
Preparation Time: 20 minutes

Quantity: 8 servings
Baking Time: 15 minutes, 400°; 30 minutes, 350°; 10 minutes, 400°

2 tablespoons flour
⅛ teaspoon salt
¾ cup sugar
1 egg
1 cup sour cream
1 teaspoon vanilla
¼ teaspoon nutmeg
3 cups apples, diced
1 9″ pie crust, unbaked
⅓ cup sugar
½ teaspoon cinnamon
¼ cup butter

1. Sift together flour, salt and sugar.
2. Add egg, sour cream, vanilla and nutmeg.   3. Beat to a thick, smooth batter; stir in apples.   4. Pour into pie shell and bake in 400° oven for 15 minutes.   5. Reduce heat to 350° and bake for 30 minutes.   6. Mix sugar, cinnamon and butter.   7. Remove pie and top with sugar mixture.   8. Return to 400° oven for 10 minutes.

Gloria Brunskill Paulsen
(Mrs. Thomas)

Crunchy Pumpkin Ice Cream Pie
An excellent fall dessert.

Planning: Must do ahead
Preparation Time: 45 minutes

Quantity: 10-12 servings
Baking Time: 10 minutes, 350°
Freezing Time: Overnight

Crust:
2 cups graham cracker crumbs
1 cup nuts, finely chopped
1 cup shredded sweetened
    coconut
1/3 cup light brown sugar, packed
1/2 teaspoon ground cinnamon
3/4 cup butter, melted

Crust:
1. In a bowl mix crumbs, nuts, coconut, sugar and cinnamon.   **2.** Add butter and toss with a fork until crumbs are moistened.   **3.** Pat half of the crumbs over the bottom and up the sides of a 9" pie plate. Sprinkle remaining crumbs on an aluminum-foil lined baking sheet. Bake 10 minutes or until crust is firm and mixture is richly browned.
4. Cool, then freeze at least one hour before filling.

Filling:
1/2 gallon vanilla ice cream
1 16-ounce can pumpkin
1/4 cup light brown sugar, packed
1 1/2 teaspoons ground cinnamon
1/2 teaspoon ground ginger
1/2 teaspoon ground nutmeg
1/4 teaspoon salt

Filling:
1. In a large bowl, beat half of the ice cream with an electric mixer until smooth.   **2.** Spread in prepared, chilled pie shell and return to freezer.
3. In the same bowl beat the pumpkin with the sugar, cinnamon, ginger, nutmeg, and salt; then beat in remaining ice cream.   **4.** Freeze until firm enough to mound in pie plate.   **5.** Sprinkle half of the remaining crumbs over the plain vanilla ice cream in pie shell.
6. Spoon pumpkin mixture over crumbs, mounding well.   **7.** Cover pie with plastic wrap and freeze overnight or until firm.   **8.** Transfer pie from freezer to refrigerator 30 minutes before serving; sprinkle with remaining crumbs.

Marty McNutt Port
(Mrs. Dale)

Amaretto Coconut Cream Pie
A tropical delight.

Planning: Must do ahead
Preparation Time: 45 minutes

Quantity: 12 servings
Baking Time: 15 minutes, 300°
Chilling Time: Until ready to serve

Crust:
1 cup graham cracker crumbs
¼ cup sugar
¼ cup butter

Crust:
1. Grease bottom of 10" springform pan. **2.** Combine crumbs, sugar and butter and press evenly on bottom of pan to form crust. Set aside.

Filling:
1¼ cups shredded sweetened
   coconut
1 cup sugar
4 eggs
2 tablespoons unflavored gelatin
⅓ cup cold water
½ cup Amaretto
⅛ teaspoon almond extract
1 quart whipping cream
12 fresh strawberries

Filling:
1. Evenly distribute coconut on baking sheet and toast in oven until golden brown, about 15 minutes, stirring frequently. Set aside. **2.** Using electric mixer at medium speed, beat sugar and eggs in large bowl until fluffy.
3. Sprinkle gelatin over cold water in heatproof measuring cup or bowl and let stand about 5 minutes to soften.
4. Set cup in small pan of hot water over direct heat until gelatin is completely dissolved. **5.** Fold gelatin, Amaretto and almond extract into egg mixture. Let stand until slightly thickened. **6.** Beat whipping cream until soft peaks form. **7.** Fold coconut (reserving small amount for garnish) into thickened egg mixture. **8.** Fold in whipped cream and blend thoroughly.
9. Pour into springform pan and chill.
10. Before serving, remove sides of pan, sprinkle top of pie with reserved coconut and garnish with strawberries.

Marty McNutt Port
(Mrs. Dale)

Strawberry Puffs with Raspberry Cassis Sauce

A colorful, attractive dessert.

Planning: Puffs can be made ahead and frozen
Preparation Time: 30 minutes

Quantity: 10-11 servings
Baking Time: 25 minutes, 400°

1 cup water
6 tablespoons butter
1 cup flour
1/2 teaspoon salt
3/4 cup eggs (about 4 to 5 large eggs)

1. Heat water and butter in a saucepan until the water boils. Add flour and salt all at once and stir quickly with a wooden spoon until the batter is stiff, leaves the sides of the pan and forms a ball. Remove from heat. **2.** Add the eggs one at a time, stirring vigorously after each addition. **3.** Using a tablespoon, scoop out a ball the size of a tangerine. Place on a lightly greased baking pan, leaving enough room between each for expansion. (approximately 2") **4.** Bake 35 minutes at 400.° Cool. **5.** Slit puffs, scoop out middle, and return to oven (with oven off) to dry.

Raspberry Cassis Sauce:
3 cups frozen raspberries, thawed but not drained
1/2 cup creme de cassis
2 tablespoons sugar

Sauce:
1. Place sauce ingredients in blender and process 1 minute. **2.** Strain through a sieve to remove seeds.

Assembly:
1/2 gallon vanilla ice cream
1 quart strawberries, washed, hulled and sliced
1 2 3/4-ounce package sliced almonds, toasted

Assembly:
1. To serve, place bottom half of puff in a stemmed goblet or glass dessert bowl. **2.** Put a rounded scoop of ice cream on puff bottom; cover with strawberry slices. **3.** Put top of puff on and spoon 2 to 3 tablespoons of sauce over. **4.** Top with a generous sprinkle of toasted almonds.

Susan Walker Crouse
(Mrs. James)

Almond Cream Puff Ring

Planning: Must do ahead
Preparation Time: 1 hour

Quantity: 10 servings
Baking Time: 40 minutes, 400°

Cream Puff Ring:
1 cup water
1/2 cup butter
1/4 teaspoon salt
1 cup flour
4 eggs

Cream Puff Ring:
1. Three hours before serving, heat water, butter and salt until butter melts and water boils, in a 2-quart saucepan.   2. Remove saucepan from heat and stir in flour all at once until mixture forms a ball and leaves sides of pan.
3. Add eggs one at a time, beating after each addition until the mixture is smooth and satiny.   4. Cool slightly.
5. Preheat oven to 400.° Lightly grease and flour cookie sheet.   6. Using a 7" plate as a guide, trace a circle in flour on the cookie sheet.   7. Drop batter by heaping tablespoons into 10 mounds, inside circle to form a ring.   8. Bake ring 40 minutes or until golden at 400.° Turn off oven; let ring set in oven 15 minutes. Remove and cool.   9. When ring is cool, slice horizontally in half with serrated knife.

Almond Filling:
1 3 1/2-ounce package instant vanilla pudding
1 cup whipping cream, whipped
1 teaspoon almond extract

Almond Filling:
1. Prepare pudding according to package directions but use only 1 1/4 cups milk.   2. Fold in whipped cream and almond extract.   3. Spoon filling into bottom half of ring. Replace top. Refrigerate.

Chocolate Glaze:
1/2 cup semi-sweet chocolate chips
1 teaspoon butter
1 1/2 teaspoons milk
1 1/2 teaspoons light corn syrup

Chocolate Glaze:
1. In a double boiler, over hot water, heat chocolate chips with butter, milk and corn syrup until smooth, stirring constantly.   2. Spoon chocolate glaze over top of ring before serving.

Marcy O'Bryon Coontz
(Mrs. James)

Chocolate Mousse ❧

Planning: Can do ahead
Preparation Time: 15 minutes

Quantity: 6 servings
Chilling Time: At least 3 hours

1 6-ounce package chocolate chips
2 tablespoons Kahlua
1 tablespoon orange juice
2 egg yolks
2 eggs
1 teaspoon vanilla
¹/₄ cup sugar
1 cup whipping cream

1. Melt chocolate chips, Kahlua and orange juice over low heat. 2. Put 2 yolks and 2 eggs in blender with vanilla and sugar. Blend 2 minutes. 3. Add cream; blend 30 seconds. 4. Add melted chocolate mixture and blend until smooth. 5. Pour in small dishes. 6. Refrigerate at least three hours before serving.

*Cindy Poyser Spragg
(Mrs. John)*

Orange Delight

Planning: Must be prepared one day
  ahead
Preparation Time: 20 minutes

Quantity: 18 servings
Baking Time: 20 minutes, 325°
Chilling Time: 24 hours

Crust:
3 egg whites
¹/₂ cup sugar
¹/₄ teaspoon cream of tartar
1 cup crispy rice cereal, crushed
1 cup nuts, chopped (pecans better
  than walnuts)

Crust:
1. Beat egg whites. 2. Add sugar slowly with cream of tartar. 3. Fold in crushed cereal and nuts. 4. Spread in 9" x 13" buttered pan and bake at 325° for 20 minutes. Cool.

Topping:
¹/₂ pint cream, whipped and
  sweetened or 8-ounce carton of
  whipped topping, thawed
1 3¹/₂-ounce package instant
  vanilla pudding
³/₄ cup coconut, shredded
2 cups mandarin oranges, drained

Topping:
1. Whip cream. 2. Add dry pudding, coconut and mandarin oranges.
3. Spread over crust and refrigerate 24 hours.

Diane Drewis Good

Cranberry Pudding

Planning: Serve warm from oven
Preparation Time: 25 minutes

Quantity: 9 servings
Baking Time: 35 minutes, 375°

Cranberry Mixture:
1 cup sugar
2 tablespoons flour
$^1/_2$ cup boiling water
2 cups cranberries

Cranberry Mixture:
1. Cook sugar, flour, and water until thickened. **2.** Add cranberries. Turn off heat, cover, and let stand while fixing batter.

Cake Mixture:
$^1/_3$ cup butter
$^1/_2$ cup sugar
1 egg, beaten
rind of 1 lemon, grated
1$^1/_2$ cups flour
2 teaspoons baking powder
$^1/_2$ teaspoon salt
$^1/_2$ cup milk

Cake Mixture:
1. Cream butter and sugar. **2.** Add remaining ingredients and mix.
3. Place cranberry mixture in greased 8" baking pan. Cover with batter.
4. Bake 35 minutes at 375.° Cool 2 minutes before removing from pan.

Sauce:
$^1/_2$ cup sugar
$^1/_2$ cup whipping cream
$^1/_4$ cup butter

Sauce:
1. Heat sauce ingredients to boiling.
2. Cook 5 minutes, stirring often.

Sue Feeney Schermer
(Mrs. Richard)

Holiday Nut Roll

Planning: Can be frozen
Preparation Time: 1 hour

Quantity: 6-8 rolls
Cooking Time: 1/2 hour
Chilling Time: 2 hours

1 16-ounce bag marshmallows
1 12-ounce can evaporated milk
1 16-ounce box graham crackers, crushed
3 pounds dates, whole
2 1/2 to 3 quarts nuts—whole almonds, pecans and English walnuts (use lots of whole almonds)

1. Melt marshmallows and evaporated milk in a large metal pan.   2. When melted, add crushed graham cracker crumbs.   3. Mix and add 3 pounds of dates and nuts, (enough to make it look like a nut roll).   4. Shape into rolls the diameter of a small orange and about 7 inches long. (Size is up to individual taste.)   5. Wrap in waxed paper and then in aluminum foil. Refrigerate or freeze.   6. Serve cold. Slice and serve plain or with a tablespoon of whipping cream.

Hint: Give these as gifts wrapped with a plaid ribbon. They are nice sliced on a Christmas cookie tray, or served as a dessert with whipped cream.

Susan Walker Crouse
(Mrs. James)

Amaretto Sauce ❧

Nice to accompany a wine and cheese party as a little dessert.

Planning: Can be made ahead
Preparation Time: 10 minutes

Quantity: 2 1/2 cups
Chilling Time: Until ready to serve

1 8-ounce carton ricotta cheese
1 8-ounce package cream cheese
1/2 cup sugar
4 egg yolks
2 tablespoons heavy cream
3 tablespoons almond flavored liqueur
fresh fruit

1. Soften cheeses.   2. Use blender or food processor to mix together ricotta cheese and cream cheese.   3. Add rest of ingredients and continue beating until smooth.   4. Pour into a 3-cup serving dish and chill.   5. When ready to serve, arrange fresh fruit around the sauce. Firm fruit such as bananas, apples, grapes, pineapple, and peaches work well.

Gini Naber Langlas
(Mrs. David)

Glazed Pears

A spectacular dessert that guests will rave about.

Planning: Can be made ahead
Preparation Time: 45 minutes

Quantity: 6-8 servings
Cooking Time: 30 minutes
Cooling Time: 1 hour

3 cups water
1 cup sugar
4 tablespoons lemon juice
4 cloves
6 to 8 large pears
1 12-ounce jar orange marmalade
medium bunch of either red or
    green seedless grapes
1 16-ounce can apricot halves,
    drained

1. In large heavy pan heat water, sugar, 2 tablespoons lemon juice and cloves, until boiling. 2. Peel and core pears from the bottom, leaving stem. Cut a thin slice from bottom of pear so pear will stand upright. Rub with lemon juice to prevent browning. 3. Reduce heat and add pears. 4. Cover and simmer over low heat until pears are tender (about 20 minutes). Turn pears frequently. 5. Remove pears to serving dish, standing upright. 6. Remove cloves from syrup. Reduce syrup until approximately 1 1/2 cups. 7. Stir in marmalade. 8. Remove from heat and cool 1 hour. 9. To serve, garnish with grapes and apricot halves. Pour syrup over all.

Peg Zeis McGarvey
(Mrs. Thomas)

Watermelon Granite ❧

Good for brunch.

Planning: Must be frozen
Preparation Time: 15 minutes

Quantity: 8-10 servings
Chilling Time: 3-4 hours

2 1/2 cups water
2 1/2 cups sugar
1/2 cup lemon juice
1 teaspoon almond extract
2 1/2 cups watermelon, diced and
    seeded
watermelon juice

1. Bring to boil the water and sugar. Simmer 5 minutes. 2. Cool. 3. Add lemon juice, almond extract, watermelon cubes and any juice left from the dicing. 4. Put all through the blender and freeze in a 2-quart ring mold, stirring once or twice. 5. Unmold at serving time by dipping briefly in hot water, placing a platter over the mold and inverting.

Leila Clark Girsch
(Mrs. Brian)

Cranberry Pear Coupes

A California favorite.

Planning: None
Preparation Time: 20 minutes

Quantity: 6 servings
Cooking Time: 25 minutes

2 cups water
1 cup sugar
1 teaspoon vanilla
6 small ripe pears
1 1/2 cups fresh or frozen
    cranberries
1 tablespoon Kirsch
6 scoops vanilla ice cream

1. Heat water, sugar and vanilla in medium saucepan to boiling. Boil about 5 minutes, stirring occasionally. Sugar should dissolve. 2. Pare, core and halve pears. Add to syrup, and simmer, covered, over low heat until tender (5 to 10 minutes). 3. Remove with slotted spoon; drain well. Refrigerate. 4. Add cranberries to syrup; heat to boiling and boil 10 minutes. 5. Puree cranberries and syrup in blender. Strain to remove seeds. Add Kirsch. 6. At serving time, stand 2 pear halves upright in each of 6 stemmed goblets. Place ice cream scoops between pear halves. Spoon cranberry puree over pears and ice cream. (Trim pears to fit goblet if necessary.)

Hint: Scald pears 1 to 2 minutes for easy peeling. They may be tinted pale green or pink if desired. Optional garnishes: nut, cherries or seedless grapes.

Mary Jean Adams Clark
(Mrs. Craig)

Country Vanilla Ice Cream

Planning: Must do ahead
Preparation Time: 15 minutes

Quantity: One gallon
Freezing Time: 30-45 minutes

4 eggs
2 1/4 cups sugar
5 cups milk
4 cups whipping cream
4 1/2 teaspoons vanilla
1/2 teaspoon salt

1. Beat eggs at high speed on electric mixer; add sugar gradually and continue to beat until mixture is very stiff.
2. Add remaining ingredients and mix well. 3. Pour into ice cream freezer and freeze according to manufacturer's directions.

Junean Goschke Witham
(Mrs. Dick)

Champagne Sherbet

Planning: Must be prepared ahead
Preparation Time: 20 minutes

Quantity: 1¼ quarts
Freezing Time: 4 hours

1 cup heavy cream
¾ cup sugar
1½ cups champagne
1 10-ounce package frozen
   strawberries, thawed
2 egg whites
¼ teaspoon cream of tartar
few drops red food coloring

1. Combine cream and ½ cup of the sugar. 2. Cook and stir over medium to low heat until sugar dissolves. Cool. 3. Stir in the champagne and undrained berries. 4. Pour into 8" x 8" x 2" pan. Cover; freeze firm. 5. Beat egg whites and cream of tartar to soft peaks. 6. Slowly add remaining sugar, beating to soft peaks. 7. Break up frozen mixture. 8. Turn into chilled mixer bowl and beat smooth with electric mixer. 9. Fold in egg whites. 10. Tint with food coloring. 11. Return to pan. Cover and freeze firm.

Marty McNutt Port
(Mrs. Dale)

Apple-Raspberry Sorbet

Planning: Can be made up to one
   week in advance
Preparation Time: 2 hours

Quantity: 8-10 servings
Cooking Time: 5 minutes

⅔ cup sugar
⅔ cup water
1 10-ounce package frozen
   raspberries, undrained
3 large golden delicious apples,
   peeled, cored and sliced
juice of ½ lemon
2 tablespoons calvados

1. Combine sugar and water in small saucepan and stir over medium-high heat until sugar is dissolved. 2. Bring to boil and boil for 5 minutes. Cool, cover and chill. 3. Puree raspberries in a food processor or blender. 4. Pass through a strainer to remove the seeds. 5. Combine pureed raspberries, apples, sugar syrup, lemon and calvados and blend well. 6. Freeze in an ice cream maker or a metal pan in the freezer. 7. If frozen in the freezer remove after frozen, partially thaw, beat in a food processor using a steel knife and re-freeze.

Several League Members

SPECIAL OCCASIONS

SPECIAL OCCASIONS

Chinese Dinner

Susie's Egg Rolls

Chinese Hot Mustard

Sweet Sour Sauce

Suan-La-T'ang

Steamed White Rice or Fried Rice

Shredded Beef over Rice Noodles

Shrimp with Snow Peas

Deep Fried Won Tons with Date Filling

Robert Mondavi Johannesburg Reisling

B & G Vouvray

Susie's Egg Rolls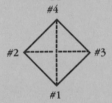

Planning: Can be frozen, uncooked
Preparation Time: 1 hour

Quantity: 15 egg rolls
Cooking Time: 3-5 minutes

2 tablespoons peanut oil
1 1/2 cups finely chopped celery
1/2 pound lean ground pork
2 cups cooked chicken, shredded
1 cup finely chopped bamboo
   shoots
1/2 cup finely chopped water
   chestnuts
1/3 cup finely chopped dried
   oriental mushrooms, soaked
   and drained
3 green onions, chopped
1 1/2 cups fresh bean sprouts,
   chopped
3 cloves garlic, minced
1 tablespoon dry sherry
1 1/2 teaspoons salt
1/2 teaspoon sugar
1/2 teaspoon pepper
1 tablespoon cornstarch dissolved
   in 2 tablespoons stock or cold
   water
15 egg roll wrappers
1 egg, beaten

1. Sauté celery and ground pork in peanut oil for about 5 minutes.   2. Add next 12 ingredients and sauté 5 minutes more.   3. Stir in cornstarch mixture and cook until thickened slightly.
4. Transfer cooked egg roll filling to a bowl and cool.   5. Fill egg rolls as follows: Place filling in egg roll wrapper as shown. Then fold #1 upward, #'s 2 and 3 inward and #4 downward, sealing flaps with beaten egg.

```
        #4
         /\
        /  \
       /:   \
  #2 <------- #3
       \:   /
        \  /
         \/
        #1
```

6. Deep fry 3 to 5 minutes or until lightly browned.   7. Uncooked egg rolls can be frozen and deep fried at a later time.   8. Serve hot with sweet-sour sauce and hot chinese mustard.

Cathy Zach Shaw
(Mrs. John)

Sweet Sour Sauce ✿

Planning: Can be made a day in advance
Preparation Time: About 10 minutes

Quantity: ¹/₂ cup
Cooking Time: 5 minutes

¹/₂ **cup red wine vinegar**
³/₄ **cup sugar**
1 teaspoon soy sauce
1 tablespoon and 1 teaspoon
cornstarch, dissolved in 2
tablespoons cold water

1. In a saucepan, mix vinegar, sugar, and soy sauce. 2. Bring to a boil over high heat. 3. Stir in cornstarch dissolved in water and cook stirring constantly, until thickened, not longer than 1 minute.

Jane Rife Field
(Mrs. Hugh)

Chinese Hot Mustard ✿

Planning: Make at least 2 hours before serving
Preparation Time: 5 minutes

Quantity: ³/₈ cup
Cooking Time: None

¹/₄ **cup dry mustard**
¹/₄ **cup boiling water**
1 tablespoon salad oil
¹/₂ **teaspoon salt**
ground turmeric

1. Blend mustard and water. 2. Add salad oil and salt. 3. For more yellow color add a little ground turmeric. 4. Make at least 2 hours before serving.

Jane Rife Field
(Mrs. Hugh)

Suan-la-T'ang
Sour-and-Hot-Soup

Planning: Can be made ahead and reheated
Preparation Time: 1 hour

Quantity: 8 servings
Cooking Time: 15 minutes

6 dried Chinese mushrooms, 1" to 1½" in diameter

3 squares, 3" each, fresh Chinese bean curd, about ½" thick

1 8-ounce can bamboo shoots

½ pound boneless pork

1½ quarts chicken stock, fresh or canned

1½ teaspoons salt

1½ tablespoons soy sauce

¼ teaspoon ground white pepper

3 tablespoons white vinegar

3 tablespoons cornstarch mixed with 5 tablespoons cold water

1 egg, lightly beaten

2 teaspoons sesame seed oil

1 scallion, including the green top, finely chopped

1. In a small bowl, cover the mushrooms with ½ cup of warm water and let them soak for 30 minutes. Discard the water. With a cleaver or knife, cut away and discard the tough stems of the mushrooms and shred the caps by placing one at a time on a chopping board. Cut them horizontally into paper-thin slices, and then into thin strips. **2.** Drain the pieces of bamboo shoot and bean curd, and rinse them in cold water. Shred them as fine as the mushrooms. **3.** With a cleaver or sharp knife, trim the pork of all fat. Then shred it, too, by slicing the meat as thin as possible and cutting the slices into narrow strips about 1½" to 2" long. **4.** Have the above ingredients, stock, salt, soy sauce, pepper, vinegar, cornstarch mixture, egg, sesame seed oil and scallions within easy reach. **5.** Combine in heavy 3-quart saucepan the stock, salt, soy sauce, mushrooms, bamboo shoots and pork. Bring to a boil over high heat, then immediately reduce the heat to low, cover the pan and simmer for 3 minutes. **6.** Drop in the bean curd, and the pepper and vinegar. Bring to a boil again. **7.** Give the cornstarch mixture a stir to recombine it and pour it into the soup. **8.** Stir for a few seconds until the soup thickens, then slowly pour in the beaten egg, stirring gently all the while. **9.** Remove the soup from the heat and ladle it into a tureen or serving bowl. **10.** Stir in the sesame seed oil and sprinkle the top with scallions. Serve at once.

Several League Members

Steamed White Rice

Planning: Can be made ahead and
reheated in the microwave
Preparation Time: 30 minutes

Quantity: 4-6 servings
Cooking Time: 25 minutes

2 1/2 cups water
1/2 teaspoon salt
1 cup long grain white rice

1. Bring water and salt to a boil.
2. Stir in rice, cover, reduce heat to
simmer and cook 20 minutes.
3. Remove from heat and let stand,
covered, until serving time.

Jane Rife Field
(Mrs. Hugh)

Fried Rice

Planning: Can be made ahead and
frozen
Preparation Time: 30 minutes

Quantity: 5-6 servings
Cooking Time: 20 minutes

6 slices bacon, chopped
2 tablespoons chopped onion
1 4-ounce can mushrooms
4 cups cold cooked rice
2 tablespoons soy sauce
1 egg, well beaten
2 tablespoons parsley
1/8 teaspoon pepper

1. Fry bacon in electric skillet, remove. 2. Brown onion and mushrooms. 3. Add rice and soy sauce.
4. Cook over low heat 5 to 10 minutes,
stirring with a fork. 5. Add egg, parsley and pepper. 6. Add bacon stirring
constantly. 7. Add soy sauce to taste.

Shirley Crandell Mast
(Mrs. Kenneth)

Shredded Beef over Rice Noodles

Planning: Uses a wok or electric skillet
Preparation Time: 2 hours

Quantity: 8 servings
Cooking Time: 15 minutes

2 pounds sirloin steak
6 tablespoons soy sauce
2 teaspoons cornstarch
4 teaspoons freshly grated ginger root
2 teaspoons rice wine
1 teaspoon sugar
¹/₂ cup chicken broth
2 tablespoons water
2 tablespoons soy sauce
1 teaspoon cornstarch
¹/₂ cup peanut oil
2 cloves garlic, crushed
8 dried whole red peppers
2 tablespoons hot bean sauce
3 teaspoons hoisin sauce
3 carrots, scraped and cut into julienne strips
2 stalks celery, cut in julienne strips
4 3-ounce packages rice noodles cooked in boiling salted water until just tender

1. Partially freeze steak; slice diagonally across the grain into 3″ x ¹/₄″ strips.
2. Combine next 5 ingredients in a bowl. **3.** Add the steak, and mix well; let stand 15 minutes. **4.** Combine chicken broth, water, 2 tablespoons soy sauce, and 1 teaspoon cornstarch, mixing well; set aside. **5.** Pour ¹/₂ cup oil around top of preheated wok.
6. Allow to heat at medium high (325°) for 30 seconds. **7.** Add beef mixture and garlic; stir-fry minutes or until beef is browned. **8.** Remove and drain on paper towels. **9.** Reserve 4 tablespoons drippings in wok. **10.** Add red peppers and stir-fry 1 minute. **11.** Add bean sauce and hoisin sauce; stir-fry 15 to 20 seconds. **12.** Add vegetables and increase heat to high (350°), and stir-fry 1 minute. **13.** Add broth mixture, and cooked until slightly thickened.
14. Add beef, and mix well; remove from heat, and keep warm. **15.** Serve with noodles.

Several League Members

Shrimp with Snow Peas

Planning: Uses a wok or electric skillet
Preparation Time: 45 minutes

Quantity: 8 servings
Cooking Time: 20 minutes

2 pounds unpeeled medium-sized fresh shrimp
1 teaspoon salt
2 teaspoons sesame oil
4 teaspoons cornstarch
1/2 cup chicken broth
6 tablespoons oyster sauce
1/2 cup peanut oil
4 cloves garlic, crushed
4 teaspoons freshly grated ginger root
1 pound fresh snow peas or 2 6-ounce packages frozen snow peas, thawed
4 teaspoons rice wine

1. Peel and devein shrimp; rinse and pat dry. 2. Sprinkle shrimp with salt and toss with sesame oil; dredge in 3 teaspoons cornstarch. Set aside. 3. Combine the chicken broth, oyster sauce, and remaining 1 teaspoon cornstarch, and mix well; set the mixture aside. 4. Pour peanut oil around top of preheated wok, coating sides; allow to heat at medium high (325°) for 1 minute. 5. Add garlic and ginger root, and stir-fry 30 seconds. 6. Add shrimp, and stir-fry 1 1/2 minutes. Remove and drain on paper towels. 7. Add snow peas to wok, and stir-fry 30 seconds. 8. Add broth mixture, stirring constantly until slightly thickened. 9. Stir in shrimp and rice wine. 10. Serve immediately.

Several League Members

Deep Fried Won Tons with Date Filling

Planning: Can be assembled one day ahead and refrigerated; can be fried 3 to 4 hours ahead
Preparation Time: 2 hours

Quantity: 5 dozen won tons
Cooking Time: 45-60 minutes

one recipe won ton wrappers or 1 pound ready-made egg-roll wrappers, cut into squares

The filling:
1 8-ounce package pitted dates
1/2 cup finely chopped walnuts
2 teaspoons freshly grated orange rind
1 to 2 tablespoons orange juice or cold water (if needed)
3 cups peanut oil, or flavorless vegetable oil
powdered sugar

1. Prepare ahead to make the filling: with a cleaver or sharp knife, chop the pitted dates finely, adding a teaspoon or so of orange juice or water if they are too sticky to cut. Combine the dates, walnuts and grated rind in a small bowl. Knead the mixture with your fingers until it can be gathered into a ball. If the mixture is dry, moisten it with orange juice or water. Roll a tablespoon of filling between the palms of your hands to form cylinders 1" long and about 1/3" in diameter. **2.** To assemble the won tons: place a cylinder of filing diagonally across each wrapper, just below the center. With a finger dipped in water, moisten the lower point of the wrapper. Fold the point over the filling and tuck it underneath. Roll up the resulting tube until all the dough surrounds the filling. Stick a finger into each end of the tube and give it a twist to seal the ends. **3.** To cook: pour the oil into a 12" wok or deep-fryer and heat the oil until a haze forms above it or it reaches 375° on a deep-frying thermometer. Deep-fry the won tons, 8 to 10 at a time, turning them occasionally, for 2 to 3 minutes, or until they are golden brown and crisp. As they are finished cooking, transfer them to paper towels to drain and cool. Just before serving, sprinkle the won tons with powdered sugar.

Jane Rife Field
(Mrs. Hugh)

French Dinner

Cream of Cauliflower Soup

Scallops, Normandy Style

Sorbet Citron

Filets with Sauce Bearnaise

Potatoes Parmesan

Mandarin Orange Lettuce Salad

Almond Crepes

B & G Vouvray

St. Emillion Grand Crev

Cream of Cauliflower Soup

Planning: Can be made 2 to 3 days ahead, up to the point where sour cream is added
Preparation Time: 1 1/2-2 hours

Quantity: 10-12 servings
Cooking Time: 40 minutes

2 tablespoons oil or shortening
1/2 cup chopped onion
1 cup finely chopped celery
1 small cauliflower, cut into flowerets
2 tablespoons fresh chopped parsley
8 cups chicken stock (preferably homemade)
1/4 cup butter
3/4 cup flour
2 cups milk
1 cup half and half
1 tablespoon salt or to taste
1 cup sour cream

Bouquet Garni*:
1/2 teaspoon peppercorns
1 teaspoon tarragon
1/2 bay leaf

1. Heat oil in an 8 to 10-quart stockpot over medium heat. **2.** Add onion and sauté until transparent, stirring frequently. **3.** Add celery and carrot and cook two minutes more, stirring occasionally. **4.** Add cauliflower and 1 tablespoon parsley. Cover and reduce to low and cook for 15 minutes, stirring occasionally to prevent sticking.
5. Add chicken stock and bouquet garni and bring to boil over medium heat. Reduce heat and simmer 5 minutes.
6. Melt butter in a 2-quart saucepan. Stir in flour and cook two or three minutes. Add milk and cook and stir until thickened and boiling. **7.** Remove from heat and stir in half and half. **8.** Stir milk sauce into simmering soup, season to taste with salt and pepper, and simmer gently 15 to 20 minutes. Soup can be made ahead to this point. **9.** Just before serving, remove bouquet garni. Mix a few tablespoons of soup with sour cream. Stir sour cream mixture into soup along with remaining chopped parsley. Serve.

Hint: *Bouquet Garni is made by placing the ingredients into a cheesecloth bag or a steeper.

Jane Rife Field
(Mrs. Hugh)

Scallops, Normandy Style

Planning: Can be prepared ahead; requires 10 to 12 scallop shells or heat-proof serving dishes
Preparation Time: About 1 hour

Quantity: 10-12 servings
Cooking Time: About 15 minutes

2 to 2¹/₂ **pounds bay scallops or sea scallops**
16 **shallots, finely minced**
³/₄ **cup unsalted butter**
1 **cup dry white wine**
1 **cup dry vermouth**
1¹/₄ **cups heavy cream**
salt and pepper
lemon juice to taste
20 to 24 **shrimp, cooked, shelled and deveined**
fresh parsley, finely chopped
lemon slices

1. Wash scallops well in salt water and pat dry with towels. Cut sea scallops in half. **2.** In a large skillet, sauté the shallots in butter until soft but not brown. **3.** Add the scallops (1 pound at a time) and gently sauté 1 to 2 minutes, turning them often. Do not overcook! **4.** Remove the first pound of scallops to a dish and cook the remaining scallops in the same pan. **5.** When the second batch of scallops have been cooked remove from pan and set aside. Keep warm as possible without further cooking. **6.** Strain scallop cooking liquid and return strained liquid to frying pan. **7.** Add wine and vermouth to cooking liquid, raise the heat under the pan, and reduce to a glaze. **8.** Add the cream, bring to a boil and cook 3 to 4 minutes until reduced slightly and well flavored. **9.** Adjust seasoning with salt, pepper and a few drops of lemon juice. **10.** Butter scallop shells or dishes to be used and heat shells for 5 minutes in a 350° oven. **11.** Return scallops to hot sauce, reheat slightly, spoon into hot shells, garnish with shrimp, chopped parsley and lemon slice. **12.** Serve at once.

Jane Rife Field
(Mrs. Hugh)

Potatoes Parmesan

Planning: Can be made ahead and reheated
Preparation Time: 1 1/2 hours

Quantity: 10-12 servings
Baking Time: 45 minutes, 350°

3 pounds new potatoes
3/4 cup butter, melted
1/3 cup grated Parmesan cheese
fresh parsley, chopped

1. Place peeled potatoes in a 9″ x 13″ baking dish.   2. Toss with melted butter and sprinkle with Parmesan cheese.
3. Bake at 350° for 45 minutes, tossing every 15 minutes (uncovered).   4. Toss with chopped fresh parsley and serve.

Several League Members

Mandarin Orange Lettuce Salad
Attractive and delicious.

Planning: Can be made ahead, but toss at the last minute
Preparation Time: 15-20 minutes

Quantity: 8 servings
Chilling Time: Until ready to serve

Dressing:
2 teaspoons salt
1 teaspoon paprika
1 teaspoon pepper
1/4 teaspoon dry mustard
1/4 teaspoon powdered sugar
1/4 cup vinegar
1 cup salad oil
Salad:
6 pieces bacon, crisply fried and crumbled
1/4 cup toasted almonds
1 8-ounce can mandarin oranges, drained
2 large bibb or Boston lettuce heads

1. Combine all dressing ingredients and shake well. Chill until ready to use.
2. Combine salad ingredients in large salad bowl. (For variation, you may also add chopped celery, green onions and green grapes.)   3. When ready to serve, toss salad ingredients with small amount of dressing.   4. Use dressing sparingly as this recipe makes enough dressing for several salads and can be kept refrigerated for several weeks.

Susan Marty Fereday
(Mrs. Mike)
Margie Lahey Skahill
(Mrs. Timothy)

Filets with Sauce Bearnaise

Planning: Filets can be done ahead, but sauce must be made just before serving

Preparation Time: 1 1/2 hours

Quantity: 8-10 servings

Baking Time: 10-12 minutes, 450°

8 to 10 6-ounce filets of beef tenderloin
2 tablespoons oil
2 tablespoons butter

1. To prepare filets ahead, either grill them over a charcoal fire or sauté them over high heat in 2 tablespoons oil and 2 tablespoons unsalted butter for 5 minutes per side. 2. Transfer filets to a cookie sheet and refrigerate. 3. To serve, place filets in 450° oven for 10 to 12 minutes or until warmed through. 4. Cover with sauce and serve at once.

Sauce:
1 teaspoon dried tarragon
2 teaspoons dried chervil (or parsley)
1 tablespoon chopped green onions
3 large cloves garlic, chopped
2 peppercorns, crushed
2 tablespoons white wine vinegar
2/3 cup vermouth
3 egg yolks
1 tablespoon water
8 ounces unsalted butter, softened
salt, pepper, freshly squeezed lemon juice, to taste

Sauce:
1. Combine tarragon, chervil, onions, garlic, peppercorns, white wine vinegar and vermouth in saucepan. 2. Cook the liquid over high heat until it is reduced to half its original quantity. 3. Strain reduced cooking liquid pressing on solids in the strainer to release flavors. 4. Combine reduced liquid, egg yolks, and water in a saucepan and cook over hot, not boiling water, whisking briskly until the mixture is light and fluffy. 5. The water over which the egg mixture is cooking should never boil or the eggs will curdle. 6. Add the butter, piece by piece, to the egg mixture stirring briskly all the time as the sauce begins to thicken. 7. Season to taste with salt, pepper and a few drops of lemon juice. 8. Serve with Potatoes Parmesan and watercress and serve at once.

Jane Rife Field
(Mrs. Hugh)

Almond Crepes

Planning: Can be made several days
in advance
Preparation Time: 3 hours

Quantity: 10-12 servings
Chilling Time: 30-60 minutes
Cooking Time: Crepes—2-3 minutes
each; Filling— about 20 minutes
Baking Time: 20-25 minutes, 350°

Crepes:
²/₃ **cups unbleached flour, sifted**
2 **tablespoons sugar**
¹/₈ **teaspoon salt**
2 **eggs**
2 **egg yolks**
1¹/₃ **cups milk**
4 **tablespoons unsalted butter,
melted**

Crepes:
1. Place ingredients into a blender.
2. Blend for thirty seconds, scrape
down side with spatula and blend for
thirty seconds more. **3.** Pour into a
stainless steel bowl and refrigerate for
30 minutes to 1 hour. **4.** Heat a heavy
bottomed 6″ skillet over medium high
heat and grease lightly with unsalted
butter. **5.** Add 2 tablespoons batter, lift
skillet from heat and tilt from side to
side until batter covers the bottom of
the pan evenly. **6.** Return to the heat
and cook until the underside of the
crepe is lightly browned about 1¹/₂ to 2
minutes. **7.** Loosen the sides of the
crepe and invert the skillet onto paper
towels. **8.** Crepes can be refrigerated
for about 3 days or frozen indefi-
nitely. **9.** Store crepes between layers
of paper towels.

Continued...

Almond Cream Filling:

1 1/2 cups sugar
1/4 to 2 tablespoons unbleached
 flour
1 1/2 cups whole milk
3 eggs
3 egg yolks
5 tablespoons butter
1 tablespoon vanilla
1/4 teaspoon almond extract
1 cup toasted slivered almonds

Garnish:

grated unsweetened chocolate
powdered sugar
whipping cream, whipped

Almond Cream Filling:

1. Mix sugar and flour well in a sauce-pan. **2.** Add milk and cook and stir until thick, then cook and stir 2 minutes longer. Remove from heat. **3.** Beat eggs with egg yolks with a wire whip. **4.** Stir some of the hot sauce into the eggs and then return all to the hot mixture. **5.** Return the custard to the heat and bring just to a boil, stirring constantly. **6.** Remove from heat, stir in butter, vanilla, almond extract and almonds. Cool to room temperature. **7.** Fill each crepe with about 2 tablespoons filling on the unbrowned side and roll up. **8.** Place folded side down in a buttered 9" x 13" baking dish. **9.** Brush with melted butter and heat 20 to 25 minutes at 350° or until hot. **10.** Sprinkle with grated chocolate; sift powdered sugar over and serve with a dollop of whipped cream.

Jane Rife Field
(Mrs. Hugh)

Sorbet Citron

Planning: Can be made up to one week in advance
Preparation Time: 1¹/₂ hours

Quantity: 10-12 servings
Cooking Time: 5 minutes

2¹/₂ **cups water**
¹/₂ **cup sugar**
3 **strips lemon rind**
²/₃ **cup lemon juice, freshly squeezed**
1 **egg white, beaten to soft peaks**

1. Boil water, sugar, and zest gently for 5 minutes. **2.** Remove from heat, cool and remove rind. **3.** Add lemon juice, place in metal container, cover and place in freezer.* **4.** When mixture is nearly firm, remove from freezer and break up crystals with a fork or a food processor. **5.** Fold in egg white. Return to freezer. **6.** For ease in serving, remove from freezer 10 to 15 minutes before serving. **7.** Serve in chilled stemware.

Hint: *The sorbet can also be frozen in an ice cream freezer.

Jane Rife Field
(Mrs. Hugh)

Italian Dinner

Funghi Marinati

Pesto

Pollo con Pepperoni

Dadini di Patate Arrosto

Insalata di Lattuga e Gorgonzola

Insalata di Mostaccioli

Granite

Soave

Trebbiano

Funghi Marinati (Marinated Mushrooms)

Planning: Can be made ahead
Preparation Time: 30 minutes

Quantity: 6 servings
Cooking Time: 30 minutes

²/₃ **cup olive oil**
¹/₂ **cup water**
juice of 2 lemons
1 bay leaf
2 garlic cloves, bruised with the
flat of a knife
6 whole peppercorns
¹/₂ **teaspoon salt**
1 pound small whole fresh
mushrooms
lettuce leaves

1. Combine the olive oil, water, lemon juice, bay leaf, bruised garlic cloves, peppercorns and salt in a 10" to 12" enameled or stainless steel skillet, and bring to a boil over moderate heat. Reduce the heat, cover and simmer for 15 minutes. **2.** Strain this marinade through a sieve and return to the skillet; bring to a simmer over low heat.
3. Drop the mushrooms into the marinade and simmer for 5 minutes turning them from time to time. **4.** Let the mushrooms cool in marinade. Serve them at room temperature or refrigerate and serve cold. They will keep in refrigerator for at least 2 days. **5.** Before serving, drain carefully and arrange on lettuce leaves such as romaine.

Hint: Serve with bread sticks and chunks of mild cheeses.

Gail Weber Riley
(Mrs. Thomas)

Pesto

Planning: Proper ingredients are essential—try and use virgin olive oil and good imported cheeses
Preparation Time: 45 minutes

Quantity: 6 servings
Cooking Time: None

2 cups basil leaves, fresh (if possible)
1/2 cup olive oil
2 tablespoons pine nuts (or whole walnuts if pine nuts are not available)
2 cloves garlic
1 teaspoon salt
1/2 cup freshly grated Parmesan cheese
2 tablespoons freshly grated Romano pecorino cheese
3 tablespoons butter, softened
pasta

1. Put the basil, olive oil, pine nuts, garlic cloves and salt in a blender and mix at high speed. Stop from time to time and scrape the ingredients down toward the bottom. 2. When the ingredients are evenly blended, pour into a bowl and mix in the two cheeses. When the cheeses are evenly blended, add the softened butter. 3. Cook enough pasta for 6 servings, al dente. (Do not overcook.) 4. Add one or two tablespoons of the hot pasta water to the pesto and stir well. 5. Toss the pesto with the pasta until the pasta is evenly coated. 6. Divide among 6 heated plates and serve immediately.

Hint: Serve with hot Italian bread. Pesto keeps well refrigerated for several weeks and also freezes well.

Gail Weber Riley
(Mrs. Thomas)

Pollo con Pepperoni (Chicken Braised with Tomatoes and Green Peppers)

Planning: Can prepare vegetables
 ahead
Preparation Time: 1¹/₂ hours

Quantity: 6 servings
Cooking Time: 1 hour

2 green peppers
4 medium firm ripe tomatoes
2¹/₂ to 3 pounds chicken, cut up
salt
freshly ground pepper
¹/₄ cup olive oil
¹/₄ cup finely chopped onions
¹/₂ teaspoon garlic, finely
 chopped

1. Skin the peppers by searing them one at a time on a long kitchen fork and turning them over a gas flame, or by placing them under the broiler 3" from the heat, turning them until they blister and lightly blacken. Use a small sharp knife to peel off the loose skin; quarter and seed the peppers; remove the white pith and cut into ¹/₄" strips. Set aside.
2. Scald the tomatoes in briskly boiling water for 10 seconds; plunge them into cold water. Cut off the stem and peel off the skin. Quarter the tomatoes and cut away the pulp and seeds, leaving just the shells. Slice the shells into ¹/₄" strips and set aside on paper towels to drain.
3. Wash the chicken and pat dry with paper towels. Salt and pepper each piece of chicken.   **4.** In a large heavy skillet, heat the oil over moderate heat. Brown the chicken, a few pices at a time, starting them skin side down and cooking until golden brown.   **5.** Pour off almost all fat from the skillet, leaving just a film. Add the onions and garlic and cook over moderate heat for about 3 minutes. Toss in peppers and cook for 2 minutes; add tomatoes and cook for another 2 minutes.

Continued...

6. Return the chicken pieces to the pan and spread the vegetables over and around them. 7. Cover the pan tightly and simmer over low heat, basting every 10 minutes. Chicken should be done in about 30 minutes.

Hint: To serve place chicken on individual warmed dinner plates, accompanied with potatoes or rice. Hot Italian bread also goes well with this course.

Gail Weber Riley
(Mrs. Thomas)

Dadini di Patate Arrosto (Diced Pan-Roasted Potatoes)

Planning: May do earlier in the day and then reheat in microwave berfore serving
Preparation Time: 40 minutes

Quantity: 6 servings
Cooking Time: 30 minutes

1¹/₂ pounds boiling potatoes
5 tablespoons vegetable oil
2 tablespoons butter
2 teaspoons salt

1. Peel potatoes and dice into ¹/₂" cubes. 2. Heat oil and butter in a heavy skillet over medium-high heat. When butter foam subsides, put in the potatoes; toss until well coated with the cooking fat. Turn the heat down to medium and let potatoes cook until a golden crust has been formed on one side. Add the salt, turn them and continue cooking and turning until every side has a nice crust. 3. After 20 to 25 minutes, test them with a fork to see if they are tender. If not, turn heat to low and cook until tender.

Gail Weber Riley
(Mrs. Thomas)

Insalata di Lattuga e Gorgonzola (Romaine Lettuce Salad with Gorgonzola and Walnuts)

Planning: Must soak lettuce ahead; mix just before serving
Preparation Time: 20 minutes

Quantity: 6-8 servings
Chilling Time: 30 minutes

1 head romaine lettuce
5 tablespoons olive oil
1 tablespoon red wine vinegar
1/2 teaspoon salt
freshly ground pepper
1/4 pound Gorgonzola
1/2 cup walnuts, coarsely chopped

1. Pull off and discard any of the romaine's bruised or blemished outer leaves. Detach the rest from the core, and tear them by hand into bite-sized pieces. Soak in several changes of cold water. Dry thoroughly. 2. Put the olive oil, vinegar, salt and a few grindings of pepper into the salad bowl. Lightly beat this mixture with a fork.
3. Add half the Gorgonzola to the dressing and mash it well with a fork.
4. Add half the chopped walnuts, all the lettuce, and toss thoroughly.
5. Top salad with the remaining half of the Gorgonzola, cut into small nuggets, and the rest of the chopped walnuts.

Gail Weber Riley
(Mrs. Thomas)

Insalata di Mostaccioli

A zesty pasta salad.

Planning: Must be made ahead
Preparation Time: 30 minutes

Quantity: 12 servings
Chilling Time: 24 hours

1 pound package mostaccioli
2 teaspoons oil
1 cucumber, seeded and cut up
1 medium onion, diced
¹/₂ jar pimento, drained
2 teaspoons parsley

Dressing:
2 tablespoons prepared mustard
1 teaspoon salt
1 teaspoon garlic salt
1 teaspoon pepper, coarsely
   ground
1¹/₂ cups sugar
¹/₄ cup oil
³/₄ cup cider vinegar

1. Cook mostaccioli in boiling water with 2 teaspoons oil for 15 minutes; drain and cool. (Do not overcook.) **2.** Add cucumber, onion, pimento and parsley. **3.** Mix dressing ingredients in blender and add to mostaccioli with all other ingredients. **4.** Chill in refrigerator for 24 hours.

Mary Manning Bracken
(Mrs. Robert)

Granite (Flavored Ices)

Planning: Must do ahead
Preparation Time: 5 minutes

Quantity: 6 servings, 1 1/2 pints of
  each liquid
Cooking Time: 8 minutes
Chilling Time: 3-4 hours

Select one of the following flavors:
Lemon Ice:
2 cups water
1 cup sugar
1 cup lemon juice

Orange Ice:
2 cups water
3/4 cup sugar
1 cup orange juice
juice of 1 lemon

Coffee Ice:
1 cup water
1/2 cup sugar
2 cups strong espresso coffee

1. In a 2-quart saucepan, bring the water and sugar to a boil over moderate heat, stirring only until the sugar dissolves. Timing from the moment the sugar and water begin to boil, let the mixture cook for exactly 5 minutes. Immediately remove the pan from the heat and let the syrup cool to room temperature. **2.** Depending on which of the flavored ices you want to make, stir in the lemon juice, or the orange and lemon juices, or espresso coffee. Pour the mixture into an ice cube tray from which the dividers have been removed. **3.** Freeze the granite for 3 to 4 hours, stirring it every 30 minutes and scraping it into the ice particles that form around the edges of the tray. The finished granite should have a fine, snowy texture. For a coarser texture that is actually more to the Italian taste, leave the ice cube divider in the tray and freeze the granite solid. Then remove the cubes and crush them in an ice crusher.

Hint: Serve this as a palate cleanser between salad and entree or as a dessert with Amaretto-flavored cookies.

Gail Weber Riley
(Mrs. Thomas)

South of the Border Cocktail Buffet

Margaritas

Guacamole

Mexican Hot Dip

Enchiladas con Salsa Verde

Aji de Gallina

Sopaipillas

Flan

Margaritas ❧

Planning: Can be made ahead and frozen

Preparation Time: 10 minutes

Quantity: Five 6-ounce servings

1 6-ounce can frozen limeade
6 ounces tequilla
2 ounces triple sec
1 tablespoon sugar
1 tablespoon freshly squeezed
   lemon juice
ice
salt

1. Combine first 5 ingredients in a blender **2.** Fill the blender with ice and blend mixture until very well blended. **3.** Serve in glasses with edges that have been dipped in water and then salt.

Terry Rosenberg Poe
(Mrs. Stan)

Guacamole

Planning: Can be done 5 to 6 hours ahead

Preparation Time: 15-20 minutes

Quantity: 12-20 servings
Chilling Time: 1 hour

2 very ripe avocados, mashed
1 small onion, finely chopped
1 teaspoon chopped green chilies
1 tablespoon lemon juice or to
   taste
1 teaspoon snipped coriander
   leaves or ¼ teaspoon ground
   coriander
1 medium tomato, chopped
salt and pepper to taste
tortilla chips

1. Mix avocados, onion, chilies, lemon juice and coriander. **2.** Stir in tomato and season to taste with salt and pepper. **3.** Cover and refrigerate at least 1 hour. **4.** Serve with tortilla chips.

Jane Rife Field
(Mrs. Hugh)

Mexican Hot Dip

Planning: Can be made ahead 2 or 3 days and baked right before serving
Preparation Time: 1 hour

Quantity: 12-20 servings
Baking Time: 30 minutes, 350°

1 8-ounce package cream cheese, softened
1 15-ounce can chili without beans
½ jar Mexican salsa, medium or mild
8 ounces grated Cheddar cheese
1 5½-ounce can ripe olives, drained and chopped
2 to 3 green onions, chopped
nacho chips

1. Layer in a 10″ pie plate or quiche pan:
a. cream cheese
b. chili
c. ½ jar of salsa
d. grated Cheddar cheese
e. chopped olives
f. green onions, chopped   2. Bake at 350° for 20 to 30 minutes or until bubbles begin to form.   3. Let stand 5 minutes.   4. Serve with nacho chips.

Linda Olson Boles
(Mrs. Harold)
Jane Rife Field
(Mrs. Hugh)

Enchiladas con Salsa Verde

Planning: Can assemble a day ahead
Preparation Time: 1 1/2 hours

Quantity: 6-8 servings
Baking Time: 20 minutes, 350°

Cheese Filling:
2 cups shredded Monterey Jack
    cheese
1 cup Cheddar cheese
1 medium onion, chopped and
    sautéed in 2 tablespoons butter
1/2 cup sour cream
2 tablespoons snipped parsley
1 teaspoon salt
1/4 teaspoon pepper

Cheese Filling:
1. Mix together the first seven ingredients. 2. Set aside.

Green Sauce:
10-ounces frozen chopped
    spinach, thawed and
    squeezed dry
2 tablespoons butter
2 tablespoons flour
1/4 teaspoon salt
1/2 cup milk
1 1/2 cups chicken broth
1 to 2 tablespoons chopped
    canned chilies
1 small onion, sauteed in
    2 tablespoons butter
1 clove garlic, finely chopped
3/4 teaspoon ground cumin
2/3 cup sour cream
shredded cheese

Green Sauce:
1. Heat butter over low heat until melted. 2. Blend in flour and salt. 3. Cook over low heat, stirring until smooth and bubbly. 4. Add milk and 1/2 cup of the chicken broth and heat to boiling, stirring constantly. 5. Boil and stir one minute. Stir in remaining chicken broth. 6. Cook and stir over low heat until hot and remove from heat. 7. Stir in spinach and remaining ingredients.

To Assemble:
1. Heat eight 6" tortillas in a hot skillet until softened. 2. Cover to prevent drying. 3. Dip each tortilla in green sauce to coat both sides. 4. Spoon about 1/4 cup filling into the tortilla and roll up. 5. Place enchiladas seam side down in a greased baking dish and cover with sauce. 6. Bake covered 15 minutes at 350° 7. Uncover and bake 5 to 10 minutes more or until bubbly. 8. Cool 5 to 10 minutes before serving. 9. Garnish with shredded cheese.

Gail Weber Riley
(Mrs. V. Thomas)

Aji de Gallina

Planning: Can be made ahead
Preparation Time: 3-4 hours

Quantity: 12-20 servings
Cooking Time: 1-2 hours

1 4-pound stewing hen
salt and pepper to taste
1/2 pound onions, chopped
2 teaspoons fresh garlic, mashed
6 banana peppers, pureed
1 teaspoon turmeric
1/2 cup oil
4 sliced bread, crusts removed
1/2 pound walnuts
1 cup grated Parmesan cheese
1 can evaporated milk
1 teaspoon seasoned salt
boiling potatoes
hard-boiled egg sliced
black olives

1. Boil the stewing hen with salt and pepper until tender.   **2.** When the chicken cools, bone it, and reserve the meat and broth separately.   **3.** Soak bread in reserved broth.   **4.** In a Dutch oven, sauté onion, garlic, banana peppers, and turmeric in oil until soft. **5.** Add the soaked bread and cook for ten minutes.   **6.** Add the nuts, cheese, and reserved chicken and cook over medium low heat for another 10 minutes.   **7.** Add the milk and seasoned salt and cook and stir until creamy. **8.** Serve over boiled potatoes. Garnish with hard boiled egg slices and black olives.

Hint: To serve as an appetizer, serve in chafing dish with French bread or crackers.

Martha Morote Ives
(Mrs. James)

Sopaipillas

Planning: Can be done a few hours ahead and reheated
Preparation Time: 45 minutes

Quantity: 12-20 puffs
Cooking Time: 2-3 minutes

2 cups flour
3/4 teaspoon salt
1/2 teaspoon baking powder
1 tablespoon shortening
1 1/2 teaspoons dry yeast
1/4 cup lukewarm water (105° to 115°)
1/2 cup and 1 tablespoon milk, scalded and cooled to room temperature (water can be substituted for milk here)
honey
maple syrup
cinnamon/sugar

1. Combine dry ingredients and cut in shortening.   2. Dissolve yeast in 1/4 cup warm water and let stand 10 minutes.   3. Add yeast to scalded milk (or water).   4. Make a well in the center of the dry ingredients, add the liquid and work into the dough.   5. On a floured surface knead the dough 15 to 20 times and set aside for about 10 minutes.
6. Roll the dough to 1/4" thickness.
7. Cut into small squares or triangles.
8. Fry in hot oil 2 to 3 minutes or until lightly browned.   9. Fry only a few at a time so the sopaipillas will puff and become hollow.   10. Drain on paper towels and serve hot with honey, maple syrup or cinnamon sugar.

Hint: The sopaipillas can be made 3 to 4 hours ahead and reheated for 8 minutes in a 350° oven, uncovered, but they are best served freshly cooked.

Several League Members

Flan

Planning: Must be made ahead
Preparation Time: 2 hours

Quantity: 12 servings
Baking Time: 45-50 minutes, 325°

1 cup sugar
1/2 cup water
1 1/2 cups milk
1 1/2 cups light cream
8 eggs
1 cup sugar
1 teaspoon vanilla

1. Over medium high heat lightly swirl saucepan containing 1 cup sugar and 1/2 cup water.   **2.** Cook, swirling frequently, until the mixture becomes tea colored. (Do not stir while cooking.) **3.** When the liquid becomes tea colored, it should be poured at once into a 2-quart mold (2-quart souffle dish). **4.** Tilt and turn the mold in such a way that the caramel coats the bottom and sides of the mold and keep turning the dish until the caramel sets. Set aside. **5.** Scald the milk and cream.   **6.** Whip the eggs and sugar until well blended. **7.** Add scalded liquid to egg mixture and beat well. Add vanilla.   **8.** Strain liquid into the prepared pan and bake in a hot (not boiling) bath at 325° oven for 45 to 50 minutes or until the custard is set.   **9.** Chill at least 4 hours before serving.   **10.** Run a knife around the edges and invert before serving.

Several League Members

Testers, Proofreaders and Contributors

The following women generously donated their time, expertise and financial support to the task of double testing each of the 1,000 recipes submitted:

Beverages & Appetizers

Gail Kugath Anfinson
Mary Kay Gallagher Beecher
Nancy McEvoy Burns
Kathie Sullivan Cahill
Sharon Gossman Fereday
Karen Karman Gartelos
Dianne Rowland Gearhart
Gina Swaim Greene
Joanne Strand Hansen
Ellen Hansen Hansen
Gina Zattoni Hunsinger
Janis Eicher Jennings
Amy Miller Lockard
Julie Yarger Manning
Becky Peet Martens
Leslie Nelson Martin
Linda Bjornstad Martin
Barbara Burnham Paxson
Terry Rosenberg Poe
Sandy Smith Ritland
Marie Shipman Spears
Marilyn Daily Strubel
Connie Knutson Tiede
Kathleen Wettengel Welch

Soups & Sandwiches
Eggs, Cheese & Pasta

Barb Alt Dodd
Barb Stoen Dowd
Ellie Kennedy Everitt
Marsha Kohler Fisher
Judy Larson Fogdall
Mary Waldon Gabrick
Angela Hamer
Noreen Hermansen
Betty Bergan Hurley
Joyce Johnson Johnson
Ann Awtry Kem
Donna Sawchuk Lesyshen
Marty McNutt Port
Susan Willett Sawyer
Jane Manlove Slykhuis
Nancy Swisher Thomas
Dee Reinhart Vandeventer
Linda Gilliam Waldon
Elizabeth Cooper Yagla
Ann Stanton Zellhoefer

Breads

Nancy Brody Bamsey
Linda Monroe Hoel
Amy Carmack Iversen
Cindy Weaver Olson
Anna Griffith Randall
Pam Childs Sears
Cathy Foster Young

254

Salads, Dressings & Condiments Vegetables

Bonnie Nelson Anderson
Sharon Armfield-Penn
Ruth Lutz Buck
Vee Hazen Carlson
Judy Levine Clauson
Barbara Alt Dodd
Pam Nockels Dowie
Cathy Ercius Enstrom
Susan Marty Fereday
Norma Smith Hassman
Carol Irgens Hellman
Patti Welch Holm
Terri Whitney Jackson
Mary Strack Kabel
Gini Naber Langlas
Marsha Green Lind
Linda Hexom Lott
Linda McConnelee McCausland
Kay Hill Meany
Nancy Shields Miller
Mary Ann Marchese Moore
Karen Rasmussen Mukai
Jane Schneider Overbeeke
Carol Riekens Pierce
Linda Johnston Rust
Chris Fauerby Smith
Cindy Poyser Spragg
Carol Hayes Steckelberg
Connie Stroh Werner
Joan Barz Westemeier

Entrees

Linda Lichty Anderson
Doris Wiernsberger Bragdon
Mary Manning Bracken
Dorothy Miller Brecunier
Donna Robinson Brown
Jane Walker Christensen
Patricia Callan Clark
Phyllis Dolan Cooper
Susan Walker Crouse
Betty Landgraf Dalton
Ann Felcher Enderlein
Cindy Martin Gilliam
Kay Putney Glessner
Diana Lichty Hansen
Mary Lutgen Lichty
Regena McKone Lindeman
Barbara Dunn McDonald
Gale Gruver Moyer
Mary Longfellow Nilsson
Cheri French O'Connor
Thieleane Stevens Raecker
Betty Jean Hoeg Schukei
Margie Lahey Skahill
Mary Ehm Strattan
Patti Corkery Sulentic
Helen Johnson Swisher
Patricia Spraggins Welton
Carol Boudreaux Williams

Desserts

Mary Ludlow Alfrey
Judy Mathews Arnold
Linda Mast Bohlen
Carol Hinson Driver
Diane Drewis Good
Joan Dawson Huhn
Cindy Horton Kline
Barbara Martin Krizek
Linda Konrardy Langham
Kris Garetson McIntee
Mary Esther Harper Pullin
Beverly Greiner Rutten
Mary Ellen Hammond Warren
Sandy Berkenes Warren

Special Occasions

Jane Rife Field
Terri Whitney Jackson
Gail Webber Riley
Nancy Buscemi Sulentic
Terri Dennis Walker
Mary Ellen Hammond Warren
Carol Rappolt Waterbury
Cathy Foster Young

Testing Contributors

Pamela Deutsch Bargfrede
Nancy Irwin Berg
Mary Boucher Brixius
Patricia Staley Early
Cindy Holmstron Frederick
Laura McQuown Fisher
Pat Behrens Jacobs
Marcia Brown Jones
Judy Dethmer Klepfer
Debbie McDonald
Deborah Vonnahme Pedersen
Karin Rhodes Sigl
Teeney Weekley

The following women enthusiastically and expeditiously proofread the thousands of words and ingredients to provide the most accurate description of our recipes:

Deborah Prust Adams
Bonnie Nelson Anderson
Mary Kay Gallagher Beecher
Mary Boucher Brixius
Betty Landgraf Dalton
Susan Marty Fereday
Cheryl Hansen Galehouse
Molly Pitcher Greenwood

Judy Brush Griffith
Susan Nejdl Junaid
Cathie Pederson Miehe
Deborah Vonnahme Pedersen
Susan Young Peters
Kathy Walden Schreiner
Dianne Brink Warren
Kate Della Maria Weidner

A special thank you to our typist, Jeanne Regan Heuer, who efficiently computerized our manuscript.
A special acknowledgement to the Black Hawk County Porkettes for their proud "tale of an Iowa pig."

256

INDEX

A

WCF Publications
Junior League of Waterloo-Cedar Falls, Inc.
Box 434
Waterloo, Iowa 50704

Please send me _____ copies of PIG OUT at the
$17.95 mail order price, which includes all charges
for postage, handling and applicable sales taxes.
(Payable in U.S. dollars only.)

Gift wrapping available _____ @ $1.00 per book

Enclosed is my check or money order in the amount
of $_____.

Name _____

Address _____

City _____

State _____ Zip _____

Make checks payable to WCF Publications

Fill out the mailing label at right to ensure accurate delivery of your order.

From:
WCF Publications
Junior League of Waterloo-Cedar Fall, Inc.
Box 434
Waterloo, Iowa 50704

PIG OUT

MAILING LABEL – PLEASE PRINT

NAME

ADDRESS

STATE

ZIP

WCF Publications
Junior League of Waterloo-Cedar Falls, Inc.
Box 434
Waterloo, Iowa 50704

Please send me _____ copies of PIG OUT at the
$17.95 mail order price, which includes all charges
for postage, handling and applicable sales taxes.
(Payable in U.S. dollars only.)

Gift wrapping available _____ @ $1.00 per book

Enclosed is my check or money order in the amount
of $_____.

Name _____

Address _____

City _____

State _____ Zip _____

Make checks payable to WCF Publications

Fill out the mailing label at right to ensure accurate delivery of your order.

From:
WCF Publications
Junior League of Waterloo-Cedar Fall, Inc.
Box 434
Waterloo, Iowa 50704

PIG OUT

MAILING LABEL – PLEASE PRINT

NAME

ADDRESS

STATE

ZIP

I would like to have the following stores and/or gift shops in my area handle PIG OUT:

Store Name _____

Address _____

City _____ State _____ Zip _____

Store Name _____

Address _____

City _____ State _____ Zip _____

I would like to have the following stores and/or gift shops in my area handle PIG OUT:

Store Name _____

Address _____

City _____ State _____ Zip _____

Store Name _____

Address _____

City _____ State _____ Zip _____

WCF Publications
Junior League of Waterloo-Cedar Falls, Inc.
Box 434
Waterloo, Iowa 50704

Please send me _____ copies of PIG OUT at the
$17.95 mail order price, which includes all charges
for postage, handling and applicable sales taxes.
(Payable in U.S. dollars only.)

Gift wrapping available _____ @ $1.00 per book

Enclosed is my check or money order in the amount
of $_____.

Name _____

Address _____

City _____

State _____ Zip _____

Make checks payable to WCF Publications

Fill out the mailing label at right to ensure accurate delivery of your order.

From:
WCF Publications
Junior League of Waterloo-Cedar Fall, Inc.
Box 434
Waterloo, Iowa 50704

PIG OUT

NAME

ADDRESS

STATE

ZIP

MAILING LABEL – PLEASE PRINT

WCF Publications
Junior League of Waterloo-Cedar Falls, Inc.
Box 434
Waterloo, Iowa 50704

Please send me _____ copies of PIG OUT at the
$17.95 mail order price, which includes all charges
for postage, handling and applicable sales taxes.
(Payable in U.S. dollars only.)

Gift wrapping available _____ @ $1.00 per book

Enclosed is my check or money order in the amount
of $_____.

Name _____

Address _____

City _____

State _____ Zip _____

Make checks payable to WCF Publications

Fill out the mailing label at right to ensure accurate delivery of your order.

From:
WCF Publications
Junior League of Waterloo-Cedar Fall, Inc.
Box 434
Waterloo, Iowa 50704

PIG OUT

NAME

ADDRESS

STATE

ZIP

MAILING LABEL – PLEASE PRINT

I would like to have the following stores and/or gift shops in my area handle PIG OUT:

Store Name _____

Address _____

City _____ State _____ Zip _____

Store Name _____

Address _____

City _____ State _____ Zip _____

I would like to have the following stores and/or gift shops in my area handle PIG OUT:

Store Name _____

Address _____

City _____ State _____ Zip _____

Store Name _____

Address _____

City _____ State _____ Zip _____